# Finite Element Analysis
# on Microcomputers

# Finite Element Analysis on Microcomputers

### Nicholas M. Baran

**McGraw-Hill Book Company**

New York   St. Louis   San Francisco   Auckland   Bogotá
Hamburg   London   Madrid   Mexico   Milan
Montreal   New Delhi   Panama   Paris   São Paulo
Singapore   Sydney   Tokyo   Toronto

**Library of Congress Cataloging-in-Publication Data**

Baran, Nicholas.
  Finite element analysis on microcomputers.

  Includes index.
  1. Finite element method—Data processing.
  2. Microcomputers—Programming.  I. Title.
  TA347.F5B355  1987    620'.001'515353    87-3251
  ISBN 0-07-033694-6

1234567890    DOC/DOC    893210987

ISBN 0-07-033694-6

The editors for this book were Betty Sun and Marci Nugent, the designer was Naomi Auerbach, and the production supervisor was Richard Ausburn. It was set in Century Schoolbook by the McGraw-Hill Book Company Professional & Reference Division composition unit.

Printed and bound by R. R. Donnelley & Sons Company.

In memory of my father, Paul Alexander Baran, 1910–1964

# Contents

# Preface

This book is an introductory text on finite element analysis with an emphasis on microcomputers. The intent of the book is to provide a practical text geared toward finite element users rather than toward students of finite element theory.

Examples in the text were developed using three microcomputer finite element programs: ANSYS-PC/LINEAR, Revision 4.2-A2, and ANSYS-PC/THERMAL, Revision 4.2.-0, both from Swanson Analysis Systems, Inc., and MSC/pal 2, Version 1.0, from The MacNeal-Schwendler Corporation. More recent versions of these software packages may now be available which may have different performance characteristics. The book's currency should not be affected, however, since the emphasis is on finite element concepts rather than specific software applications.

It should be noted that most of the computer-generated graphics from MSC/pal 2 were generated with the high-resolution Japanese IBM 5550 Kanji Model Computer and the IBM 5577 printer, thanks to Ken Blakely of The MacNeal-Schwendler Corporation. The graphics from ANSYS-PC/LINEAR and ANSYS-PC/THERMAL were generated with the much lower resolution IBM PC color graphics adapter and the IBM ProPrinter. The difference in quality of these graphics is not intended in any way to reflect on the actual products represented. ANSYS-PC/LINEAR and ANSYS-PC/THERMAL also support high-resolution graphics, but no equipment of this kind was available for use with these products.

Many generous people contributed to this project. Above all, I would like to thank Ken Blakely of The MacNeal-Schwendler Corporation and Laurie Scott of Swanson Analysis Systems, Inc. Without their generous help and cooperation, this book would not have been possible. I would also like to thank Dave Dietrich and Robert Gorman of Swanson Analysis Systems, Inc., and Mark Baker for reviewing parts of the manuscript. In addition, thanks are due Mike Bussler of Algor Interactive Systems, Jim Leung of Celestial Software, Richard Ay of COADE/McGraw-Hill, and Susan Tellep of Control Data. I am also indebted to Jan Benes and Tomas Frank, who both had a great deal to do with the publication of this book. Finally, I would like to thank my sponsoring editor, Betty Sun, for her unswerving encouragement throughout. And, to my wife Esther, thanks for the support.

*Nicholas M. Baran*

# Trademark List

| | |
|---|---|
| ANSYS | Swanson Analysis Systems, Inc. |
| ANSYS-PC/LINEAR | Swanson Analysis Systems, Inc. |
| ANSYS-PC/THERMAL | Swanson Analysis Systems, Inc. |
| MSC/pal 2 | The MacNeal-Schwendler Corporation |
| MSC/AutoFEM | The MacNeal-Schwendler Corporation |
| NASTRAN | The MacNeal-Schwendler Corporation |
| IMAGES 3D | Celestial Software, Inc. |
| SUPERSAP | Algor Interactive Systems, Inc. |
| SAP-86 | Number Crunching Systems, Inc. |
| SAP 80/81 | Computers and Structures, Inc. |
| VAX 11-780 | Digital Equipment Corp. |
| IBM PC | International Business Machines, Inc. |
| Apple Macintosh | Apple Computer, Inc. |
| FASTBACK | Fifth Generation Systems, Inc. |
| Apollo Domain | Apollo Computer, Inc. |
| Sun-3 | Sun Microsystems, Inc. |
| Cyber 180 | Control Data, Inc. |
| FINITE/GP | COADE/McGraw-Hill, Inc. |
| MARC | MARC Analysis, Inc. |
| GT-STRUDL | Georgia Institute of Technology |
| STARDYNE | System Development Corp. |
| IRMA Board | Digital Communications Associates |
| CROSSTALK | Microstuf, Inc. |
| Microsoft Mouse | Microsoft, Inc. |
| AutoCad | AutoDesk, Inc. |

# Introduction

This is a book for practicing engineers using the finite element method in their daily work. In addition to the basic concepts of the finite element method, the book provides the engineer with practical techniques and guidelines for obtaining accurate and useful results from finite element analysis. Microcomputer-based finite element programs are becoming increasingly popular in the industry, and, therefore, the emphasis in this book is placed on the use of the microcomputer for analysis work. However, the concepts and techniques presented are equally applicable to mainframe- and minicomputer-based programs.

The finite element method is probably the most widely used form of computer-based engineering analysis. Most engineers, from all disciplines, come across the finite element method at some point in their careers. The method is used for analyzing a broad range of engineering structures and components, from the human body to the wings of an airplane.

With the advent of the microcomputer, more and more engineers are gaining access to finite element analysis programs and are using them to solve an increasingly broad range of problems. While the finite element method is extremely useful, like any other tool, it can be misused, leading to inaccurate or inefficient results. Unfortunately, there are few, if any, books on the market that provide practical guidelines for *users* of the finite element method. There are a number of excellent books on the theory of the finite element method which generally provide a highly mathematical and rigorous treatment of the subject and are useful for those who plan to specialize in finite element analysis or intend to write their own finite element programs.

However, the great majority of engineers who use the finite element method are neither finite element specialists nor programmers interested in designing their own finite element programs. Most users employ finite element analysis as a tool for analyzing the adequacy of a structure or component under a variety of loading conditions. Many users use finite element analysis fairly infrequently and need a practical reference guide to refresh their memories on the important concepts and methodologies of finite element analysis. Others have just started working in industry and have never had a finite element class in college. This book is intended to fill the need for a practical guide that provides the methods and techniques necessary for effective and accurate use of finite element analysis. Some of the basic questions answered by this book are listed below:

1. What is *finite element analysis*, and how is it used?

2. What finite element codes are available, and where do microcomputers fit in?

3. What factors do I need to be aware of when I design my finite element model (e.g., element types, loading conditions, material properties, geometry, and boundary conditions?)

4. Is my problem suitable for running on a microcomputer? Can I download and/or upload programs from the mainframe?

5. What can go wrong with my analysis? How do I correct inaccurate results?

6. How do I interpret the results of my analysis?

Chapter 1 starts with a basic introduction to the finite element method and includes a series of examples of typical problems. Chapter 2 covers the types of structures and components that can be analyzed using the finite element method and how the various types of elements can be applied. The various types of loading conditions are also discussed. In Chap. 3, we take a look at the differences between mainframe, mini, and microcomputers and survey the major finite element codes in use today.

Starting with Chap. 4, we begin actually working through some finite element problems. We discuss basic modeling techniques: what to watch out for when designing a finite element model, what to avoid, and how to increase efficiency and accuracy. Chapters 5 and 6 work step by step through a finite element analysis. Chapters 7, 8, and 9 present a series of examples from the main areas of finite element analysis: statics, dynamics, and thermal (heat transfer) analyses.

It is assumed that the reader has a solid background in strength of materials and engineering mechanics. No knowledge of the finite element method is required. In order to use microcomputer-based finite element programs effectively, it is necessary to be familiar with the computer's operating system and with a simple text editor. These topics are discussed further in Chap. 3 and in App. A.

# 1

# Overview of Finite Element Analysis

Finite element methods are predominantly used to perform computer-based analyses of the static, dynamic, or thermal behavior of physical systems, structures, and components. They are used primarily when hand calculations cannot provide sufficiently accurate or detailed results or when the system to be analyzed is so complex that hand calculations are not appropriate. With the reduced cost of processing on microcomputers and "friendlier" software, finite element analysis has also become a viable alternative for solving small engineering problems that were previously solved "by hand."

Finite element analysis is broadly defined as a group of numerical methods for approximating the governing equations of any continuous system. In this book, we will consider its application to solids.

This chapter presents a basic introduction to the concepts and terminology of finite element analysis. Before discussing the theory of finite elements, it is important to emphasize that a thorough theoretical understanding of the finite element method is not a prerequisite to using finite element programs. The principle of finite elements, as one would expect, is a rigorous mathematical theory based on the calculus of variations, energy theorems, the principle of elasticity, and other equations of physics and engineering. It is not the purpose of this book to derive the theory of finite elements. There are many excellent texts available that cover the theory thoroughly, some of which are listed in the references at the end of this chapter.

Mastery of the finite element theory is absolutely essential if you are writing your own finite element programs. As a user of finite element programs, however, it is sufficient to have a rudimentary understanding of the basic concepts of the finite element method, which we will try to impart in this chapter. On the other hand, it is imperative as a user to understand the physical problem you are attempting to solve and how to use the finite element program and interpret its results correctly. The ultimate goal of this book is to impart this understanding.

In this chapter, we will first discuss the basic theory of finite element analysis. We will then work through the solution of a simple structural problem using the finite element method, both by hand and using a finite element computer program. This exercise will help clarify how finite element programs work and how they are used.

## 1.1 The Basic Concept of the Finite Element Method

The theory of finite elements is sometimes called the "theory of piecewise continuous approximations." In general, the objective of finite element analysis is to approximate with a sufficient degree of accuracy the values of the unknowns of a governing differential equation at selected points on the domain of a continuous physical system or structure. A mathematical model of the physical system or structure, divided into *nodes* and *finite elements*, is created, and the governing equations are applied to it and solved for each node.

The governing differential equation can define a wide variety of physical phenomena. Poisson's equation, for example, is a second-order partial differential equation which governs deflections of a membrane, bending of a prismatic beam, heat conduction with sources, and many other physical phenomena. The main function of the finite element program is to reduce the differential equation to a set of simultaneous algebraic equations which can be readily solved by a computer. The solution of these equations yields directly, or by means of minor additional computation, the desired unknown quantities, such as deflections, temperatures, or stresses.

The steps involved in a finite element analysis are shown in Table 1.1. The first step is to create the finite element model. The finite element model is a geometrical representation of the actual physical structure or body being analyzed. The model is created by dividing the structure into a number of subregions called "elements." The values of the unknown quantities are to be computed at selected points in the elements, usually at the corners. These points are called "nodes." Figure 1.1 shows an arbitrary shape divided into nodes and elements. The process of dividing up the body is often called "discretization" and is normally performed by the user. As we shall see in later chapters, discretization of the body or structure is the most important phase of the analysis and greatly affects the accuracy of the results.

TABLE 1.1.   The steps in a finite element analysis

1. User creates the finite element model
   a. Define geometry, nodes, and elements
   b. Specify material properties, loading conditions, and boundary conditions
2. Finite element program performs analysis
   a. Formulate equation
   b. Solve equation
3. Finite element program reports results
   a. Compute node and element values (displacements, temperatures, stresses, reaction forces, etc.)
   b. Postprocess results (plots, code checks, etc.)

In addition to defining the location of nodes and elements, the user usually supplies the geometrical properties of the elements, material properties, boundary conditions, and loading conditions relevant to the analysis. Some finite element programs include or allow the use of databases that automatically supply the properties of standard structural elements.

It is important to emphasize that the finite element model is a mathematical simulation of the actual physical structure or body that it represents. The physical properties must be specified. If the structure is composed of I beams, for example, the elements must be assigned the geometrical properties of the I beam. If the body is made of steel, the material properties of

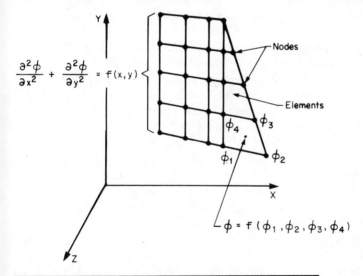

Figure 1.1    An arbitrary shape divided into nodes and elements. The shape is governed by the partial differential equation shown. The value of this equation at any point in an element is a function of the values of the nodes $\phi_i$ bounding the element.

steel must be assigned to the elements of the body. If the body is pinned at a support point or rigidly fixed, this support condition must be represented in the finite element model. Finally, the applied loads must be modeled. For example, a seismic analysis might require a lateral acceleration of 3 G to be applied to the model. A heat transfer analysis might require a temperature change in the working fluid of 300° over a period of 10 seconds. A static analysis may simply include the dead load of the structure.

In the second step of the analysis, the finite element program applies the governing partial differential equation and its boundary conditions in the form of an *equivalent integral formulation*. This is a procedure involving minimization of a functional (variational calculus) and energy conservation laws. For example, most finite element programs for structural analysis use the principle of virtual displacements to express the differential equations of equilibrium in their equivalent integral formulation. Further discussion of this procedure can be found in Bathe and Wilson, *Numerical Methods in Finite Element Analysis* (Ref. 1). Finite element programs are designed to work with specific differential equations. A program designed to solve heat transfer problems cannot solve structural analysis problems. However, many programs include several "modules," each designed to solve a certain type of problem.

After the finite element model is completely defined, the main numerical, or "number-crunching," phase of the analysis is performed by the finite element program. The program treats the nodal displacements as variables of an interpolation function, usually a polynomial, to give an analytical expression for displacement at any point inside the element. This is conceptually illustrated in Fig. 1.1. A polynomial (sometimes differential) function must be formulated for each element in the body. The polynomials are then substituted into the integral formulation of the partial differential equation resulting in a set of simultaneous algebraic equations which are solved to give the nodal values of the unknowns.

This may be the final step in the analysis or may be followed by additional computation where the nodal values are used to calculate other quantities. For example, in most finite element programs for structural analysis, the calculated nodal values are the displacements of the body. These displacements can then be used to calculate the strains and stresses in each element.

So far, we have discussed the concept of finite element analysis in very general terms. As we mentioned earlier, implementation of the finite element concept varies depending on the type of problem that is to be solved. Most finite element programs for microcomputers are designed to solve statics and dynamics problems in the elastic range. The primary reason for this is that these types of problems are the most straightforward to solve with finite element analysis and therefore require less processing time and memory capacity than problems in, for example, heat transfer, fluid flow, and nonlinear analysis. We will discuss in greater detail the issues of computer processing speed and storage in Chap. 3.

It is interesting to note that the finite element method was originally formulated strictly for structural analysis. It was not until some 10 years after its first application that finite element analysis was generalized to analyze any boundary value problem. More on the history of the finite element method is included at the end of this chapter.

## 1.2 An Example of the Finite Element Concept

To illustrate the concept of finite element analysis in more physical terms, we will work through the finite element analysis of a simple truss by hand. While the truss is a simple structure, the method of solution of a truss problem by finite element analysis is applicable to any finite element structure. The truss problem is therefore an excellent vehicle for learning the basic concepts and terminology of the finite element method.[1]

A simple three-member truss is shown in Fig. 1.2. Each member of the truss is itself a natural element of the finite element model. It is not necessary to divide a truss member into smaller elements since it can take only axial loads and therefore has a constant stress at any cross-section along its length. Breaking up a member of a truss into smaller elements would accomplish nothing. As we shall see, another simplification with the truss element is that it is possible to obtain an exact solution of the forces and displacements without resorting to integral formulations or energy methods. The objective of our analysis is to determine the displacements of the structure when subjected to the load $P$.

Before working with the truss in Fig. 1.2, let us examine a single truss member (bar) as shown in Fig. 1.3. A node is located at each end of the bar. Since the bar is pinned at each end and cannot take loads in the $Z$ direction, each end of the bar can displace in only two directions, $X$ and $Y$. This means that each node has 2 degrees of freedom, often abbreviated DOF.

The number of degrees of freedom per node varies for different elements. For example, a beam in a two-dimensional frame would have 3 DOF at each node since a rotation due to moment loading would be included. In the most general case, a node may have 6 DOF: one rota-

---

[1] A similar analysis may be found in Robert D. Cook, *Concepts and Applications of Finite Analysis*, 2d ed., Wiley, New York, 1981, pp. 21–29. Acknowledgment is also due Mike Bohn of the University of California Extension Center, Berkeley.

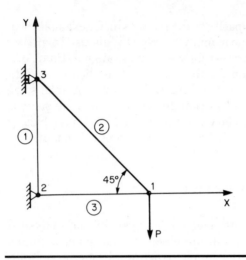

**Figure 1.2**    A simple planar three-member truss. The circled numbers denote the elements; the numbers at the points are the node numbers.

tion and one displacement in each of the three coordinate axes. This is shown in Fig. 1.4.

Referring to Fig. 1.3, the displacements at node 1 are denoted $u_1$ and $u_2$ in the positive $X$ and $Y$ directions. At node 2, they are denoted $u_3$ and $u_4$. Corresponding forces are applied at each node, $F_1$ and $F_2$ at node 1, $F_3$ and $F_4$ at node 2. The bar has a uniform cross-sectional area $A$ and Young's modulus $E$.

The general relationship between force and displacement is given by the equation

$$\varepsilon F \nabla = [K]\varepsilon\, U \nabla \tag{1.1}$$

where $\varepsilon F \nabla$ = applied force vector
$[K]$ = stiffness of the structure in the direction of the applied force
$\varepsilon U \nabla$ = displacement vector

In the case of the planar truss element, this relationship is expressed in matrix notation as

$$\begin{Bmatrix} F_1 \\ F_2 \\ F_3 \\ F_4 \end{Bmatrix} = \begin{bmatrix} k_{11} & k_{12} & k_{13} & k_{14} \\ k_{21} & k_{22} & k_{23} & k_{24} \\ k_{31} & k_{32} & k_{33} & k_{34} \\ k_{41} & k_{42} & k_{43} & k_{44} \end{bmatrix} \begin{Bmatrix} u_1 \\ u_2 \\ u_3 \\ u_4 \end{Bmatrix} \tag{1.2}$$

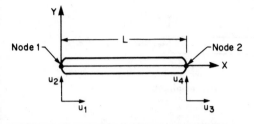

**Figure 1.3**   A single truss member of length $L$ and displacements $u_1$. Each displacement represents 1 DOF. Therefore, the truss member has 4 DOF.

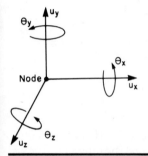

**Figure 1.4**   A node can have 6 DOF in the general case; one rotation and one translation in each of the three axes.

where $k_{ij}$ is the stiffness influence coefficient (force at the $i$th node due to the $j$th displacement). The matrix of $k_{ij}$ terms is called the "stiffness matrix." If you are unfamiliar with matrix algebra, Strang, *Linear Algebra and Its Applications* (Ref. 2), is an excellent text on the subject. For the purposes of this book, all you need to know is that Eq. (1.2) is equivalent to a set of four linear simultaneous equations of the form

$$F_1 = k_{11}u_1 + k_{12}u_2 + k_{13}u_3 + k_{14}u_4$$
$$F_2 = k_{21}u_1 + k_{22}u_2 + \ldots$$

Notice that Eq. (1.2) represents four linear equations. This is because there are 4 DOF. *There is always the same number of linear equations as there are nodal degrees of freedom.*

If we set the displacement $u_j$ to 1 and all other displacements to 0, the $j$th column of $k_{ij}$ is the set of nodal forces which act on the bar to maintain static equilibrium. To see this, assume $u_2 = u_3 = u_4 = 0$. Then Eq. (1.2) reduces to

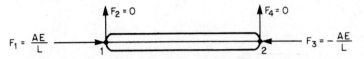

**Figure 1.5**    Loads required to maintain the horizontal truss element in equilibrium when subjected to a unit horizontal displacement $(u_1 = 1$ at node 1, $u_2 = u_3 = u_4 = 0)$.

$$\begin{Bmatrix} F_1 \\ F_2 \\ F_3 \\ F_4 \end{Bmatrix} = \begin{bmatrix} k_{11} \\ k_{21} \\ k_{31} \\ k_{41} \end{bmatrix} \{u_1\} \qquad (1.3)$$

From basic mechanics of materials (Ref. 3), the change in length of a rod subjected to an axial force is given by the equation

$$u = \frac{FL}{AE}$$

where the notation is consistent with our previous definitions. This equation is actually derived from the theory of elasticity and the differential equation of a beam. For more complex systems and geometries, we would not have the luxury of applying a simple linear equation as we do with a truss or frame.

A unit displacement of $u_1$ will cause a compressive strain in the bar equal to $-1/L$, and, from the above equation, the axial force in the bar is $AE/L$. The loads required to maintain equilibrium are shown in Fig. 1.5. Expressing these forces in the first column of the stiffness matrix, we have

$$k_{i1} = \begin{bmatrix} \dfrac{AE}{L} \\ 0 \\ -\dfrac{AE}{L} \\ 0 \end{bmatrix} = \frac{AE}{L} \begin{bmatrix} 1 \\ 0 \\ -1 \\ 0 \end{bmatrix} \qquad (1.4)$$

If we set $u_4$ to 1 and the other displacements to 0, there is no stress in the bar since truss members can take only axial loads. Therefore, $k_{i4}$ is simply equal to 0. This is also the case with $k_{i2}$. The displacement of $u_3$ causes a tensile strain in the bar giving the same result as $u_1$ except with the signs reversed. The stiffness matrix for the bar is

$$k_{ij} = \frac{AE}{L} \begin{bmatrix} 1 & 0 & -1 & 0 \\ 0 & 0 & 0 & 0 \\ -1 & 0 & 1 & 0 \\ 0 & 0 & 0 & 0 \end{bmatrix} \qquad (1.5)$$

This is an exact solution of the forces and displacement relationships for this simple truss element.

Deriving Eq. (1.5) was straightforward because the bar in Fig. 1.3 is parallel to the $X$ axis. For our three-member truss problem, this simplification does not apply to all the elements. Therefore, we need a means to express the stiffness matrix for elements at some angle θ to the $X$ and $Y$ axes.

Figure 1.6 shows the truss element oriented at an angle θ to the $X$ axis. In this case, the vertical forces $F_2$ and $F_4$ will contribute a vertical component to each displacement and will therefore have nonzero values. Setting $u_3$ to 1 and the remaining displacements to 0, we can generate $k_{i3}$ of the stiffness matrix. The component of $u_3$ normal to the bar does not contribute to the strain in the bar. Therefore, the strain is $u_3(\cos θ)/L$, and the axial force is $AE(\cos θ)/L$. Applying simple trigonometry, we obtain the values for the forces

$$F_3 = \frac{AE(\cos^2 θ)}{L}$$

$$F_4 = \frac{AE(\cos θ)(\sin θ)}{L}$$

$$F_1 = -F3$$

$$F_2 = -F4$$

Therefore

$$k_{i3} = \frac{AE}{L} \begin{bmatrix} -\cos^2 θ \\ -\cos θ \sin θ \\ \cos^2 θ \\ \cos θ \sin θ \end{bmatrix} \qquad (1.6)$$

The other columns can be obtained in similar fashion, giving the following stiffness matrix:

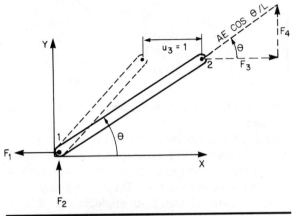

**Figure 1.6** The truss member is oriented at an angle $\theta$ to the $X$ axis. In this case, node 2 experiences a unit horizontal displacement ($u_3 = 1$) while the other displacements are held to 0. Both vertical and horizontal forces now contribute a component to maintaining equilibrium.

$$k_{(i,j)} = \frac{AE}{L} \begin{bmatrix} c^2 & cs & -c^2 & -cs \\ cs & s^2 & -sc & -s^2 \\ -c^2 & -cs & c^2 & cs \\ -sc & -s^2 & sc & s^2 \end{bmatrix} \quad (1.7)$$

where $c = \cos\theta$ and $s = \sin\theta$. If $\theta$ is 0, Eq. (1.7) reduces to Eq. (1.5), the stiffness matrix for the truss member parallel to the $X$ axis.

We have now developed the general stiffness matrix for a two-dimensional truss element. This stiffness matrix can be applied to any planar truss problem. In general, a stiffness matrix is generated for each element of the truss by applying Eq. (1.7). Then, equations of equilibrium are generated for each node in the truss, and the element stiffness matrices are assembled into a global stiffness matrix, along with the force and displacement matrices. These simultaneous equations are then solved by applying the boundary conditions of the problem. We will work through this procedure using the three-member truss as an example. While this may seem like a tedious exercise, it is helpful in gaining a clearer understanding of the basic principles of finite element analysis. In fact, the procedure we will work through is the basis of all finite element programs.

Returning to our three-member truss, Fig. 1.7a shows the truss geometry and elements. Elements 1 and 3 have a length $L$, while element 2 has a length of $L_2 = \sqrt{2}L$. To simplify the calculations, element 2 has a Young's modulus of $E_2 = \sqrt{2}E$ while elements 1 and 3 have a modulus of $E$.

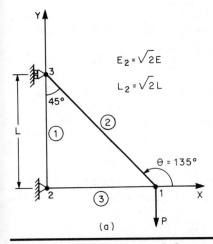

**Figure 1.7** (*a*) The geometry and elements of the three-member truss. To simplify calculations, assume Young's modulus of element 2, $E_2$ is $\sqrt{2} \times E$, the modulus for elements 1 and 3.

Figure 1.7*b* shows the applied forces and reactions acting on the truss. Note that these forces are the externally applied forces. The forces $\{F\}_i$ that we calculated for the element stiffness matrix are the nodal forces caused by the displacements of the elements. For equilibrium, the sum

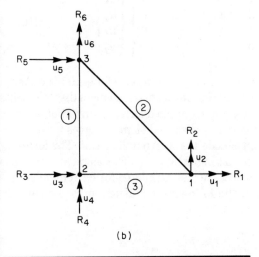

**Figure 1.7** (*b*) The external forces and reactions and the nodal displacements that generally apply to the three-member truss.

of the applied forces and the nodal forces must be zero. We will solve
these equilibrium equations, but first we must calculate the stiffness
matrices for each element, applying Eq. (1.7).

For element 1, $\theta = 90°$, $c = 0$, and $s = 1$. Substituting into Eq. (1.7)
yields

$$\begin{Bmatrix} F_3 \\ F_4 \\ F_5 \\ F_6 \end{Bmatrix} = \frac{AE}{L} \begin{bmatrix} 0 & 0 & 0 & 0 \\ 0 & 1 & 0 & -1 \\ 0 & 0 & 0 & 0 \\ 0 & -1 & 0 & 1 \end{bmatrix} \begin{Bmatrix} u_3 \\ u_4 \\ u_5 \\ u_6 \end{Bmatrix} \qquad (1.8)$$

For element 2, $\theta = 135°$, $c = 1/\sqrt{2}$, and $s = -1/\sqrt{2}$. The angle between
the $X$ axis and the element is measured counterclockwise, as in the
derivation of Eq. (1.7).

The stiffness matrix for element 2 is

$$\begin{Bmatrix} F_1 \\ F_2 \\ F_5 \\ F_6 \end{Bmatrix} = \frac{AE_2}{2L_2} \begin{bmatrix} 1 & -1 & -1 & 1 \\ -1 & 1 & 1 & -1 \\ -1 & 1 & 1 & -1 \\ 1 & -1 & -1 & 1 \end{bmatrix} \begin{Bmatrix} u_1 \\ u_2 \\ u_5 \\ u_6 \end{Bmatrix} \qquad (1.9)$$

For element 3, $\theta = 0°$, and the stiffness matrix reduces to Eq. (1.5):

$$\begin{Bmatrix} F_3 \\ F_4 \\ F_1 \\ F_2 \end{Bmatrix} = \frac{AE}{L} \begin{bmatrix} 1 & 0 & -1 & 0 \\ 0 & 0 & 0 & 0 \\ -1 & 0 & 1 & 0 \\ 0 & 0 & 0 & 0 \end{bmatrix} \begin{Bmatrix} u_3 \\ u_4 \\ u_1 \\ u_2 \end{Bmatrix} \qquad (1.10)$$

We can now generate a set of equilibrium equations for each node. As we
mentioned earlier, the nodal forces resulting from the element displacements
are equal and opposite to the externally applied forces acting at each node.
A conceptual representation of the applied and element forces is shown in
Fig. 1.8a. A free-body diagram of node 1 is shown in Fig. 1.8b. The forces $R_2$
and $R_1$ are the external forces acting on node 1. The element forces are
expressed in the stiffness matrices we just calculated for each member.

For equilibrium of node 1, the following equations must be solved:

$Y$ direction: $R_2 - F_{2(\text{element 3})} - F_{2(\text{element 2})} = 0$

$X$ direction: $R_1 - F_{1(\text{element 3})} - F_{1(\text{element 2})} = 0$

The forces $F_2$ and $F_1$ are found in the element stiffness matrices. Note
the minus sign on the element forces. We are solving for the forces

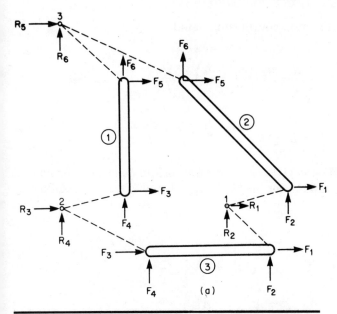

**Figure 1.8** (a) The relationship between the external forces acting on the nodes $R_1$ and the element forces resulting from the displacements $F_1$. At each node, the sum of the applied forces and the element forces must be 0.

acting on the pin. The element forces in the stiffness matrix are acting on the element. Solving for $R_2$, inspection of Eq. (1.10) shows that $F_2$ for element 3 is 0, as we would expect from the free-body diagram. Therefore, referring to Eq. (1.9) and recalling that $E_2/L_2 = E/L$,

$$R_2 = F_{2(\text{element 2})}$$

$$= \frac{AE}{L}\left(\frac{u_1}{2} + \frac{u_2}{2} + \frac{u_5}{2} - \frac{u_2}{6}\right) \qquad (1.11)$$

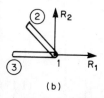

(b)

**Figure 1.8** (b) The free-body diagram for node 1. The node is acted on by the external forces $R_2$ and $R_1$ and the internal forces caused by the displacements of elements 2 and 3 ($F_1$ and $F_2$ for each element).

Solving the $X$-direction equilibrium equation,

$$R_1 - \frac{AE_2}{L_2}\left(\frac{u_1}{2} - \frac{u_2}{2} - \frac{u_5}{2} + \frac{u_6}{2}\right) - \frac{AE}{L}(-u_3 + u_1) = 0$$

$$R_1 = \frac{AE}{L}\left[\left(\frac{3}{2}\right)u_1 - \frac{u_2}{2} - u_3 - \frac{u_5}{2} + \frac{u_6}{2}\right] \qquad (1.12)$$

Equations (1.11) and (1.12) are the equilibrium equations for node 1. We proceed similarly for nodes 2 and 3 and obtain the following equations.

Node 2:

$$Y\text{ direction: } R_4 = \frac{AE}{L}(u_4 - u_6) \qquad (1.13)$$

$$X\text{ direction: } R_3 = \frac{AE}{L}(-u_1 + u_3) \qquad (1.14)$$

Node 3:

$$Y\text{ direction: } R_6 = \frac{AE}{L}\left[\frac{u_1}{2} - \frac{u_2}{2} - u_4 - \frac{u_5}{2} + \left(\frac{3}{2}\right)u_6\right] \qquad (1.15)$$

$$X\text{ direction: } R_5 = \frac{AE}{L}\left(\frac{u_1}{2} + \frac{u_2}{2} + \frac{u_5}{2} - \frac{u_6}{2}\right) \qquad (1.16)$$

We now have expressions for all the external forces in the problem. Combining Eqs. (1.11) through (1.16), we obtain the global stiffness matrix and load and displacement vectors:

$$
\begin{Bmatrix} R_1 \\ R_2 \\ R_3 \\ R_4 \\ R_5 \\ R_6 \end{Bmatrix} = \frac{AE}{L}
\begin{bmatrix}
\frac{3}{2} & -\frac{1}{2} & -1 & 0 & -\frac{1}{2} & \frac{1}{2} \\
-\frac{1}{2} & \frac{1}{2} & 0 & 0 & \frac{1}{2} & -\frac{1}{2} \\
-1 & 0 & 1 & 0 & 0 & 0 \\
0 & 0 & 0 & 1 & 0 & -1 \\
-\frac{1}{2} & \frac{1}{2} & 0 & 0 & \frac{1}{2} & -\frac{1}{2} \\
\frac{1}{2} & -\frac{1}{2} & 0 & -1 & -\frac{1}{2} & \frac{3}{2}
\end{bmatrix}
\begin{Bmatrix} u_1 \\ u_2 \\ u_3 \\ u_4 \\ u_5 \\ u_6 \end{Bmatrix} \qquad (1.17)
$$

Equation (1.17) represents the set of linear algebraic equations to be solved for the unknown displacements. Again, since there are three nodes, there are 6 DOF in the problem and therefore six linear equations. As we established earlier, the set of forces $R_i$ are the external forces including the support reactions. In this problem, there are three unknown reactions: $R_3$, $R_4$, and $R_5$. Force $R_2$ is the external force $-P$ (force is negative due to sign convention). Forces $R_1$ and $R_6$ are 0.

At this point, boundary conditions must be applied to the problem. Some of the degrees of freedom of the structure must be 0. Otherwise, the entire structure could move as a rigid body, and there would be no unique solution to Eq. (1.17). The truss is pinned to its support at node 2. Therefore, $u_3 = u_4 = 0$. The truss is supported by a roller at node 3 so that $u_5 = 0$. Substituting these values into Eq. (1.17) and rearranging $k$ and $u$ give the following equation:

$$
\begin{Bmatrix} R_1 = 0 \\ R_2 = -P \\ R_6 = 0 \\ R_3 \\ R_4 \\ R_5 \end{Bmatrix}
= \frac{AE}{2L}
\begin{bmatrix}
3 & -1 & 1 & -2 & 0 & -1 \\
-1 & 1 & -1 & 0 & 0 & 1 \\
1 & -1 & 3 & 0 & -2 & -1 \\
-2 & 0 & 0 & 1 & 0 & 0 \\
0 & 0 & -2 & 0 & 2 & 0 \\
-1 & 1 & -1 & 0 & 0 & 1
\end{bmatrix}
\begin{Bmatrix} u_1 \\ u_2 \\ u_6 \\ 0 \\ 0 \\ 0 \end{Bmatrix}
\tag{1.18}
$$

The first three linear equations involving $u_1$, $u_2$, and $u_6$ can be solved by themselves using gaussian elimination or Cramer's rule:

$$
\begin{Bmatrix} 0 \\ -P \\ 0 \end{Bmatrix}
= \frac{AE}{2L}
\begin{bmatrix}
3 & -1 & 1 \\
-1 & 1 & -1 \\
1 & -1 & 3
\end{bmatrix}
\begin{Bmatrix} u_1 \\ u_2 \\ u_6 \end{Bmatrix}
\tag{1.19}
$$

Solving Eq. (1.19) yields

$$u_1 = -\frac{PL}{AE}$$

$$u_2 = -\frac{4PL}{AE} \tag{1.20}$$

$$u_6 = -\frac{PL}{AE}$$

Equation (1.19) is called a "reduced-stiffness matrix." The technique of reordering the global stiffness matrix and eliminating the reactions from the resulting equations is common to most finite element programs in order to reduce the amount of computation. The reactions can now be solved for by back-substitution into either Eq. (1.18) or the equilibrium equations. The accuracy of the displacement values can be easily checked by substituting these values into the equilibrium equations and verifying that the sum of the forces is 0.

We have completed the finite element analysis of a three-member truss. While we solved the problem by hand, adding a few more elements would make hand calculations very difficult. And, in most cases, finite element problems involve considerably more than three elements. Obviously, the assembly and solution of simultaneous equations is an ideal application for a computer. In the next section, we will solve the same problem using a finite element program.

### 1.3   Using a Finite Element Program to Solve the Problem

There are four basic steps involved in the use of finite element programs:

1. Define the physical problem.
2. Create the finite element model.
   a. Define geometry, nodes, and elements.
   b. Define material properties and loading and boundary conditions.
3. Perform the analysis using the finite element program.
4. Interpret the results.

The complexity of these steps is directly proportional to the complexity of the physical problem. Clearly, solution of the three-member truss problem should be almost trivial using a finite element program. And, indeed, it is. But, as in the case of our hand calculation in the last section, the basic approach is representative of any finite element analysis.

The first step is to define the physical problem. We wish to perform a static analysis of a three-member truss as shown in Fig. 1.7$a$. In our example, truss elements 1 and 3 are 100 in, and element 2 is 141.42 in ($\leqslant \overline{2L}$). Young's modulus is $10 \times 10^6$ lb/in$^2$ for elements 1 and 3, and $14.142 \times 10^6$ lb/in$^2$ ($\leqslant \overline{2E}$) for element 2. All elements have a cross-sectional area of 1.0 in$^2$. A vertical downward load of 100 lb is applied at node 1. As in the hand calculation, node 2 is constrained in the $X$ and $Y$ directions, and node 3 is constrained in the $X$ direction. In terms of our hand calculation,

$$L = 100 \text{ in}$$
$$E = 10.0 \times 10^6 \text{ lb/in}^2$$
$$A = 1.0 \text{ in}^2$$
$$P = 100 \text{ lb}$$
$$u_3 = u_4 = u_5 = 0$$

With this information, we have defined the physical problem. We have specified the geometry, material properties, loading conditions, and boundary conditions for the problem and are ready to create the finite element model. Figure 1.9 shows the input file for the three-member truss problem using the finite element program ANSYS-PC/LINEAR. We will cover in detail this and other microcomputer finite element programs in later chapters. For our purposes here, the listing in Fig. 1.9 is typical of step 2 in a finite element analysis: creating the finite element model.

While various finite element programs handle the data input step differently, the sequence of commands in Fig. 1.9 is typical of the "creation phase" of finite element analysis. Each line is annotated with a comment

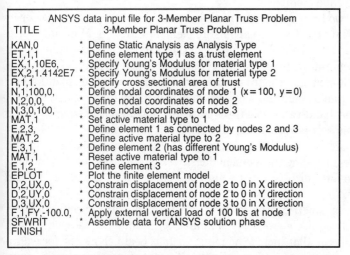

```
            ANSYS data input file for 3-Member Planar Truss Problem
  TITLE              3-Member Planar Truss Problem
  KAN,0          * Define Static Analysis as Analysis Type
  ET,1,1         * Define element type 1 as a trust element
  EX,1,10E6,     * Specify Young's Modulus for material type 1
  EX,2,1.4142E7  * Specify Young's Modulus for material type 2
  R,1,1.         * Specify cross sectional area of trust
  N,1,100,0,     * Define nodal coordinates of node 1 (x = 100, y = 0)
  N,2,0,0,       * Define nodal coordinates of node 2
  N,3,0,100,     * Define nodal coordinates of node 3
  MAT,1          * Set active material type to 1
  E,2,3,         * Define element 1 as connected by nodes 2 and 3
  MAT,2          * Define active material type to 2
  E,3,1,         * Define element 2 (has different Young's Modulus)
  MAT,1          * Reset active material type to 1
  E,1,2,         * Define element 3
  EPLOT          * Plot the finite element model
  D,2,UX,0,      * Constrain displacement of node 2 to 0 in X direction
  D,2,UY,0       * Constrain displacement of node 2 to 0 in Y direction
  D,3,UX,0       * Constrain displacement of node 3 to 0 in X direction
  F,1,FY,-100.0, * Apply external vertical load of 100 lbs at node 1
  SFWRIT         * Assemble data for ANSYS solution phase
  FINISH
```

**Figure 1.9**  ANSYS-PC/LINEAR data input file for three-member planar truss. Each command is annotated with comments and further explained in the main text. This listing is normally input for the ANSYS preprocessor called PREP7.

explaining the command. We will examine the listing in Fig. 1.9 line by line.

After assigning a title to the problem, the first step is to define the type of analysis to be performed. In this case, we are performing a static analysis. As we mentioned earlier, many programs provide "modules" for different types of analysis. ANSYS-PC/LINEAR provides static and modal analysis modules.

The next step is to define the type or types of elements to be used in the analysis. Most finite element programs provide a number of different element types. Typical element types are truss, beam, plate, and shell. Many programs have considerably larger element "libraries," including elements for special types of problems and structures. We will consider element types in greater detail in Chap. 2.

More than one element type can be used in a single analysis. For example, you could analyze a testing table with legs modeled as beam elements and the tabletop modeled as a series of plate elements. This is possible because the stiffness matrix for each element is assembled separately as we saw in the hand calculation of the truss problem. In this simple example, we are using a truss element. In ANSYS, this element is called STIF1. Since there is only one element type in this analysis, there is only one ET (element type) command. If we had a second element type, there would be another ET command line. For example, the command ET,2,42 would specify an element of type 2, called STIF42, which is an axisymmetric, two-dimensional, solid element.

The next two lines specify the modulus of elasticity in terms of material types. Material type 1 will be applied to elements 1 and 3. Material type 2 will be applied to element 2. Again, since element stiffness matrices are assembled separately, more than one material property may be used in a finite element model. In the truss example, we could assume elements 1 and 3 are made from aluminum, while element 2 is made from copper. Consistent with the hand calculation, we have not included the weight of the members themselves in this example. Normally, the density of the element material would be included unless it is negligible in comparison to the applied loads. Including the element densities adds another term to the load vector in the force-displacement equations. This term is usually called the "mass matrix."

Next, the geometric properties of the elements are specified. Truss elements just require a cross-sectional area since they can take only axial loads. In elements that include bending, such as beam elements, for example, additional terms are required for the moment of inertia, the maximum fiber distance, and torsional stiffness. In ANSYS, each set of geometric properties is denoted as a real constant R. Since we are using only one element of constant cross-sectional area, we have one set of real constants (R, 1).

The lines starting with the letter $N$ define the location of each node in global coordinates. We will discuss coordinate systems further in Chap. 2. In this example, each node is defined separately. As we shall see, it is possible to generate sets of nodes spaced incrementally from previously defined nodes. It would be quite inconvenient if we had to define nodes individually in a model requiring 500 nodes.

After the nodes are defined, the active material type is set to 1. While this material type remains active, defined elements will be assigned this material type. Next we define the "element connectivities" for element 1. Element 1 is connected by nodes 2 and 3. The material type is then set to 2, and element 2 is defined. We then reset to material type 1 and define element 3. We could have defined elements 1 and 3 consecutively and then defined element 2, but then the numbering sequence would be different from our hand calculation example.

At this point, the geometry is defined, and it is useful to produce a plot of the model on the screen to ensure that there are no errors using the EPLOT command. Most finite element programs on microcomputers provide an interactive method of displaying the created model on the screen.

Next, the boundary conditions of the problem are defined. The lines starting with the letter *D* define each displacement or degree of freedom that is to be constrained to 0. Boundary conditions usually include zeroed

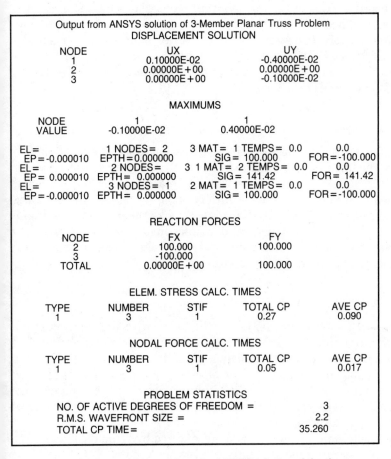

Output from ANSYS solution of 3-Member Planar Truss Problem
DISPLACEMENT SOLUTION

| NODE | UX | UY |
|---|---|---|
| 1 | 0.10000E-02 | -0.40000E-02 |
| 2 | 0.00000E+00 | 0.00000E+00 |
| 3 | 0.00000E+00 | -0.10000E-02 |

MAXIMUMS

| NODE | 1 | 1 |
|---|---|---|
| VALUE | -0.10000E-02 | 0.40000E-02 |

| EL = | 1 NODES = 2 | 3 MAT = 1 TEMPS = 0.0 | 0.0 |
|---|---|---|---|
| EP = -0.000010 | EPTH = 0.000000 | SIG = 100.000 | FOR = -100.000 |
| EL = | 2 NODES = | 3 1 MAT = 2 TEMPS = 0.0 | 0.0 |
| EP = 0.000010 | EPTH = 0.000000 | SIG = 141.42 | FOR = 141.42 |
| EL = | 3 NODES = 1 | 2 MAT = 1 TEMPS = 0.0 | 0.0 |
| EP = -0.000010 | EPTH = 0.000000 | SIG = 100.000 | FOR = -100.000 |

REACTION FORCES

| NODE | FX | FY |
|---|---|---|
| 2 | 100.000 | 100.000 |
| 3 | -100.000 | |
| TOTAL | 0.00000E+00 | 100.000 |

ELEM. STRESS CALC. TIMES

| TYPE | NUMBER | STIF | TOTAL CP | AVE CP |
|---|---|---|---|---|
| 1 | 3 | 1 | 0.27 | 0.090 |

NODAL FORCE CALC. TIMES

| TYPE | NUMBER | STIF | TOTAL CP | AVE CP |
|---|---|---|---|---|
| 1 | 3 | 1 | 0.05 | 0.017 |

PROBLEM STATISTICS

| | |
|---|---|
| NO. OF ACTIVE DEGREES OF FREEDOM = | 3 |
| R.M.S. WAVEFRONT SIZE = | 2.2 |
| TOTAL CP TIME = | 35.260 |

**Figure 1.10** Partial printed output from the ANSYS solution of the three-member truss problem.

degrees of freedom, and, in some cases, initial displacements assigned to nodes.

Finally, we apply the vertical load of 100 lb at node 1. A wide variety of loading conditions can be applied to a structure, including pressure loads, initial temperatures, accelerations, and initial displacements. We will discuss boundary and loading conditions in greater detail in Chap. 2.

The input file is then executed by the ANSYS program to produce the results shown in Fig. 1.10. A plot of the deformed shape superimposed on the original model is shown in Fig. 1.11. To check these results, we can substitute the values for $P$, $A$, $E$, and $L$ into Eq. (1.20), which gives the same results as those shown in Fig. 1.10. The output in Fig. 1.10 also gives the external reactions at nodes 2 and 3 and the axial stress SIG and the axial force FOR in each element. The elastic and thermal strains EP and EPTH, respectively, do not apply to this problem. Notice that ANSYS also reports the amount of processor time required to compute the element stresses and nodal forces, the total active degrees of freedom in the problem, and the total processor time for the entire analysis. The term R.M.S. WAVEFRONT SIZE involves the equation solver used by ANSYS and affects the computer time required for the solution. We will discuss this topic further in Chaps. 3 and 4.

## 1.4   A Broader View

Thus far, we have concentrated on a very narrow and simple application of the finite element method, primarily to gain a conceptual understanding of how the method works. In "real life," the finite element method is used to solve a wide variety of engineering problems, ranging from simple truss deflection analyses, like the one above, to highly complex problems in structural dynamics involving several thousand degrees of freedom. In this section, we will take a look at some examples of other finite element applications.

### 1.4.1   A Seismic Analysis of a Light Tower

Figure 1.12 shows a model of a light tower with the light assembly inclined at an angle of 40°. The light tower is subjected to the horizontal ground-acceleration time history of the 1940 El Centro earthquake, which is shown in Fig. 1.13. The objective of the analysis is to determine the transient response of the light tower under the imposed accelerations. The analysis is performed using MSC/pal 2 from The MacNeal-Schwendler Corporation.

The model consists of nine nodes connected by beam elements. Node 1 is the base node and is rigidly fixed to the ground. The other nodes

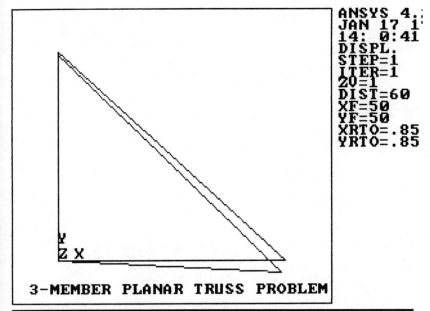

**Figure 1.11** A plot from the ASNYS program showing the three-member truss in its deformed shape superimposed on its original shape. These types of plots are extremely helpful in understanding the physical behavior of the structure under the prescribed loading conditions.

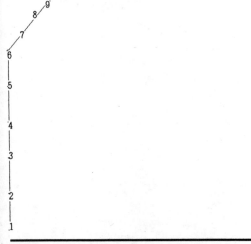

**Figure 1.12** The finite element model of a light tower. The light assembly weighs 40 lb and is inclined at 40° from the vertical axis of the main post. The tower is analyzed using the MSC/pal 2 program.

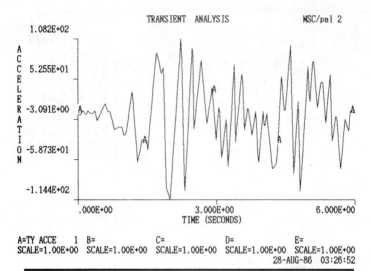

**Figure 1.13** The time history for 6 seconds of the ground acceleration during the El Centro earthquake of 1940. This ground acceleration is input as the dynamic loading condition in the light tower example.

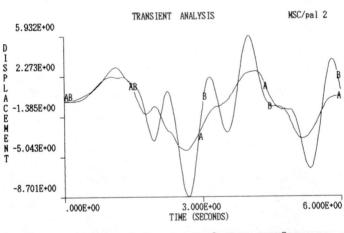

**Figure 1.14** The transient response of the light tower and the ground to the time history of Fig. 1.13. Notice that curve A represents the displacement of the ground (node 1), while B represents the displacement of the tower (nodes 1 through 9).

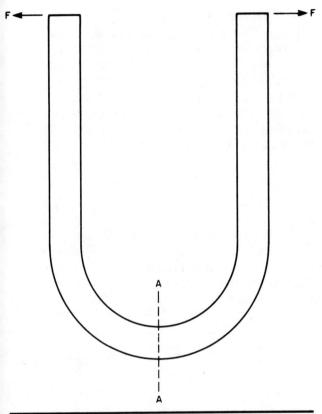

**Figure 1.15**   A schematic of a U-shaped steel bar analyzed for stress at cross-section *A–A* when subjected to equal and opposite tensile forces at its ends.

each have 3 DOF, $X$ and $Y$ translations, and a $Z$ rotation. In the analysis, the acceleration time history of Fig. 1.13 is input as the loading condition of the problem, and the displacements of the light tower are computed as a function of time. The displacements of the light tower and the ground are shown in Fig. 1.14. Normally, the analysis would also include stress results to check the adequacy of the light installation under the prescribed loads.

In contrast to the static analysis in our truss example, this problem consists of time-varying loads, and the numerical solution is much more complex. Rather than solving simultaneous linear algebraic equations, dynamic analyses require the solution of coupled ordinary differential equations. We will discuss seismic and dynamic analysis in greater detail in Chaps. 2 and 8.

### 1.4.2  Static Analysis of a U-Shaped Bar

Figure 1.15 shows a U-shaped bar, loaded at its ends by equal and opposite forces. The model consists of half of the bar since it is symmetrical about cross-section $A$–$A$. The objective of the analysis is to obtain the stress at cross-section $A$–$A$ due to the tensile loads.

The model is shown in Fig. 1.16. It consists of 153 nodes and 64 elements. Three-dimensional, isoparametric 8-node elements are used in this problem, and there are 444 active DOF. The analysis is performed with ANSYS-PC/LINEAR.

### 1.4.3  Intersecting Cylinders

As a final example, Fig. 1.17 shows a finite element model (MSC/pal 2) of intersecting cylinders, typical of a nozzle-pipe configuration. The inter-section is analyzed for stress under internal pressure. Note that the element mesh is more refined in the area of the intersection. Stresses will be higher in the area of the intersection, and more accurate results can be obtained by increasing the number of elements. We will look closely at the issue of mesh refinement in Chap. 4.

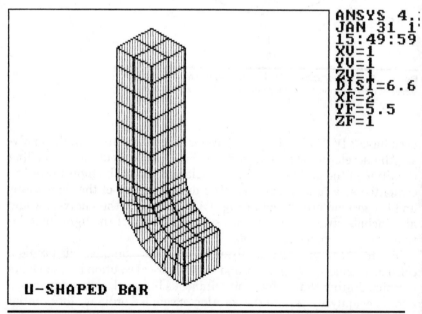

**Figure 1.16**  The finite element model of half of the U-shaped bar. Due to its symmetry, only half of the bar is modeled, saving storage space and execution time. Notice that the plot uses hidden lines for the rear elements of the structure.

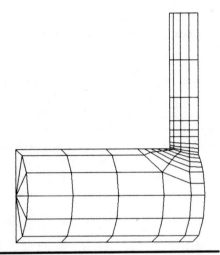

**Figure 1.17**  Intersecting cylinders modeled using the MSC/pal 2 program. Notice that the mesh is more refined at the point of intersection where stress concentrations would be expected to occur.

## 1.5  A Brief History

Finite element analysis was first termed as such by R. W. Clough in a paper on plane stress analysis, published in 1960 (Ref. 4). However, the roots of finite element analysis go back to the Ritz method of numerical analysis, first introduced in 1909. Using minimization principles from the calculus of variations, R. Courant applied the Ritz method to obtain "piecewise approximations" of solutions for problems of equilibrium and vibrations in 1943 (Ref. 5), and further development of these ideas continued through the 1940s and early 1950s. By 1953, engineers began to use computers to solve structural problems.

The paper by M. J. Turner, R. W. Clough, H. C. Martin, and L. J. Topp, published in 1956, is considered a major turning point in the development of finite element analysis (Ref. 6). The paper dealt with the "stiffness and deflection of complex structures" and contributed to much broader interest in numerical analysis among engineers. By 1960, when the term "finite element" was coined, numerical analysis of engineering structures using high-speed digital computers was advancing rapidly in the aeronautics and space industries.

But it was only in 1963 that finite element analysis was actually recognized as a variation of the Rayleigh-Ritz method used in variational calculus (Ref. 7). This recognition established finite element analysis as a serious academic discipline and led to much broader research and to its application to heat transfer and fluid mechanics problems, in addition to structural problems.

By the early 1970s, finite element analysis was established as a general numerical technique for solving any system of differential equations and found application in a broad range of disciplines. However, until very recently, finite element analysis was limited to expensive mainframe computers and was therefore primarily used by the aeronautics, automotive, defense, and nuclear industries. With the dramatic decline of hardware and processing costs, finite element analysis is accessible to virtually every engineer and scientist and is gaining widespread acceptance as a powerful and economical analytical tool.

## References

1. Bathe, K.-J., and E. L. Wilson: *Numerical Methods in Finite Element Analysis*, Prentice-Hall, Englewood Cliffs, N.J., 1976.
2. Strang, G.: *Linear Algebra and its Applications*, Academic Press, New York, 1976.
3. Timoshenko, S. P., and J. M. Gere: *Mechanics of Materials*, Van Nostrand, New York, 1972.
4. Clough, R. W.: "The Finite Element Method in Plane Stress Analysis," *Proceedings of the Second Conference on Electronic Computation*, American Society of Civil Engineers, New York, 1960, pp. 345–377.
5. Courant, R.: "Variational Methods for the Solution of Problems of Equilibrium and Vibrations," *Bulletin of the American Mathematical Society*, vol. 49, 1943, pp. 1–23.
6. Turner, M. J., R. W. Clough, H. C. Martin, and L. J. Topp: "Stiffness and Deflection Analysis of Complex Structures," *Journal of Aeronautical Sciences*, vol. 23, no. 9, 1956, pp. 805–823.
7. Melosh, R. J.: "Basis for Derivation of Matrices for the Direct Stiffness Method," *Journal of American Institute for Aeronautics and Astronautics*, vol. 1, 1965, pp. 1631–1637.

# 2

# Elements, Loads, and Boundary Conditions

Finite element analysis enables us to mathematically simulate physical structures and their loading conditions. The accuracy of an analysis, however, depends entirely on the information entered by the finite element user or analyst. The analyst must define the structure's geometry and select the types of elements that most accurately resemble the behavior of the actual structure. The material of the structure and the boundary conditions and loads must be modeled accurately. In short, the user must understand the physics of the problem and supply the finite element program with accurate physical data.

In this chapter, the input data required by finite element programs are described. This includes geometric coordinate systems, material properties, the most common element types, boundary conditions, and the basic types of loading considered in this book. In addition, we review the topic of stress and strain, which is helpful in understanding the behavior of the various element types. We will also briefly look at the typical output from finite element programs. Interpretation of the results from a finite element analysis is discussed in greater detail in Chap. 6.

## 2.1 Units

Most engineers in the United States still use the English system of units, while most other countries use the Système Internationale (SI) metric system of units. Fortunately, any consistent set of units can be used with finite element programs.

Consistency of units cannot be overemphasized. If the dimensions of the finite element model are in inches and the defined loads

**TABLE 2.1 Consistent Sets of Units**

| System | Force | Mass | Length | Time | Pressure | Density | Gravity |
|---|---|---|---|---|---|---|---|
| USCS | pound (lb) | lb/G (lbm) | inch (in) | second (s) | $lb/in^2$ | $lbm/in^3$ | $386.1 \ in/s^2$ |
| fps | lb | slug | foot (ft) | s | $lb/ft^2$ | $slug/ft^3$ | $32.17 \ ft/sec^2$ |
| SI | newton (N) | kilogram (kg) | meter (m) | s | pascal (pa) | $kg/m^3$ | $9.807 \ m/s^2$ |
| cgs | dyne (dyn) | gram (g) | centimeter (cm) | s | $dyn/cm^2$ | $g/cm^3$ | $980.7 \ m/s^2$ |
| kg | kg (kp or kgf) | kg/G | m | s | $kg/m^2$ | $kg/G\text{-}m^3$ | $9.807 \ m/s^2$ |

are in pounds, the material's modulus of elasticity, for example, must be expressed in pounds per square inch ($lb/in^2$). Similarly, if loads are input in kips (1000 lb) and dimensions in feet, the modulus would have to be expressed in kips per square foot. If the analysis calls for the acceleration of gravity, this quantity must be expressed in units consistent with the geometry of the model. One of the most common user errors is to specify the geometry in inches and then to apply the acceleration of gravity in feet per second squared. Similar considerations apply to the use of the metric system. Consistent units of length, mass, force, and time must be used at all times to avoid errors. Table 2.1 gives sets of consistent units for important engineering quantities.

## 2.2 Coordinate Systems

Finite element programs use, by default, the Cartesian coordinate system for defining the node locations of the model and for data output. However, most programs also support polar, cylindrical, and spherical coordinate systems. Figure 2.1 illustrates these various coordinate systems. The user establishes the origin and axes of the selected coordinate system and can generally change the coordinate system in effect at any time during model preparation. For example, Fig. 2.2 shows a rectangular shape with a semicircle on top of it. In this case, it would be convenient to define the rectangular portion of the model in Cartesian coordinates and then switch to polar coordinates to define the circular portion.

Most finite element programs distinguish between global and local coordinate systems. The global coordinate system is the overall coordinate system for the analysis. A local coordinate system can be defined relative to the origin of the global coordinate system. This feature can be helpful in problems involving both rectangular and circular shapes. For example, in Fig. 2.2, if the origin of the global Cartesian system is selected as point $A$ (not necessarily the best choice), it would be convenient to define a local polar coordinate system with its origin at point $B$. To avoid confusion, node points defined in a local coordinate system will still be listed in the output with their global coordinate values.

Many programs include methods for translating and rotating sets of nodes or node patterns to accomplish the equivalent of a local coordinate system. We will discuss methods of generating node patterns in Chap. 4.

The coordinate systems discussed so far are *nodal coordinate systems*. In other words, the coordinates are used to specify the locations of the nodes of the finite element model. Some element types require an *element coordinate system*, which is entirely local to the element, for the purpose

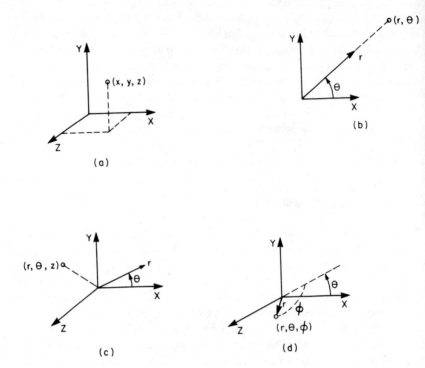

**Figure 2.1**   Coordinate systems for finite element analysis: (a) Cartesian, (b) polar, (c) cylindrical, and (d) spherical.

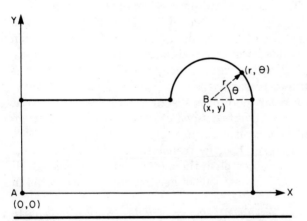

**Figure 2.2**   A shape where it is convenient to use both Cartesian and polar coordinates. Note that point $B$ is the origin of a local coordinate system relative to the global origin, point $A$.

of specifying the geometric properties of the element or for establishing the direction of applied loads. The element coordinate system for a
rectangular beam element from the MSC/pal 2 finite element program
is shown in Fig. 2.3. Further discussion of element coordinates can be
found in Chap. 4.

## 2.3  Material Properties

Finite element programs for microcomputers primarily deal with *linear,
elastic,* and *isotropic* material properties. Isotropic materials have properties that do not vary with direction. Composite fiber materials are

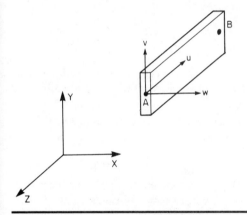

**Figure 2.3**   Element coordinate system for the rectangular beam in MSC/pal 2. The *u* coordinate
always points from the first node to the second
node.

examples of anisotropic materials, whose elastic modulus varies according to the orientation of the fibers. While some finite element programs
can handle anisotropic materials, we will not cover these materials in
this book.

A material exhibits linear, elastic behavior when its displacement
is linearly proportional to the applied force and when it returns to its
undeformed position after the force is removed. Figure 2.4 shows a typical stress-strain curve. The examples and applications of finite element
analysis in this book involve material behavior in the linear, elastic range.
Nonlinear analysis involving plastic deformation is an advanced application of finite element analysis and is generally not performed on microcomputers due to the large processing and storage requirements associ-

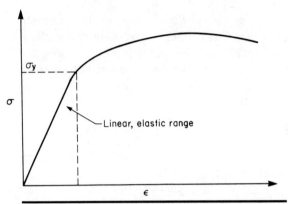

**Figure 2.4**  The stress-strain curve. This book deals with finite element analysis in the linear, elastic range.

ated with it. Fortunately, the objective of a large number of engineering analyses is to determine a structure's adequacy well within its linear, elastic range.

The material properties of interest and their general form of units for linear, elastic analysis are as follows:

1. $E$ = Young's modulus or the modulus of elasticity (force/area).
2. $G$ = shear modulus of elasticity (force/area) which is related to $E$ by the formula $G = E/2(1 + \nu)$, where $\nu$ = Poisson's ratio.
3. $\rho$ = mass density of the material (mass/volume).
4. $\nu$ = Poisson's ratio (unitless).
5. $\alpha_E$ = the coefficient of thermal expansion of the material from the formula $\epsilon = \alpha_E(\delta T)$(strain/temperature).

The following additional material properties apply to heat transfer analysis:

6. $k$ = thermal conductivity of the material (energy/distance-temperature).
7. $C_p$ = specific heat (energy/mass-temperature).
8. $\alpha_D$ = thermal diffusivity (area/time).

Typical values of these properties for some common materials are given in Table 2.2. It should be noted that problems that do not involve significant shear loading or temperature changes do not require values for $G$ and $\alpha$. We shall also see that mass density can sometimes be ignored in certain problems.

## 2.4  Stress, Strain, and Failure Criteria

The primary objective of finite element analysis is to determine the displacements and stresses of the modeled physical structure. The resultant stresses are then compared to some failure criteria to determine if the design is adequate for the applied loads. The failure criteria generally depend on the applications of the structure. In some cases, the fatigue life of the component may be the critical design parameter. In other cases, the peak load that the part can sustain is the important consideration.

Various branches of the engineering industry have organizations that establish failure criteria for that branch. For example, the *American Society of Mechanical Engineers (ASME) Pressure Vessel and Boiler Code* establishes failure criteria for the design of components and structures in nuclear power plants, petroleum and natural gas facilities, and other pressurized equipment.

It should also be noted that the results of finite element analysis may indicate an "overdesign" in which the structure or component is unnecessarily strong for the applied loads. In this case, the designer can specify a weaker, less expensive material or reduce the dimensions of parts of the structure, resulting in a more efficient and economical design.

Whatever the failure criteria, the desired output from finite element analysis of structural mechanics problems is usually stress. We discuss stress at this point to help clarify the behavior of the element types described in the next section. As mentioned in the introduction, it is assumed that the reader has a background in strength of materials, so that the objective here is to summarize the main concepts of stress rather than to explain them.

### 2.4.1  Axial or Uniform Stress

The axial stress in a beam or the hoop stress in a thin-walled pressure vessel are examples of uniform stress. Uniform stress does not vary over the cross-sectional area on which the load is applied. Axial stress in beams is defined by the familiar equation $\sigma = \pm P/A$, where $P$ is the applied load and $A$ is the cross-sectional area.

Another important form of uniform stress is called *membrane stress*. Membrane stress is caused by in-plane strains and forces acting on thin plates (hence membranes) and shells. Figure 2.5 shows membrane stresses acting on a thin plate.

### 2.4.2  Bending Stress

Bending stress varies linearly through the cross-section and, for beams, is given by the equation

**TABLE 2.2** Material Properties

| Material | Density $(\rho)$ (lb/s²/in⁴) | Modulus of elasticity $(E)$ (lb/in²) | Shear modulus $(G)$ (lb/in²) | Yield stress $(\sigma_y)$ (lb/in²) | Coefficient of thermal expansion $(\alpha E)$ (°F⁻¹) | Thermal conductivity $(k)$ (Btu/s-in-°F) | Specific heat $(Cp)$ (Btu/lbm-°F) | Thermal diffusivity $(\alpha_D)$ (in²/s) |
|---|---|---|---|---|---|---|---|---|
| Aluminum | $2.6 \times 10^{-4}$ | $10 \times 10^6$ | $4 \times 10^6$ | $20 \times 10^3$ | $12 \times 10^{-6}$ | $2.96 \times 10^{-3}$ | 0.216 | 0.138 |
| Steel | $7.3 \times 10^{-4}$ | $30 \times 10^6$ | $12 \times 10^6$ | $30\text{--}60 \times 10^3$ | $6.5 \times 10^{-6}$ | $6 \times 10^{-4}$ | 0.110 | 0.0193 |
| Magnesium | $1.7 \times 10^{-4}$ | $6 \times 10^6$ | $24 \times 10^6$ | $12\text{--}18 \times 10^3$ | $14.5 \times 10^{-6}$ | $2 \times 10^{-3}$ | 0.256 | 0.123 |
| Copper | $8.3 \times 10^{-4}$ | $15 \times 10^6$ | $6 \times 10^6$ | $10\text{--}45 \times 10^3$ | $9.3 \times 10^{-6}$ | $5.19 \times 10^{-3}$ | 0.096 | 0.160 |
| Concrete* | $2.2 \times 10^{-4}$ | $3 \times 10^6$ | — | $4\text{--}7 \times 10^{-6}$ | $1.25 \times 10^{-5}$ | 0.200 | $7.2 \times 10^{-4}$ | — |

SOURCE: Data from S. P. Timoshenko and J. M. Gere, *Mechanics of Materials*, Van Nostrand, New York, 1972.
NOTES: Poisson's ratio $v$ is taken as 0.3 for most metals. Properties vary greatly depending on composition, heat, treatment, and temperature.
*Compression only.

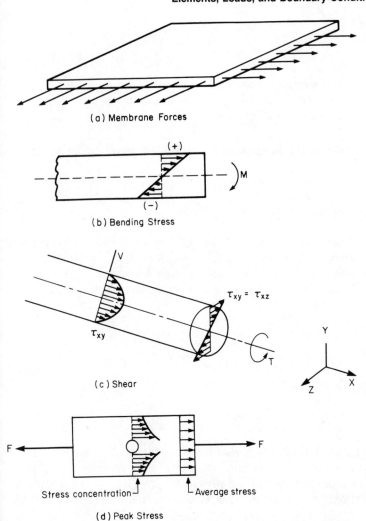

(a) Membrane Forces

(b) Bending Stress

(c) Shear

(d) Peak Stress

**Figure 2.5** Loadings and stress distributions for various shapes. The membrane forces in (a) produce uniform stress. Bending stress is maximum at the outer fiber and zero at the neutral axis. Transverse shear is zero at the surface and maximum at the center. Torsion is maximum at the surface, zero at the center. The peak stress is shown for a notched beam, looking down on the beam.

$$\sigma = \pm \frac{Mc}{I}$$

where $M$ = the bending moment
$c$ = the fiber distance from the neutral axis
$I$ = the moment of inertia

Figure 2.5*b* shows the bending stress distribution over a beam cross-section.

### 2.4.3 Shear Stress

Shear stresses can be characterized as the resultant stresses from torsion and transverse shear loads. Torsional stress is analogous to bending stress, varying linearly from zero at the center to a maximum at the surface of the part. For a circular cross-section, torsional stress is given by the equation

$$\tau = \frac{Tr}{J}$$

where $T$ = the torque
$r$ = the radius
$J$ = the polar moment of inertia

See Roark and Young, *Formulas for Stress and Strain* (Ref. 1), for torsion equations for noncircular cross-sections. Transverse shear in beams varies parabolically from zero at the surface to a maximum at the neutral axis of the beam. The maximum shear stress is given by

$$\tau = \frac{kV}{A}$$

where $k$ = a geometrical constant (see Ref. 1)
$V$ = the shear force
$A$ = the area

Figure 2.5*c* shows the stress distributions of torsion and shear on a beam cross-section.

### 2.4.4 Peak Stresses

So far, we have discussed stresses that are distributed either uniformly, linearly, or parabolically through the cross-section of the material. In addition to these stresses, there are often localized stress distributions in a component or structure due to geometric discontinuities or transient thermal loads. These types of stresses are often referred to as "peak stresses." It must be emphasized, however, that peak stresses do not necessarily cause nonlinear or plastic behavior of the material. The most common form of peak stress is caused by stress concentrations in a component. The reader is probably familiar with stress concentration factors for holes in plates or notches in beams. These holes and notches are geometric discontinuities that cause locally high stresses. Figure 2.5$d$ shows an example of local peak stress due to a notch in a rectangular beam.

Stress concentration factors are empirically and analytically derived for various geometric shapes (see Ref. 2). In fact, finite element analysis can be used to determine stress concentration factors, as we shall see in an example in Chap. 7. To determine the stress at a discontinuity using hand calculations, the nominal stress that would apply if the discontinuity did not exist is multiplied by the stress concentration factor.

Another form of peak stress arises from transient thermal loading, causing local thermal expansion or contraction of the material. For example, if the temperature of the working fluid in a nozzle changes from 500 to 70°F in several seconds, the inside surface of the material exposed to the fluid will cool much more rapidly than the outer material, causing local peak stresses. Peak stresses are also caused by impact and point loads.

### 2.4.5 Plane Stress and Plane Strain

Many three-dimensional (3-D) problems can be reduced to two-dimensional (2-D) problems by employing the concepts of plane stress and plane strain. This is, of course, extremely helpful in finite element analysis where the complexity and execution time of the analysis are highly dependent on the number of degrees of freedom in the model. Clearly, 2-D problems require fewer degrees of freedom than 3-D problems. The important concepts of plane stress and plane strain are discussed in this section.

Plane stress is a condition where stresses in one of the three orthogonal axes are zero. Referring to Fig. 2.6, a thin plate is loaded by forces in the $X$–$Y$ plane. Since the plate is thin, it is assumed that the stresses caused by these forces are *independent* of the $Z$ axis and do not vary through the thickness. The stresses on the surface in the $Z$ direction are zero. There may, however, be strains in the $Z$ direction due to Poisson's effect. The assumption of plane stress is reasonable for thin plates and is

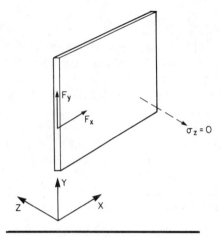

**Figure 2.6**  An example of plane stress. The thin plate has zero stress in the $Z$ direction.

used in finite element analysis primarily to analyze these types of components.

Plane strain is a condition where the strains are zero in one of the three orthogonal axes. Referring to Fig. 2.7 , this means there is no out-of-plane deformation of the cross-section. This situation is quite different from the plane stress condition. In general, there are nonzero stresses in the direction of zero strain (in this case, the $Z$ direction) in order to maintain the condition of plane strain (again, due to Poisson's effect). The assumption of plane strain is valid for long cylindrical or prismatic bodies uniformly loaded perpendicular to the axis of zero strain. A good example of a plane strain problem is the analysis of a concrete dam subjected to hydrostatic pressure. By taking a 2-D slice out of the dam and applying the assumption of plane strain, a large 3-D problem can be reduced to an easily manageable 2-D analysis.

### 2.4.6  Principal Stresses

Most finite element programs report the element principal stresses. In the most general three-dimensional state of stress, there are three principal stresses. The principal stresses are perpendicular to each other and occur on planes where the shear stress components are zero. The principal stresses represent the maximum, minimum, and intermediate stresses at a given point. In practical terms, principal stresses are generally considered in two dimensions ($\sigma_3 = 0$). For this case, the principal stresses are given in terms of the normal and shear stress components as follows:

$$\sigma_{1,2} = \frac{\sigma_x + \sigma_y}{2} \pm \sqrt{\frac{(\sigma_x - \sigma_y)^2}{2} + \tau_{xy}^2}$$

The maximum shear stress is given by

$$\tau_{\text{max}} = \frac{\sigma_1 - \sigma_2}{2}$$

A convenient vehicle for understanding the concept of principal stresses is Mohr's circle (Ref. 2).

### 2.4.7  Equations for Failure Criteria

As mentioned above, most finite element analysis results are compared to some failure criteria to determine the adequacy of the structure being

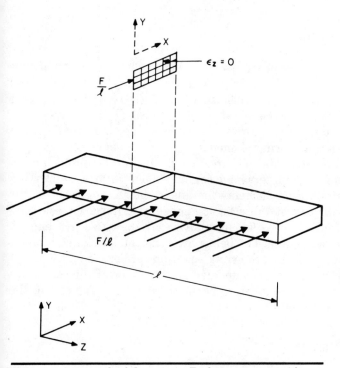

**Figure 2.7**  An example of plane strain. For long structures with uniform loading, a 2-D slice modeled with plane strain elements produces accurate results.

analyzed. One of the most common failure criteria is based on the distortion energy theory first proposed in 1904 by Huber and later by Von Mises and Hencky (Ref. 3). In fact, somehow Von Mises and Hencky seem to have received all the credit as the theory is often called the "Hencky–Von Mises theory." In any case, the result of the theory is an equation based on principal stresses. Many finite element programs report the results of this equation, usually in terms of the failure stress $\sigma_f$. Failure is predicted to occur if

**EDITOR: OFFLINE MATERIAL ON PAGE 48 IS MISSING**

There are other competing theories such as the maximum normal strain theory, the maximum normal stress theory, and the maximum shear stress theory which are elaborated upon in Collins, *Failure of Materials in Mechanical Design* (Ref. 3). In general, these various theories yield fairly similar results. Other failure criteria are specified by engineering organizations as mentioned above. Some finite element programs have postprocessing routines that compute stresses and compare them to allowable code values.

## 2.5   Element Types

As we shall see in the next chapter, some mainframe finite element programs have 60 or more element types in their element library. While specialized applications may require special elements, probably 90 percent of the world's engineering problems can be solved using 4 or 5 basic element types.

There are two main categories of elements: line elements and area elements. Beam and spring elements are line elements, for example. Plate and solid elements are area elements. Most finite element programs on microcomputers have small element libraries supporting the basic line and area elements for linear, elastic analysis. In this section, we will look at these basic elements. Criteria for selecting appropriate element types for an analysis are discussed in Chaps. 4 and 5. The elements described below are based on *small deformation theory,* meaning that the governing equations are based on the undeformed geometry and are not updated as the material deforms, since the deformations are assumed to be small relative to the size of the structure or component.

### 2.5.1   Beam Elements

Beam elements can be used for a wide variety of engineering problems. Obviously, frame and truss structures are modeled using beam elements. The geometrical properties of structural shapes such as I beams, channel sections,

T sections, and box beams are sometimes included as a database in finite element programs. But, in addition, many other shapes can be approximated by beam elements. Piping systems, cable trays or conduits, mechanical linkage systems, bolts, rods, and shafts are just some of the less obvious applications of a beam element. Tapered and unsymmetrical odd-shaped parts can often be modeled as beam elements. In general, parts with lengths much greater than their cross-sectional depth or width should be modeled as beam elements. As mentioned above, we will discuss criteria for selecting elements in greater detail in Chap. 4.

Beam elements are generally uniaxial elements that can sustain compression, tension, torsion, shear, and bending loads. Except for very short beams, shear effects are usually negligible and are usually computed only if specified by the user. The truss element is a special case of the beam element, characterized by the fact that it can take only compression and tension (axial loading).

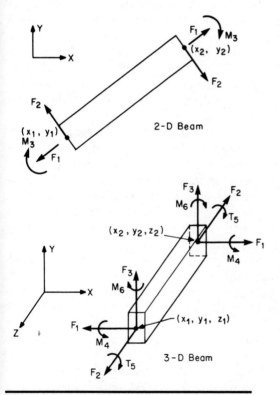

Figure 2.8 Two- and three-dimensional beam elements. The subscripts for the forces and moments indicate degrees of freedom.

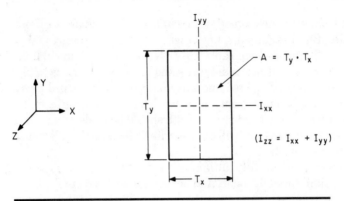

**Figure 2.9**   Beam cross-sectional properties. Because $I_{yy}$ and $I_{xx}$ are not necessarily equal, beam orientation is critical (see Chap. 4).

Beam elements can be applied in two or three dimensions, depending on the problem. Some finite element programs have separate 2-D and 3-D beam elements. Others use a 3-D element for 2-D problems simply by setting the third coordinate to 0. Figure 2.8 shows two- and three-dimensional beam elements. In the most general 3-D case, each node has 6 DOF. A 2-D beam element has 3 DOF at each node. The 2-D beam can be loaded only in tension, compression, shear, and in-plane bending. An out-of-plane load would be required for torsion. The 3-D beam can also be loaded in torsion and out-of-plane shear.

Figure 2.9 shows the cross-sectional properties of the beam element. In the case of the truss, the only cross-sectional property to be specified is the area. As we shall discuss in Chap. 4, beam orientation with respect to the model's global coordinates must be considered when designing beam finite element models unless the cross-section is axisymmetrical. An I beam, for example, has different moments of inertia about its two planar cross-sectional axes, and, therefore, its orientation is critical to the accuracy of the model. Beam elements generally have an element coordinate system or an additional reference node called a "K node" for orienting the beam (see Chap. 4).

Various finite element programs handle beam elements differently. ANSYS-PC/LINEAR, for example, has separate 2-D and 3-D "spar elements" for modeling of trusses and beams with pinned connections and provides separate 2- and 3-D beam elements along with unsymmetrical, tapered beam elements.

MSC/pal 2 provides a 3-D beam element which can be defined as a truss member by specifying "moment releases" at the nodes (see Chaps. 4 and 7). Two-dimensional problems are handled by zeroing the third coordinate. In addition, MSC/pal 2 has separate rectangular, circular, and curved beam elements.

Although beam elements vary from program to program, most programs provide sufficient flexibility to handle a broad range of beam problems.

### 2.5.2 Plate and Shell Elements

The terms "plate" and "shell" are used differently by various textbook authors and also by finite element program developers. Shells are curved surfaces but are often modeled by an assembly of flat plate elements. However, there are also curved shell elements, which are mathematically more complex than flat plate elements. In short, there are a number of theoretical approaches to the design of plate-shell elements for finite element analysis, and there is no real agreement in the literature as to the best approach. (For further discussion of plate-shell theory, see Refs. 4, 5, and 6.)

For our purposes here, we will simply refer to "plate elements," whereby it is understood that flat plates and shells such as pressure vessels and other curved, thin objects can be modeled by plate elements. Some finite element programs refer to "plate elements," others to "shell elements." In some cases, these elements are identical except that they have different names.

The main concept to be aware of is that structures modeled by plate elements must have a thickness that is much smaller than the other dimensions. Typical structures are housings and cabinets for electrical components, thin metal platforms, pressure vessels, propeller or turbine blades, and body parts for motor vehicles. Plate structures are resistant to membrane and bending loads.

Plate elements are generally three-node triangular or four-node quadrilateral elements as shown in Fig. 2.10. In general, quadrilateral plate elements are more accurate than triangular elements, and it is preferable to use quadrilaterals wherever possible. Triangular elements are mainly used at model boundaries or in geometric transition regions where quadrilaterals may not fit. We discuss modeling techniques in greater detail in Chap. 4.

In the most general case, plate elements have 6 DOF per node. In most practical applications, however, some degrees of freedom are eliminated by plane stress or plane strain assumptions. In addition, flat plate theory does not account for in-plane rotational stiffness of flat plates (see Ref. 4). Most finite element programs assign a small stiffness for in-plane rotation to avoid a zero diagonal in the element matrix, which would cause numerical difficulties.

In most plate and shell problems, in-plane rotation is not significant. In cases where in-plane rotation is significant, other element types or

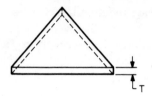

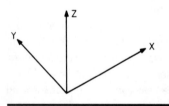

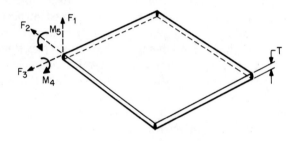

**Figure 2.10** Triangular and quadrilateral plate elements. In theory, there is no rotational stiffness; therefore, the sixth degree of freedom is not shown (see text and Ref. 7).

special modeling techniques are required. An example might be a shaft connected perpendicularly to a flat plate and rotated in torsion (see Chap. 4).

### 2.5.3  Axisymmetric and Solid Elements

Solid elements are used to model structures and components in which the thickness is substantial when compared to the other dimensions. Examples of such structures are valve and gear housings, bearing races, automotive steering knuckles, thick welded joints, and thick-walled cylinders. By using a number of solid elements through the thickness of the part, the stress distribution can be accurately obtained. The U-shaped bar of Fig. 1.16 is an example of the use of solid elements. Solid elements are also commonly used in heat transfer analysis since normally the objective is to determine the temperature and stress distribution through the wall of the component.

While some "thick" components could be modeled with beam or plate elements, the desired degree of accuracy would not be obtained since detailed stress distributions through the thickness are not considered in beam or plate elements. In fact, results are not reliable when elements based on beam and plate behavior are used to model thick components. Criteria for selecting appropriate element types are discussed in Chap. 4.

A three-dimensional solid element normally has 8 nodes, each with 3 DOF: an $X$, $Y$, and $Z$ translation. However, some programs support variable-node solid elements which can support as many as 21 nodes where a high degree of accuracy is required. Figure 2.11 shows a typical 8-node, 3-D solid element.

A special, but actually more common, application of solid elements is the axisymmetric element. In many practical applications, solid parts are "solids of revolution" and are therefore axially symmetric. This means that the geometry and material behavior are independent of the circumferential coordinate of the part. Using 2-D axisymmetric solid elements, a two-dimensional slice of the component can accurately simulate the actual 3-D problem. Again, assumptions of plane stress or plane strain may apply depending on the geometry and application. Figure 2.12 shows a typical application using axisymmetric elements.

Axisymmetric elements typically have four nodes, each with 2 DOF: an $X$ and $Y$ translation. Thus, the number of degrees of freedom is

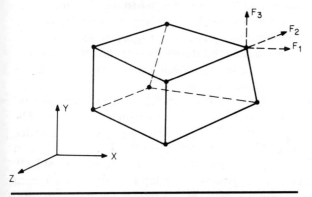

**Figure 2.11** An eight-node, three-dimensional solid element. Each node has 3 DOF.

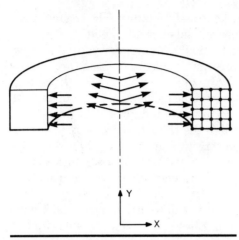

**Figure 2.12** An application of axisymmetric elements. The grid represents 2-D axisymmetric elements used to model the structure. For modeling purposes, assume axisymmetric elements occupy 1 radian of thickness.

reduced by at least a factor of 3 when going from a 3-D to a 2-D solid element analysis. Three-node elements can be used for transitions and boundaries, where necessary.

### 2.5.4   Other Element Types

The great majority of engineering problems can be solved with beam, plate, and solid elements. However, there are situations requiring additional, more specialized elements. As we mentioned earlier, some large mainframe programs support as many as 60 element types for various special applications in nonlinear analysis, electromagnetics, and other fields. For most purposes, the most useful special elements are the spring element, the damping element, and the generalized stiffness element. We will also briefly discuss the generalized mass element.

Most finite element programs support some form of a spring element to facilitate modeling of nonrigid supports or spring connections. The most common element is a uniaxial longitudinal spring element, which has two nodes and a user-defined spring constant (force per unit displacement). In this case, the element has up to 3 translational DOF at each node. Some programs include an option to define the element as a torsional spring, in which case the degrees of freedom are rotational and the spring constant is defined in terms of torque per radian.

It is up to the user to define the stiffness of the spring element. In some cases, the structure may include springs with stiffness coefficients specified by the manufacturer. In other cases, it may be necessary to analyze the support separately to determine its stiffness, which is then input as a spring element or as a generalized stiffness element, which is described shortly.

Most finite element programs also support a damping element for use in dynamic analysis. Damping elements can be used to specify a viscous damper such as a dashpot or shock absorber. For general damping of a structure or component, it is preferable to specify a critical damping percentage as discussed further in Chap. 8.

It is also possible to include a user-defined stiffness matrix in a finite element model, using a generalized stiffness element. The generalized stiffness element is a 6 × 6 matrix representing the coefficients of the 6 DOF per node. The generalized stiffness element is used primarily to reduce the size of a large finite element problem. The user-defined stiffness matrix is usually obtained from a previous analysis of part of the larger structure. By substituting the stiffness matrix for the analyzed part of the structure, the node points of the part can be eliminated, thus reducing the overall degrees of freedom of the model of the larger structure. This may be desirable in dynamic analyses where degrees-of-freedom limitations are usually more severe than in static analyses. Clearly, use of the generalized stiffness element is a fairly specialized application.

Analogous to the generalized stiffness element is the generalized mass element. In many problems, particularly in dynamics, it is often convenient to represent a concentrated weight by a lumped mass in the finite element model. An example is a large valve motor operator connected by a beam structure to a pipe. Rather than model the geometry of the motor operator, it is convenient to simply specify it as a lumped mass. An example of this type of problem is presented in Chap. 8. Mass elements can be used as a single point with 6 DOF representing a lumped mass or as a 6 × 6 mass matrix.

## 2.6  Boundary Conditions

In order to prevent the finite element model from moving freely through space (rigid-body motion), each of the possible degrees of freedom must be constrained somewhere on the model. This is done by imposing boundary conditions in the form of enforced displacements at appropriate node points on the model. The enforced displacements should correspond to the actual behavior of the physical structure in order to ensure accurate results. In this section, we will cover the basic types of boundary conditions usually applied in finite element analysis. Other modeling techniques involving boundary conditions are discussed in Chap. 4.

In general, displacement boundary conditions simulate the actual supports of the structure. There are three basic types of supports: simply supported, fixed or clamped, and roller supports. These supports are illustrated in Fig. 2.13.

A simply supported structure is free to rotate about its support point but cannot translate in any direction. These are pin, ball-joint, or knife-edge supports. To model this type of support, the translational degrees of freedom must be eliminated by specifying zero displacements in the two or three translational directions.

A fixed or clamped support restricts all translations and rotations to zero. Built-in, cantilever, and welded connections are fixed supports. All degrees of freedom must be eliminated by specifying zero displacements in all directions.

A roller support permits one free translation in the two-dimensional case but restricts the other translation and rotation to zero. Roller supports are often used to allow for thermal expansion. Sliders and rollers on tracks or guides are other examples of roller supports.

In addition to modeling of basic supports, boundary conditions are also applied to simulate other modeling assumptions that may be required. For example, in problems involving symmetry, quarter- or half-models are often used to reduce the problem size. In these cases, boundary conditions must be enforced to simulate the symmetry condition.

In some problems, it is convenient to specify an enforced displacement rather than a pressure or force. While enforced displacements are primarily used for specifying support boundary conditions, there are situations where the design calls for the structure to conform to a specific deflected shape. By enforcing the desired displacements, the resultant loads required to maintain the deflected shape can be determined in addition to the stresses. An example of this type of problem is given in Chap. 7.

The application of boundary conditions depends on the type of structure being analyzed and also on the finite element program being used. If the program supports 2-D elements, then the application of boundary conditions in the third dimension for a 2-D analysis is unnecessary. On the other hand, programs that use 3-D elements for 2-D problems require that all displacements in the third dimension are zeroed.

Engineering judgment must be applied in determining what boundary conditions best simulate the behavior of the actual structure. In some cases, it is necessary to try the analysis using different boundary conditions to determine which set of conditions produces the worst-case results. Boundary conditions are discussed further in Chap. 4. Exam-

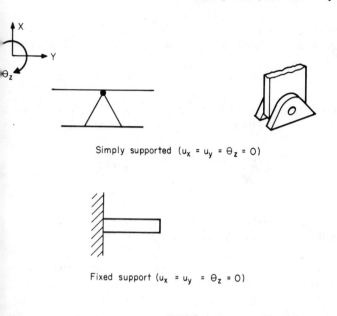

Simply supported ($u_x = u_y = \Theta_z = 0$)

Fixed support ($u_x = u_y = \Theta_z = 0$)

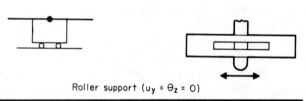

Roller support ($u_y = \Theta_z = 0$)

**Figure 2.13** Boundary conditions typically applied in finite element analysis.

ples of various applications of boundary conditions can be found throughout the example problems in this book.

## 2.7  Loading Conditions

In this section, we present an overview of static, dynamic, and heat transfer analysis. The basic governing equations are presented, and the types of loads that can be applied are summarized. More detailed coverage of these types of analysis is provided in Chaps. 7, 8, and 9, which are devoted to each type of analysis, respectively.

### 2.7.1 Static Analysis

An example of static analysis was provided in Chap. 1. The basic governing equation is

$$\varepsilon F \nabla = [ K ] \varepsilon U \nabla$$

where the terms were given in Chap. 1 [see Eq. (1.1)]. Most finite element programs support the following types of static loads:

1. Nodal forces and moments (concentrated loads)
2. Accelerations and gravity loads
3. Pressure loads
4. Line or distributed loads
5. Thermal loads (nodal temperatures)
6. Enforced displacements (See previous section.)

In our truss problem in Chap. 1, we applied a concentrated nodal force. Flat plate and axisymmetric problems may often involve pressure loads. While various types of load inputs are possible, the loads are ultimately converted to nodal forces by the finite element program. Many programs allow you to define pressure loads as force per area. However, the program will convert this pressure to an equivalent set of nodal forces. Similarly, line or distributed loads can often be specified as force per unit length but are converted to equivalent nodal forces.

Accelerations and gravity loads can be used to apply equivalent dynamic acceleration forces to a structure in a static analysis. The mass density of the finite element model must be nonzero for accelerations or gravity to have any effect. A common application of accelerations is to simulate seismic effects by an "equivalent static analysis" (see Chap. 8).

Thermal loads are simply nodal forces resulting from differential thermal expansion or contraction based on a specified reference temperature. The specified reference temperature is the thermal "stress-free temperature" of the structure. The coefficient of thermal expansion for the material must also be specified. Finite element programs that support thermal loads usually accept input of nodal temperatures. In some cases, element temperatures can be specified. As we shall see, heat transfer analysis is often the first step in performing a thermal stress analysis.

Finite element programs usually allow multiple load cases to be performed using static analysis. This means that a series of different loading conditions can be applied without having to reassemble the stiffness matrix of the model. This is convenient for running test cases using different loads. In addition, postprocessing routines may allow the results of different load cases to be combined. We will discuss combined load cases in Chaps. 6 and 7.

Static analysis is the least complicated and time-consuming form of finite element analysis. It is useful to perform a static analysis even in cases where only dynamic results are required, simply to ensure that the model is accurate and that the boundary conditions are reasonable. It is preferable to discover modeling errors in a static analysis rather than in a time-consuming dynamics run.

### 2.7.2  Dynamic Analysis

Dynamics involves the analysis of structures subjected to time-varying loads such as the forces generated by earthquakes, road traffic, or oscillating machinery. The governing equation for dynamic analysis in its general form is

$$[M]\varepsilon \ddot{U} \nabla + [C]\varepsilon \dot{U} \nabla + [K]\varepsilon U \nabla = \varepsilon F \nabla \qquad (2.1)$$

where  $[M]$  = the mass matrix of the active degrees of freedom  
$\quad\quad [C]$  = the damping matrix  
$\quad\quad \varepsilon U \nabla$  = the vector of displacements (The first and second derivatives of $U$ with respect to time are the vectors of velocity and acceleration, respectively.)  
$\quad\quad \varepsilon F \nabla$  = the vector of applied moments and forces

Equation (2.1) represents a series of ordinary differential equations, one for each degree of freedom in the structure. If there is no velocity or acceleration (time-dependent effects) associated with the problem, the general Eq. (2.1) reduces to the equation for static analysis [Eq. (1.1)].

**2.7.2.1  Modal Analysis**   There are a number of types of dynamic analysis. The most important and simplest form of dynamic analysis is modal analysis (also called "mode-frequency" or "normal-modes-analysis"). The objective of modal analysis is to determine the natural frequencies and corresponding mode shapes of the structure. This is accomplished by applying Eq. (2.1) with undamped, free harmonic vibrations, in which case, Eq. (2.1) reduces to

$$[M]\varepsilon \ddot{U} \nabla + [K]\varepsilon U \nabla = 0 \qquad (2.2)$$

since there are no forces or damping.

If there are $N$ DOF, there are $N$ ordinary differential equations in the form of Eq. (2.2). The solution of each of these differential equations yields a natural frequency $f = (1/2\pi)(\leq\overline{K/M})$ and a characteristic shape or mode shape corresponding to the natural frequency. The lowest natural frequency is called the *fundamental frequency*, and its mode shape is called the *fundamental mode of vibration*. Figure 2.14 shows the three mode shapes for a 3-DOF cantilever beam.

Without going into the mathematics (see Ref. 7), the solution of Eq. (2.2) is of the form

$$(K_{11} - M_1\omega^2)a_1 + K_{12}a_2 + \cdots + K_{1N}a_N = 0$$

$$K_{21}a_1 + (K_{22} - M_2\omega^2)a_2 + \cdots + K_{2N}a_N = 0$$

$$\vdots$$

$$K_{N1}a_1 + K_{N2}a_2 + \cdots + (K_{NN} - M_N\omega^2)a_N = 0$$

where $\omega/\pi = \leq\overline{K/M}$ or $2\pi f$ radians per second, called the *natural circular frequency*.

This set of equations represents a characteristic value or *eigenvalue* problem. The quantities $\omega^2$ represent the characteristic values or the eigenvalues. The natural frequency $f$ is simply the square root of the eigenvalue in units of cycles per second (hertz).

The mode shape for each frequency is defined by the set of characteristic amplitudes $a_1 \ldots a_N$. This set represents the characteristic vector or *eigenvector* for the particular natural frequency. Thus, the terms "eigenvector" and "mode shape" are equivalent.

It is important to realize that the mode shapes represent relative amplitudes of vibration rather than absolute displacements. Since there are no uniquely defined forces in modal analysis, the displacements are arbitrary but proportional to each other to properly define the mode shape. Finite element programs generally normalize mode shapes to create a maximum distortion of unity (1.0) for each mode. The mode shapes are also scaled for graphical output.

An important property of mode shapes (characteristic vectors) is that any two mode shapes are orthogonal to each other. This means that the scalar product of two normalized characteristic vectors is zero. Finite element programs check for orthogonality and will report an error where the scalar product is nonzero. For further discussion of orthogonality, see Biggs, *Introduction to Structural Dynamics* (Ref. 7).

As mentioned earlier, there are as many natural frequencies and mode shapes as there are active degrees of freedom. Since each mode shape represents an independent motion of the structure, superimposing the independent motions of the individual modes gives the complete motion of the struc-

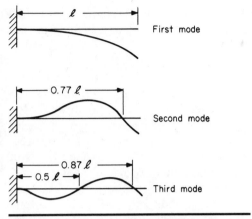

First mode

Second mode

Third mode

**Figure 2.14**  Mode shapes for a cantilever beam
(see Ref. 8).

ture. In most, though not all, problems, only the first few modes are significant. As we shall see later, the participation of each mode in the motion of the structure is determined by the product of the modal vector, the system mass matrix, and the load-direction vectors. This quantity is called the *modal participation factor*.

The number of frequencies and modes to be computed by the finite element program can be specified by the user. Master or active degrees of freedom can also be specified to reduce the size of the problem. This is discussed further in Chap. 8.

Modal analysis should always be the first step in a dynamic analysis. The mode shapes are required to solve more general dynamics problems such as transient response or response spectrum analysis. Modal analysis also provides very useful insight into the behavior of the structure and the accuracy of the finite element model. A quick look at the mode shapes tells you if the model is accurate. Unexpectedly low natural frequencies might indicate modeling errors such as incorrect material properties or boundary conditions. We present an example of modal analysis in Chap. 8.

After a modal analysis has been performed, the system's response to various dynamic loading conditions can be analyzed. The most common types of analyses are response spectrum analysis and transient and steady-state response analyses. Various finite element programs offer different capabilities for analyzing dynamic loading. Therefore, it is important to check that your dynamics applications can be solved by the finite element programs under consideration. For example, ANSYS-PC/LINEAR supports response spectrum and random-power spectral density analysis but does not support transient response analysis. The opposite is true of MSC/pal 2. IMAGES3D performs only response spectrum analysis. These various analysis types are briefly described in the next paragraphs. Further details can be found in Chap. 8.

**2.7.2.2  Response Spectrum Analysis**  Response spectrum analysis is primarily used in the analysis of structures and components subjected to ground motion caused by earthquakes. A response spectrum is a plot that represents the maximum response of a set of single-degree-of-freedom oscillators to a given dynamic input over the frequency range of interest. The response is usually measured in terms of displacement, acceleration, or velocity. Figure 2.15 shows a typical response spectrum. Response spectra, often given for a range of damping values, are empirically or analytically derived from historical earthquake data and testing results. See Biggs, *Introduction to Structural Dynamics* (Ref. 7), for further discussion of computation of response spectra. It should be emphasized that the response spectrum must be applicable to the location of the structure to be analyzed.

A structure or component can be analyzed for response to the input represented by the response spectrum, once the natural frequencies and mode shapes of the structure have been determined. For each mode shape and frequency of the structure, the response (acceleration, velocity, or displacement) of a corresponding single-degree-of-freedom system is represented by the response spectrum. The responses of the structure and of the response spectrum at that frequency are not equivalent but are related by the modal participation factor, which is a measure of the

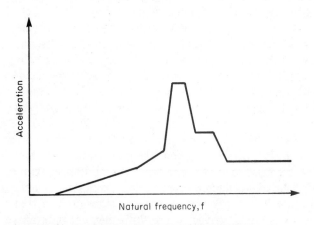

**Figure 2.15**  A typical acceleration response spectrum representing a series of 1-DOF oscillators within the frequency range of interest.

participation of the mass of the structure in that particular mode (see Ref. 7). In most cases, only the first few modes actually participate significantly in dynamic excitation.

In summary, the finite element program first calculates the frequencies and mode shapes of the structure and the modal participation factor for each mode. The response spectrum, which has been input by the user in tabular form, is then used by the finite element program to calculate the equivalent response for each mode by multiplying the response spectrum value by the modal participation factor. The total response of the structure is computed by modal superposition, using a variety of numerical methods. We present an example of response spectrum analysis in Chap. 8.

**2.7.2.3  Transient Response Analysis**  The example in Sec. 1.4.1 illustrates transient response analysis. In that example, the response of a light tower to an acceleration time history was calculated. In the case of transient response analysis, the force vector in Eq. (2.1) is a function of time, where $F(t)$ is the time-varying forcing function. A time history gives the accelerations, displacements, or forces as a function of time for a given dynamic input such as the motion of the base or support of a structure.

In a transient response analysis using modal superposition, the first step is to compute the natural frequencies and mode shapes with the structural damping set to zero as in the case of modal analysis. The response of each mode is then computed for each time interval of the enforced time history, with the user-defined damping included. Modal superposition is then applied to compute the overall system response. The mathematics of transient response analysis is extremely complex and beyond the scope of this book. The reader is referred to Biggs, *Introduction to Structural Dynamics* (Ref. 7), and to Timoshenko, Young, and Weaver, *Vibration Problems in Engineering,* fourth edition (Ref. 8).

In the case of the light tower, the time history in Fig. 1.13 is for the first 6 seconds of the El Centro earthquake. A time history can represent any set of time-varying loads. Appropriate time steps (intervals) for the time history and damping values must be supplied by the user. For this purpose, it is useful to first study the mode shapes and frequencies of the structure. Selection of transient time steps and damping is further discussed in Chaps. 4 and 8.

**2.7.2.4  Steady-State (Harmonic) Response Analysis**  Steady-state response analysis involves analyzing a structure for sinusoidally varying forces or displacements. This type of analysis is also referred to as "frequency" or "harmonic response analysis." In steady-state response analysis, the forcing function $F(t)$ is applied as a sine wave at a specific frequency. By varying the frequency of the forcing function, the structure's response to a range of forcing frequencies can be determined.

If the applied forcing frequency coincides with a resonant frequency of the structure, the response is infinite unless damping has been included. MSC/pal 2 supports frequency response analysis.

### 2.7.3  Heat Transfer Analysis

Steady-state and transient heat transfer analysis problems are mathematically analogous to problems of structural mechanics. In heat transfer, we deal with conductivity, temperature, and heat flows which correspond to stiffness, displacement, and force, respectively. A steady-state problem is analogous to a statics problem, and a transient problem corresponds to a dynamics problem.

The objective of steady-state analysis is to determine the temperature distribution of the part when it has reached thermal equilibrium with the environmental thermal conditions. For example, a nozzle and pipe intersection may have 500°F water flowing in the main pipe with 100°F water injected through the nozzle. What is the temperature distribution in the nozzle after steady state has been reached? This is a typical problem in nuclear power plants when rapid cooling of the reactor is required. Figure 2.16 shows a typical steady-state thermal distribution for the nozzle-pipe problem.

In transient analysis, the objective is to determine the thermal response of the component to time-varying changes in temperature. The analogy to dynamics problems should be evident. In our nozzle example above, a severe thermal transient occurs when the 100°F water is first injected into the main pipe. Severe thermal stresses develop in the region where the pipe and nozzle intersect. It is necessary, then, to determine the temperature and resulting stress distribution as a function of time. A transient for this situation is shown in Fig. 2.17.

The results of a heat transfer analysis give temperatures for each node of the finite element model and heat flow rates through the element. The temperature at each node represents a degree of freedom. Thus, a four-node thermal solid element has 4 DOF, 1 for each node. Once the temperature distribution is calculated, a thermal stress analysis can be performed using a statics finite element program that supports nodal temperature input and can read the node and element data from the heat transfer program.

The governing equations for heat transfer analysis depend on the type of analysis being performed. The primary forms of heat transfer are conduction, convection, and radiation. The rate equations for these heat transfer mechanisms are as follows:

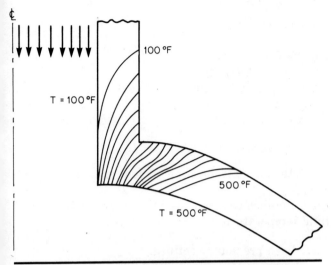

**Figure 2.16** A steady-state temperature distribution for a nozzle-pipe intersection where water flowing through the nozzle is 100°F and the water in the main pipe is 500°F. We are looking at a quarter-section of the nozzle-pipe intersection from down the pipe.

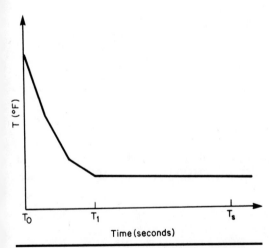

**Figure 2.17** A thermal transient. From $T_0$ to $T_1$, the temperature drops rapidly. At $T_s$, we assume steady state. An analysis would be performed at several time intervals to determine the temperature distribution of the part at these time points.

$$\text{Conduction: } Q = -kA\left(\frac{\delta T}{\delta x}\right)$$

where $Q$ = the heat flow rate (energy)
   $k$ = the thermal conductivity
   $A$ = the area through which the heat flows
   $T$ = the temperature
   $x$ = the length variable

$$\text{Convection: } Q = hA(T_w - T_\infty)$$

where $h$ = the convection heat transfer coefficient(energy/area-temperature)
   $T_w\, T_\infty$ = the difference between the surface and ambient or fluid temperatures

The other terms have been previously defined.
$$\text{Radiation: } Q = \sigma \epsilon A(T_w^4 - T^4)$$

where $\sigma$ = the Stefan-Boltzmann constant
   $\epsilon$ = the emissivity of the surface

The other terms have been previously defined. An additional important equation defines the rate of energy storage in a solid:

$$\frac{dE}{dt} = \rho V C_p \left(\frac{\delta T}{\delta t}\right)$$

where $E$ = the energy
   $t$ = the time
   $\rho$ = the density
   $V$ = the volume
   $C_p$ = the specific heat
   $T$ = the temperature

The finite element formulation of the governing heat transfer equation, as implemented in ANSYS-PC/THERMAL (Ref. 10), is presented below:

$$[C]\left\{\frac{dT}{dt}\right\} + [K]\{T\} = \{Q\} \qquad (2.3)$$

where $C$ = the matrix of specific heat terms ($C = \rho V C_p$)
   $dT/dt$ = the nodal temperature derivatives with respect to time
   $K$ = the thermal conductivity matrix composed of conductivity terms for each degree of freedom in the model

$T =$ the vector of nodal temperatures
$Q =$ the vector of heat flow rates

For example, the conductivity terms for a thin rod would be of the form $kA/L$,
where $A =$ the conducting area
$L =$ the rod length
$k =$ the thermal conductivity

Note the similarity of this formulation to the stiffness matrix terms for the truss in Chap. 1.

Radiation and heat generation are handled by special elements in ANSYS-PC/THERMAL (see Chap. 9). Modeling techniques and example problems in heat transfer analysis can be found in Chaps. 4 and 9. For further discussion of finite element methods for heat transfer analysis, see Myers, *Analytical Methods in Conduction Heat Transfer* (Ref. 9).

It should be noted that the equation for steady-state heat conduction [no time-dependent term in Eq. (2.3)] is a form of the classic Laplace and Poisson field equation (see Chap. 1), which can be used to solve problems in a variety of applications, some of which are as follows:

1. Steady-state heat conduction
2. Torsion of a shaft
3. Flow-through porous media
4. Pressurized membranes
5. Circulation of ideal fluid flow
6. Electrostatic fields
7. Diffusion

The steady-state portion of Eq. (2.3) is

$$[K]\{\,T\,\} = \{\,Q\,\}$$

[See Eq. (2.3) for definition of terms.] In the case of electrostatic fields, for example, you can substitute permittivity for conductivity and charge density for the heat flow rate. Then, the unknown becomes electric potential (voltage) instead of temperature. Thus, a program like ANSYS-PC/THERMAL can be used to solve problems involving electrostatic fields. Swanson Analysis Systems, Inc., *ANSYS-PC/ THERMAL User's Manual* (Ref. 10) gives the appropriate variables that should be substituted into ANSYS-PC/THERMAL for the above types of analysis.

## 2.8  Finite Element Analysis Output

The output from a finite element analysis depends on the types of elements that are used and the type of analysis. All finite element analyses produce a nodal solution which gives the nodal displacements or, in the case of heat transfer analysis, the nodal temperatures. External forces and reaction forces are generally reported, if applicable. A modal analysis reports the natural frequencies and mode shapes of the structure. Transient analyses report the nodal displacements for each time step of the analysis.

Element output depends on the type of element. For example, truss elements report axial force and axial stress. Beam elements report the bending moment, axial force, and axial and bending stresses. Most programs also combine bending and axial stresses to give a total compressive and tensile stress in the beam.

Plate and shell elements report membrane and bending stresses, principal stresses, and moments and pressures. Solid elements report various stress components depending on the modeling assumptions and loading (e.g., axisymmetric and plane stress).

Most programs will report the maximum stress in the structure. However, for solid elements, it is generally necessary to use a postprocessor to determine the maximum stress distribution in the model. We will discuss postprocessing in greater detail in Chap. 6.

A very desirable feature of microcomputer finite element programs is the ease with which graphical output of the results can be obtained. Deflected shapes and stress or temperature contour plots are generally much more informative than a table of element stresses and nodal forces. We will cover graphical output and general topics regarding finite element output in greater detail in Chap. 6.

## References

1. Roark, R. J., and W. C. Young: *Formulas for Stress and Strain*, 5th ed., McGraw-Hill, New York, 1975.
2. Timoshenko, S. P., and J. M. Gere: *Mechanics of Materials*, Van Nostrand, New York, 1972.
3. Collins, J. A.: *Failure of Materials in Mechanical Design*, Wiley, New York, 1981.
4. Cook, Robert: *Concepts and Applications of Finite Element Analysis*, 2d ed., Wiley, New York, 1981.
5. Zienkiewicz, O. C.: *The Finite Element Method*, 3d ed., McGraw-Hill, New York, 1979.
6. Bathe, K.-J., and Edward L. Wilson: *Numerical Methods in Finite Element Analysis*, Prentice-Hall, Englewood Cliffs, N.J., 1976.
7. Biggs, John M.: *Introduction to Structural Dynamics*, McGraw-Hill, New York, 1964.
8. Timoshenko, S. P., J. M. Young, and W. Weaver: *Vibration Problems in Engineering*, 4th ed., Wiley, New York, 1974.
9. Myers, Glen E.: *Analytical Methods in Conduction Heat Transfer*, McGraw-Hill, New York, 1971.
10. Swanson Analysis Systems, Inc.: *ANSYS-PC/THERMAL User's Manual*, March 1986 (for ANSYS Revision 4.2), Houston, Pa.

# 3

# The Hardware and Software

In this chapter, we will look at the hardware and software required for finite element analysis. Finite element analysis can be performed using a wide variety of computers and finite element programs. The choice of hardware and software is largely dependent on the type of analysis being performed and, of course, on cost and time constraints. We will examine these issues in this chapter. Before doing so, we will review the basic components of the computer and how they are used by finite element programs. A clear understanding of how finite element software utilizes the computer is helpful when making decisions as to what hardware and software should be applied to solve a particular problem.

In this book, the primary emphasis is on the use of microcomputers for solution of finite element problems. However, it is important to understand the limitations of the microcomputer and its relationship to its more powerful cousins, mini and mainframe computers. Although the boundaries between these various types of computers have become increasingly blurred as microprocessor technology has become more sophisticated, we will establish definitions of these types of computers for the purposes of this book and then examine the capabilities, advantages, and disadvantages of each type of computer. In addition, the topic of "uploading" and "downloading" analyses between micro and mainframe computers is discussed.

Having examined the hardware options, we will take a look at finite element software. Over the years, several programs have become dominant in the industry. We will present an overview of these major finite element codes and discuss how they fit in with microcomputers.

## 3.1  Review of Computer Fundamentals

In general, all computers have three main components: a central processing unit (CPU), internal read/write or random-access memory (RAM), and external storage in the form of disk or tape drives.

### 3.1.1  The CPU

The CPU is the heart of the system and executes the instructions of the computer program(s) running on the computer. The CPU is generally a single chip for which a specific instruction set is designed and incorporated into the computer's operating system. In the case of larger computers, there may be multiple CPUs with special processors for input/output (I/O) and control of peripherals such as printers, disk drives, and modems. We will discuss the differences between various computer types later in this chapter.

As an example, the IBM PC is equipped with a CPU designed and manufactured by Intel Corporation. The CPU is the Intel 8088 and is used primarily with the MS-DOS (disk operating system) from Microsoft Corporation.[1] The Intel 8088 is a 16-bit processor, meaning in loose terms that it can process 16 bits (0s or 1s) of data at one time. In addition, for mathematical, number-crunching tasks, an optional Intel 8087 numeric coprocessor is available, which is installed in an empty socket next to the main 8088 CPU. The 8087 can process 80 bits of data at one time and can therefore execute numerical calculations much faster than the 8088. Almost all finite element programs for the IBM PC or compatible microcomputer require the numeric coprocessor to be installed. Numeric coprocessors are also commonly referred to as "floating-point processors."

The CPU executes instructions according to a "machine cycle," the period of which is controlled by an oscillating crystal, called the "machine clock" or "timer." The Intel 8088 in the IBM PC operates at a clock rate of 4.77 million cycles per second (4.77 MHz). The bit size (sometimes called the "word size") and the clock rate of the CPU are the most significant, though not the only, parameters that determine the processing power and speed of the computer. The memory addressing capacity, input/output speed, and the data transfer capacity (data-bus width) are other crucial factors.

---

[1] Other operating systems such as UNIX and XENIX are available for the Intel 8088 but have remained in relative obscurity due to the popularity of MS-DOS. IBM provides its own proprietary version of MS-DOS called PC-DOS.

### 3.1.2 Memory

The internal memory capacity of the computer is measured in bytes. One byte consists of 8 bits. One byte can represent a single text character, but more are required to handle numbers. On 16-bit microcomputers, integers are stored in 2 bytes, single-precision numbers (7 or fewer digits) are stored in 4 bytes, and double-precision numbers (8 to 16 digits) are stored in 8 bytes. Most finite element programs use double-precision numbers to avoid numerical round-off errors.

Internal memory used for storing data input by the user or the computer program is "volatile" read/write or random-access memory (RAM). When the computer is turned off, information in RAM is lost. Data that is to be saved is written to an external storage device such as a disk or tape drive before shutting down the computer. Read-only memory (ROM) contains permanently coded instructions that are part of the CPU and peripheral processor instruction set.

The internal memory capacity or maximum "core" size of the computer is dependent on the amount of memory that can be addressed by the computer's CPU and also on the memory handling capacity of the computer operating system. For example, the Intel 8088 can address 1 million bytes (1 Mbyte) of memory. However, as far as the user is concerned, the MS-DOS (as of Version 3.1) can address only 640,000 bytes (640K bytes) of core memory (RAM). Additional memory may be used as an external storage device, called a "RAM disk" or "virtual memory." We will discuss RAM disks and virtual memory later in this section.

### 3.1.3 External Storage

Data is stored externally either on disk or tape drives. On larger computers, a disk or tape unit can store from 20 to more than 500M bytes of data. On microcomputers, hard-disk drives typically store from 10 to 40M bytes of data. Floppy-disk drives have a capacity ranging from 360K bytes to 1.2M bytes of data. Of course, these capacities keep increasing as storage technology improves. Compact laser (CD-ROM) disks have capacities of 500M bytes or more, but, as of this writing, are read-only, meaning that data can be written one time to disk and from then on can only be read. This type of read-only disk is useful for storing an encyclopedia or large reference tables of data such as the *American Institute of Steel Construction (AISC) Manual.*

The speed with which data can be accessed is the critical performance factor of an external storage device. Access speed is primarily a function of cost. Disk and tape drives for large computers are typically much faster than disk drives for microcomputers and also much more expensive. Floppy-disk drives are considerably slower than hard-disk drives and, of course, much less expensive.

Regardless of the external storage device used, data can be accessed much more quickly from internal memory. Internal memory has no moving parts such as drive spindle motors and read/write heads, and, therefore, data access is almost instantaneous. For this reason, the use of excess, or "expanded," internal memory as an external storage device is an effective method to improve performance. Of course, when the computer is shut down, the information in RAM must be written to disk or tape. Internal memory used as an external storage device is called "virtual memory" or a "RAM disk." Software must be specifically written for handling internal memory as a RAM disk. When a RAM disk program is executed, the internal memory is actually designated as another external storage device and "formatted" as if it were another disk or tape drive. Many larger computers have software for handling virtual memory built into the computer's operating system.

RAM disks are useful only if you have a lot of excess memory. For example, most finite element programs for the PC use 512K bytes of memory. In a machine with 640K bytes of memory, this leaves only about 100K bytes for a RAM disk since DOS uses roughly 30K bytes of RAM. For most finite element programs, 100K bytes of RAM is not adequate for storing data files during an analysis. The solution is to use an expanded-memory option such as the Intel Above Board, which can support as much as 8M bytes of additional memory. However, the finite element software must be designed to access the expanded memory.

## 3.2  Micros, Minis, and Mainframes: Some Definitions

There are three general categories of computers: mainframe, mini, and micro. Somewhere between the mini and microcomputer is the "engineering workstation," which we will discuss under the category of minicomputers. As mentioned earlier, definition of these categories is difficult and somewhat subjective due to the advances in microprocessor technology and the increasing overlap in processing power in each of these categories. However, there still remain identifiable and significant differences among these machines. The purpose here is not to establish definitive criteria for categorizing different computers but, rather, to set forth some guidelines for these categories as used in this book.

## 3.2.1   The Microcomputer

The microcomputer is strictly defined as a *single-user, single-processor* desktop system with a CPU size ranging from 8 to 16 bits.[2] The main memory capacity of the microcomputer is generally 1 Mbyte or less, and multiuser or networking capability, although available, is not practical for number-crunching tasks such as finite element analysis. For our purposes, the microcomputer is a *single-tasking machine,* meaning that one application or program is operated at one time. Again, multitasking software is available but not practical with finite element analysis. In other words, if you intend to use a microcomputer for finite element analysis, you will not, for example, be able to do word processing or spreadsheet analysis while running a finite element program in the background. Microcomputer programs are normally executed interactively, meaning that the computer executes user instructions immediately rather than in batch mode as described in the section on minicomputers.

Microcomputers generally have one or two 5¼- or 3½-in floppy-disk drives and one or two hard-disk drives with capacities ranging from 10 to 40M bytes. Virtual-memory usage is not a built-in feature of microcomputers, but it can be added with appropriate software and hardware additions. As mentioned earlier, memory-expansion boards are available which support up to 8M bytes of virtual memory.

For use with finite element analysis, microcomputers must be equipped with at least 512K bytes of main memory, graphics capabilities, at least 10M bytes of hard-disk storage (preferably more), and a numeric coprocessor. Graphics boards and monitors can range from a few hundred to several thousand dollars depending on the resolution and color capabilities required. For most purposes, the inexpensive graphics equipment is adequate. Of course, it must be ensured that the finite element software is compatible with the selected graphics hardware. Inexpensive dot matrix printers with graphics capability are generally used for printing, although plotters are available for better-quality graphics output.

For finite element analysis, the dominant microcomputers are the IBM PC AT and XT and compatible machines from other vendors. A microcomputer system suitable for finite element analysis can be purchased for less than $6000.

---

[2] This statement might provoke some controversy since some microcomputers such as the Apple Macintosh are advertised as 32-bit computers. However, the MC68000 processor in the Macintosh is considered a 16-bit processor since it can handle only 16-bit numerical operations.

### 3.2.2  Workstations and Engineering Workstations

Minicomputers are full 32-bit, multiuser, multitasking systems that can generally support up to 40 users. Memory capacities on minicomputers range from 4 to 16M bytes. Due to the large memory capacity of minicomputers, they are almost always designed to take advantage of virtual memory. Systems configured with large amounts of memory can handle multiple computational-intensive tasks such as finite element analysis and computer-aided design (CAD). Most minicomputers require special air-conditioned rooms. However, there are models available which are designed to operate in a normal office environment.

Minicomputers are equipped with disk and tape drives with storage capacities of up to 400M bytes each. Thus, a minicomputer system can be configured with gigabyte storage capacities. Most minicomputer systems can also be networked, allowing machines in different locations to share programs and files from other "nodes" (computers) on the network. Fully configured minicomputers such as the Digital Equipment Corporation VAX 11/780 range in cost from $100,000 to $500,000, depending on the amount of memory and peripherals (disks, tapes, printers, etc.) and other customer-selected options.

Programs on minicomputers can be run interactively or in batch mode. *Batch mode* means that the user prepares his or her data file (a "batch" of instructions) in advance and then submits the file to be executed by the computer. The file to be executed is placed in a queue and is executed according to its priority. A high-priority job might be completed within half an hour (including printing), while a low-priority job might run overnight. In most organizations, the charge for computer usage is assessed according to the priority of the job.

Interactive usage is more prevalent on minicomputers. In this case, the user runs the program directly from his or her terminal. Interactive usage is typical of computer-aided design (CAD) applications and is now more widely used for finite element model generation. We will discuss finite element model generation in greater detail in later chapters.

While minicomputers offer the flexibility and power to support multiple tasks and users, users often find themselves "contending" for resources on a minicomputer. A company may have its accounting system, its word processing system, and its engineering software all on one minicomputer. While one user is running a finite element analysis, another is preparing payroll. Another user might be writing a report, and so on. The end result is poor performance for all users and long waits for output from the printers.

One solution to this "resource contention" problem is to move engineering applications to a dedicated "engineering workstation." Engineer ing workstations are also full 32-bit machines but are designed for *single-user usage* rather than multiuser. However, engineering workstations are often networked with other workstations so that data can be shared among users. The main task of the dedicated engineering workstation is to execute number-crunching tasks such as finite element analysis and CAD.

A typical engineering workstation might use the Motorola 68020 32-bit processor operating at a clock rate of 16.7 MHz. Up to 16M bytes of main memory can be supported, and virtual-memory support is built into the workstation operating system. In general, engineering workstations use the UNIX operating system, which supports multitasking and virtual-memory operation. Workstations range in price from $8000 to $35,000, depending on memory, storage, and networking options. Typical engineering workstations are the Apollo Domain series or the Sun Microsystems Sun-3 series.

### 3.2.3 Mainframe Computers

Until about 1980, virtually all finite element analyses were performed on mainframe computers. Mainframe computers are large multiuser, multitasking machines that provide a central processing facility for large engineering and manufacturing companies, research and financial institutions, and other enterprises requiring high-capacity computing power. Fully configured mainframe computers can cost well over $1 million and require separate air-conditioned rooms and a high level of maintenance and vendor support.

A typical mainframe used in the engineering industry is the Cyber 180, built by Control Data Corporation. This machine has a 64-bit, single-processor CPU and supports up to 130M bytes of main memory. For number-crunching tasks such as finite element analysis, the Cyber 180 can comfortably support 40 users. The Cyber uses a unique scheme of peripheral processors for handling I/O which frees up the CPU considerably for arithmetic operations. For this reason, clock cycle rates are not a particularly meaningful benchmark of performance since tasks are distributed among multiple processors. In general, performance comparisons on multiuser systems are difficult since performance depends on the number of users and the types of applications being performed.

The primary characteristic that distinguishes the mainframe from mini and microcomputers is the processor size, which is typically 60 to 64 bits. The large processor provides the processing power required for extremely large finite element analyses involving 10,000 DOF or more in addition to the capability of supporting a large number of users. Mainframes can also support a large number of external storage units with capacities of up to 500M bytes each. A typical mainframe configuration might include 10 300-Mbyte disk drives or more. As with minicomputers, mainframe operating systems are designed to use virtual memory.

Mainframe programs are generally run in batch mode as described in the previous section. With the advent of CAD and other graphics tools, interactive usage is becoming more popular on mainframes. However, most large analysis problems are still run in batch mode on a mainframe.

Resource contention can also be a problem on mainframe computers. If a lot of engineers are performing large number-crunching analyses simultaneously, mainframe performance can also deteriorate, causing long waits for results.

## 3.3    Finite Element Programs and Hardware Considerations

In this section, we will examine how finite element codes utilize the computer hardware. With this information, we can assess the performance and efficiency issues pertaining to micro, mini, and mainframe computers. We will then take a look at micro-to-mainframe communication and how it can be implemented for finite element analysis.

### 3.3.1    Finite Element Solution Methods

As we saw in Chap. 1, the main function of the finite element program is to solve the simultaneous equations in the stiffness matrix. In static analysis, the size of the problem is primarily a function of the size of the stiffness matrix. In dynamic analyses, the problem size is a function of the stiffness, mass, and damping matrices. In heat transfer analysis, the conduction and force matrices govern the problem size. In all these cases, however, the number of degrees of freedom ultimately determines the size of the matrices and thus the size of the problem.

Recall that the number of degrees of freedom in the stiffness matrix determines the number of simultaneous equations. The number of simultaneous equations *to be solved* is a function of the number of *active degrees of freedom*. The active degrees of freedom comprise the *nonzero terms* in the stiffness matrix. We will see shortly why active degrees of freedom are significant.

As we mentioned earlier, most finite element programs use double-precision numbers, requiring 8 bytes per number. A finite element problem with 200 DOF would have a 200 × 200 stiffness matrix (200 rows and 200 columns). A 200 × 200 stiffness matrix has 40,000 terms. If each term is 8 bytes, then 320,000 bytes of memory are needed to store a 200 × 200 stiffness matrix. This is, in fact, approximately the maximum size permitted for in-core solutions on a microcomputer such as the IBM PC. Most finite element programs require about 250K bytes of memory just for loading the program. After loading the DOS and the finite element program, a PC with 640K bytes of memory has just over 320K bytes remaining to store the stiffness matrix and other coefficients from the mass matrix or the load vectors. As you can see, this explains why finite element programs require at least 512K bytes to actually run an analysis.

In view of this memory limitation, one might conclude that microcomputers can solve only finite element problems involving less than 200 DOF. This is not the case. This limitation actually means that only about 40,000 terms (coefficients) may be stored in memory at one time. Finite element programs are designed so that only *nonzero terms* or *active degrees of freedom* need to be stored in the stiffness matrix. Zero terms are discarded before loading the simultaneous equations into memory. Referring to Eq. (1.17), notice that of the 36 possible coefficients, 14 of them are zero. By applying the additional boundary conditions, we actually end up with a $3 \times 3$ matrix of only 9 terms. By eliminating the zero terms, problems with thousands of degrees of freedom can be solved. In addition, many finite element programs do not attempt to solve the entire set of equations simultaneously in core memory. The stiffness matrix is solved in blocks, and portions are swapped in and out of core memory from an external storage device.

Finite element codes use special techniques for eliminating the zero terms from the simultaneous equations. The most common technique is the bandwidth solution method. In this case, the nodes are renumbered, and, thus, the stiffness matrix is rearranged so that all the nonzero terms cluster near the diagonal of the matrix. There are numerical techniques for doing this, and they are discussed in Bathe and Wilson, *Numerical Methods in Finite Element Analysis* (Ref. 1), and Cook, *Concepts and Applications of Finite Element Analysis* (Ref. 2). The boundary of the band at the top nonzero coefficient in each column is called the "skyline" or "profile." Figure 3.1 shows a typical banded stiffness matrix. Referring to Eq. (1.17), notice that the matrix terms are *symmetric* about the diagonal. Taking advantage of symmetry, finite element codes store only the terms on and above the diagonal. The terms between the diagonal and the skyline are the only coefficients that must be stored in the stiffness matrix.

Some finite element codes use another numerical technique called the *wavefront* or *frontal solution method*. Discussion of this technique can be found in the references cited above.

As mentioned earlier, most finite element codes can work with arrays larger than core memory by solving the equations piecewise and swapping data in and out of core. This is an "out-of-core" solution method.

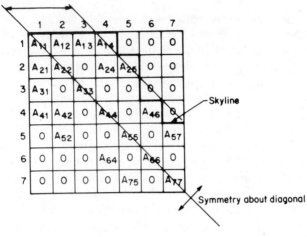

Full Array

Banded Storage

**Figure 3.1** An arbitrary banded matrix. The full array is symmetric about the diagonal, allowing the lower terms to be discarded. Only the terms between the diagonal and the skyline, indicated by the heavy line, need to be stored in the banded storage array. In this example, the semibandwidth is 4.

Some finite element programs use "in-core" equation solvers, meaning that the entire problem must fit into core memory for solution. The advantage of in-core solvers is that they execute much faster than out-of-core solvers. The obvious disadvantage is that the problem size is limited by the amount of available core memory.

## 3.3.2   Hardware Trade-Offs: Time, Cost, and Performance

There are no hard-and-fast rules for evaluating performance on micro-computers versus minicomputers or mainframes. This is because perfor-mance is so greatly affected by the particular operating environment of the computers in question. Clearly, if one were to line up an IBM PC, a VAX 11/780, and a Cyber 180 and perform an identical analysis on each without any other users or tasks sharing the systems, the Cyber would be by far the fastest, the VAX would be a strong second, and the PC would be by far the slowest. In real life, however, mini and mainframe computers are used by multiple users performing a variety of tasks. These types of computers are not cost-effective unless they are heavily utilized. While minis and mainframes have far more memory than microcomput-ers, this memory must be shared among multiple users and tasks.

During peak usage, turn-around time on a mainframe or minicom-puter can actually be longer than on a PC. Users can wait several hours for output from a fairly small finite element analysis run (the term "run" refers to an analysis, task, or job performed on a computer). The primary advantage of the PC is that the resource contention problem simply does not exist. A single-user, single-tasking machine will always give consistent performance. Finite element packages with out-of-core equation solvers can solve large finite element problems on a micro-computer if you are willing to wait. However, microcomputers should be equipped with hard disks of 30 or 40M bytes storage capacity if you plan to run large problems.

Table 3.1 shows the wall-clock times for a range of finite element analysis runs using ANSYS-PC/LINEAR on an IBM-compatible PC and on a VAX 11/780. It is evident that the VAX is always the faster machine. But these times indicate that the PC gives acceptable results for even

**TABLE 3.1   Comparisons of Static and Dynamic Analyses Run on a VAX 11/780 and on a Leading Edge PC (Time in Minutes)**

| Analysis type | Active DOF | VAX time | PC time |
|---|---|---|---|
| Static | 12 | 1 | 2 |
| Dynamic | 17 | 1 | 2 |
| Static | 40 | 1 | 2 |
| Static | 360 | 3 | 10 |
| Static | 444 | 3 | 10 |
| Static | 588 | 5 | 22 |
| Static | 1074 | 9 | 41 |
| Static | 1860 | 9 | 58 |
| Dynamic | 588 | 6 | 69 |

SOURCE: Courtesy of Swanson Analysis, Houston, Pa.
NOTE: VAX times will vary depending on computer usage.

large analyses involving close to 2000 active DOF. It is important to realize that the VAX times can vary considerably according to usage. The finite element run that takes 9 minutes on a VAX in Table 3.1 might take an hour during peak usage, waiting in a queue to be printed.

Central processing, multiuser, mini and mainframe computers offer few advantages to finite element users. Since finite element analysis is usually performed by one engineer rather than by a team effort, a single-user machine is ideal for this purpose. With the advent of 32-bit engineering workstations which can run finite element problems of virtually any size or complexity, the role of minis and mainframes in engineering analysis is diminishing and will continue to do so.

For finite element analysis, the ideal machine is currently the engineering workstation (unless you can afford a CRAY Supercomputer). Engineering workstations are about twice as expensive as microcomputers, and software and peripherals generally cost more. However, for $8000 to $20,000, the engineering workstation offers considerably more power and performance than a microcomputer.

The fact is, however, that many engineering firms have considerable investments in both minis and mainframes along with microcomputers. Microcomputers offer flexibility and ease of use for small- to medium-sized problems in statics, dynamics, and heat transfer. Micros can alleviate the bottleneck on the mini or mainframe by allowing engineers to work on problems independently, leaving the larger machine for large, nonlinear heat transfer or dynamics analyses. In addition, microcomputers can be equipped with adequate graphics capabilities for a few hundred dollars. Obtaining similar graphics capability on minis and mainframes is considerably more expensive. As we shall see, easy access to graphics greatly simplifies finite element analysis and contributes to more accurate and useful results. Finally, microcomputers offer flexibility in software selection. Engineers can take advantage of a wide variety of productivity tools such as CAD software, report generators, database and spreadsheet programs, and so on, for a reasonable cost.

### 3.3.3  Uploading and Downloading

A popular approach to large finite element problems is to prepare the model and input data on a microcomputer and then to "upload" it to the mini or mainframe for execution. One advantage to this approach is that the user can use the microcomputer graphics capability to ensure that the finite element model is accurate and then load the checked data file onto the larger computer for the actual analysis. In this manner, the user avoids having to repeat the analysis due to simple modeling errors and therefore saves both processing time and labor time involved in preparing the analysis. Since most mainframes and mini systems include fees or charges for terminal and processor usage, project costs can be reduced by doing all the preparation work on the microcomputer. A second advantage is that the microcomputer is not tied up for long periods running the analysis. This means that the microcomputer user can work on another problem while the mainframe is executing the submitted analysis.

Most, if not all, finite element programs for microcomputers have some capability of translating data files into formats readable by mini and mainframe finite element programs. As we shall see in the next section on software, some finite element programs on micros are actually smaller versions of mainframe and mini programs. In any case, the file must be in the proper format for the mainframe finite element software before it is uploaded.

The most common method of uploading a file from the micro to the mainframe (or mini) is to set up the microcomputer as a remote terminal of the mainframe. This can be accomplished either by a direct serial connection between the micro and mainframe or by using telecommunications software and dialing into the mainframe using a modem. In either case, the micro and mainframe must be properly equipped to support this operation.

The direct connection requires a special board for the PC such as the IRMA board (from Digital Communications Associates) which links the PC to IBM mainframes. Other computer manufacturers now have hardware options allowing PCs to be linked to their minis or mainframes. With such direct connections, it is a straightforward matter of transmitting the prepared data file from the microcomputer disk drive to the mainframe.

If the mainframe and micro are not directly connected but are equipped with communications hardware and software, another solution is to dial into the mainframe from the micro using a communications software package such as Crosstalk. In this case, the micro user makes the connection with the mainframe and logs in as a remote terminal. The data file on the micro can then be sent via modem to the mainframe. One method for sending the file is to enter the mainframe text editor and open a new file. You can then use the communications software (Crosstalk, for example) to send the microcomputer disk file line by line to the mainframe editor. The editor reads each line into the file you opened just like it would if you were typing in the file from the keyboard. This method is a bit tedious and usually requires some experimentation with the communications software and the mainframe editor. However, it is a workable method for uploading files.

The communications approach is often used for "timesharing" on a service bureau mainframe computer. For example, your company may not own a large computer and primarily relies on microcomputers for day-to-day analysis work. When a problem is too large or time-consuming for the micro, you can dial up a service bureau and submit your checked data file for analysis on the service bureau mainframe.

Downloading files from the mainframe to the micro is a similar process. With the direct connection, the software supports this operation. Using communications software, the easiest method is to "capture" the mainframe file on the screen of the microcomputer. Logged in as a remote terminal, set your communications software to capture-to-disk mode and simply list the mainframe file on the screen using the mainframe text editor. The capture feature will save all data appearing on the screen into a file on the microcomputer disk drive. In this way, output files from the mainframe can be captured on the PC for postprocessing or printing. However, in many cases, output files from mainframe jobs are so large that, at standard phone line communication rates, the downloading time is prohibitively long. Generally, microcomputers are used more for uploading and as remote terminals for the mainframe.

There are other communications "protocols" which can be used to transfer files to and from the mainframe. Kermit, X.PC, and Xmodem are popular data transfer protocols. Of course, both the mainframe and micro must support these protocols if they are to be used successfully. File transfer is easier with these protocols than with the communications software described above. The direct connection approach provides the easiest method for linking the micro and mainframe, but it is also the most expensive.

### 3.3.4   Summary

At this point, the reader may be looking for some definitive guidelines for determining whether to use a microcomputer for a specific problem. Theoretically, microcomputers can solve almost any finite element problem. Out-of-core-based finite element programs can solve as large a problem on a micro as they can on a mainframe; it just takes longer. If you can run your problem over your lunch hour or even overnight, you can run some very large problems on a microcomputer. As of this writing, however, nonlinear and creep analysis, thermal-electric and magnetics analysis, substructuring, superelements, and other advanced applications of finite element analysis are not available on the microcomputer.

There are, of course, problems in heat transfer and dynamics that will simply take too long to execute on a microcomputer. In these cases, you are better off using an engineering workstation or a mini or mainframe. The best approach is to start using the microcomputer for smaller problems (2000 DOF or fewer) and see how long these analyses take. You will then be able to judge what your limitations are and at what point you need to use a more powerful machine. These issues depend heavily on the types of problems you are solving, on what kind of software you have, and, of course, on how quickly you need results.

## 3.4   Finite Element Software

As mentioned in Chap. 1, finite element programs did not become commercially available until the early 1970s and, at first, were relegated to powerful mainframes in the aerospace, nuclear, defense, and automotive industries. During those early years of finite element analysis, several finite element codes became entrenched as the standard codes for certain industries. Gradually, these codes have evolved into general-purpose finite element programs that dominate the finite element software market.

While the focus here is on microcomputers, it is important to be aware of the major mainframe finite element codes since most codes on microcomputers can "communicate" with these mainframe codes.

In the following sections, we will present a survey of the major mainframe finite element codes on the market today and then take a look at some of the codes available on microcomputers. It should be emphasized that this survey is not comprehensive and may overlook some very worthy finite element programs. It is, however, intended to give the reader a general overview of what software is available by presenting descriptions of codes which are widely used in the engineering profession.

### 3.4.1   Mainframe-Mini Finite Element Codes

In this section, the major mainframe-mini finite element codes are discussed. Further information on these programs can be obtained from the vendors referenced at the end of this chapter. General information on a wide variety of finite element software can be obtained from software catalogs provided by mainframe service bureaus. Service bureaus usually have large libraries of finite element programs which can also be leased or purchased directly from their vendors.

### 3.4.2   SAP IV

Two of the pioneers in the development of finite element analysis are Professors Klaus-Jürgen Bathe and Edward L. Wilson. Bathe, Wilson, and Fred E. Peterson developed the SAP series of finite element programs in the early 1970s at the University of California at Berkeley. Early versions of SAP were research versions and not released to the public.

Sponsored by grants from the National Science Foundation, SAP IV, "A Structural Analysis Program for Static and Dynamic Response of Linear Systems," was released to the public domain in 1973. This program became the basis of more finite element codes than any other program in existence. Many companies took the SAP IV program and modified it for their specific applications. Service bureaus such as Boeing Computer Services developed their own versions of SAP IV for their clients. And now, versions of SAP IV have appeared on microcomputers, as we shall see in the next section.

In its original form, SAP IV did not support graphics and was a "batch-oriented program," meaning that the user prepared an input file for batch processing, as described earlier in this chapter. The program is written in Fortran and runs without modification on the CDC 6400, 6600, and 7600 computers. The documentation and source code can still be obtained in the public domain (Ref. 3).

SAP IV initially contained the following element types:

a. Three-dimensional truss element

b. Three-dimensional beam element

c. Plane stress and plane strain element

d. Two-dimensional axisymmetric solid

e. Three-dimensional solid

f. Variable-number-nodes thick shell and three-dimensional element

g. Thin plate or thin shell element

h. Boundary element

i. Pipe element (tangent and bend)

These elements are described in greater detail in Bathe, Wilson, and Peterson, *SAP IV* (Ref. 3).

The SAP IV program in its original form performed linear static, modal, and dynamic analyses, including response history and response spectrum analyis. Modified versions have included heat transfer analysis, nonlinear analysis and larger element libraries. Most modified versions have also added some form of graphics capability.

In general, SAP IV has been used primarily by structural and civil engineers for structural static and dynamic analyses. However, piping systems and mechanical components can also be analyzed with SAP IV.

### 3.4.3  ANSYS

The ANSYS finite element program from Swanson Analysis, Inc. (Ref. 4), was developed in the late 1960s and has been in production use since 1970. Initially, the program was primarily used in the nuclear industry, but in recent years it has found usage in the automotive, aerospace, and construction fields, among others. The program has been under continuous development and currently supports over 60 different element types for static, dynamic, nonlinear, and heat transfer analysis. ANSYS includes elements similar to those listed in the description of SAP IV plus a wide variety of specialized elements for advanced applications, including electro-magnetics, large deflection analysis, and thermoelectric and thermal-hydraulics analysis. ANSYS is probably most noted for its nonlinear and heat transfer capabilities.

Until 1981, ANSYS was primarily operated in batch mode on main-frame computers such as the Cyber 170. In recent years, the program, which is written in Fortran, has been ported to a wide variety of minis, workstations, and mainframes, and it supports interactive capabilities. ANSYS supports both screen and printed graphics including superim-posed deflected shapes and stress contour plots.

The program's extensive capabilities are well suited for advanced applications in many engineering disciplines. While ANSYS can be used for basic linear, structural analysis, there are cheaper and less complex codes available, including Swanson's own ANSYS-PC/LINEAR version, which we will discuss in the section on microcomputers.

### 3.4.4 MSC/NASTRAN

MSC/NASTRAN from The MacNeal-Schwendler Corporation (Ref. 5) represents the other finite element "heavyweight" along with ANSYS. In its early development, NASTRAN was primarily used in the aerospace industry, and, like ANSYS in the nuclear industry, became the industry standard. Also in similar fashion, NASTRAN has undergone extensive development over the years and is now used in a wide variety of engi-neering disciplines.

NASTRAN supports some 20 standard element types plus user-defined element options for nonstandard analyses. The Direct Matrix Abstraction Program (DMAP) allows users to solve problems using their own customized analysis routines within NASTRAN. This feature, of course, is intended for advanced finite element users. Nonlinear analysis, aeroelasticity, and heat transfer analysis are supported by NASTRAN in addition to statics and dynamics. Interactive graphics capabilities are supported by NASTRAN along with a variety of pre- and postprocessing utilities. NASTRAN is primarily operated in batch mode and runs on most mainframe and minicomputers and engineering workstations.

Like ANSYS, NASTRAN has powerful capabilities for almost any engineering application. Again, there are less complex and expensive finite element codes for standard linear static and dynamics analyses. The MacNeal-Schwendler Corporation also markets a finite element program for microcomputers called MSC/pal 2, which we will discuss in the next section.

### 3.4.5   Other General-Purpose Finite Element Programs

There are a number of other general-purpose finite element programs that are widely used in the industry. The MARC finite element program from MARC Analysis Research Corporation is a general-purpose finite element program with particular emphasis on nonlinear and heat transfer applications (Ref. 6). The MARC program features a separate interactive graphics and model generator called MENTAT. MARC is a direct competitor of ANSYS and NASTRAN.

GTSTRUDL and STARDYNE are established finite element programs specializing in linear static and dynamic structural analysis, respectively (Refs. 7 and 8). These are examples of programs with less advanced capabilities than ANSYS, NASTRAN, or MARC but with enough flexibility and power to meet most requirements for basic linear structural analysis.

### 3.4.6   Special-Purpose Finite Element Programs

Special-purpose finite element programs are designed for special applications which require limited element types, materials, and loading conditions. While general-purpose codes can also be used for most special applications, special-purpose programs are generally more convenient for the user since they are designed for the specific application.

As an example, dynamic analysis of piping systems is a common special application for which there are a number of special-purpose finite element codes. These codes have built-in elements for various piping types, sizes, and configurations, thus saving the analyst considerable effort in specifying material and geometric properties.

Special finite element programs for offshore oil platform analysis, soil-structure interaction, and the analysis of electromagnetic devices are other examples of special-purpose finite element programs. Service bureau software catalogs are an excellent source of information on special-purpose finite element codes.

## 3.5   Microcomputer Finite Element Codes

In this section, we will consider some of the finite element codes available on the microcomputer. While most microcomputer finite elementcodes are intended for linear static and dynamic analysis, there are also heat transfer finite element programs available on the micro. Again, the purpose here is to give an overview of some of the more widely used microcomputer finite element programs rather than a comprehensive survey.

The ASME *Mechanical Engineering Magazine,* January 1985 (Ref. 9) presents an informative survey of microcomputer finite element codes.

### 3.5.1   ANSYS-PC/LINEAR and ANSYS-PC/THERMAL

As mentioned in the section on mainframe codes, ANSYS is one of the two largest finite element mainframe programs. ANSYS-PC/LINEAR and ANSYS-PC/THERMAL (Ref. 4) are reduced versions of the mainframe ANSYS code. The major difference from the mainframe code is the reduced number of available element types and analysis options. While the mainframe code supports over 60 element types and 7 analysis options, ANSYS-PC/LINEAR supports 13 element types and 2 analysis options, static and modal (natural frequency) and response spectrum analysis. PC/THERMAL supports 8 element types including a radiation element and 2-D and 3-D solid elements.

An attractive feature of the ANSYS-PC versions is that they are fully compatible with the ANSYS mainframe code. Models can be prepared on the micro, checked for accuracy, and then run on the ANSYS mainframe version, if desired. On the other hand, the programs may be used independently on the microcomputer. ANSYS uses a wavefront solution technique which solves the equations of the stiffness matrix in core but swaps terms to and from disk. Because of this technique, the ANSYS-PC versions support unlimited problem sizes. Of course, you will be limited by your patience and the microcomputer's hard-disk storage capacity.

While ANSYS supports interactive processing, it is really a batch-oriented program. Data can be input directly from the keyboard, but it is generally more convenient to prepare a complete input file using a text editor. ANSYS supports full graphics capabilities including deflected shapes superimposed on the original shape. Stress contour plots can be generated using the ANSYS postprocessor.

ANSYS-PC/LINEAR performs statics and modal analyses of structures using truss, beam, plate, or solid elements. In addition, generalized stiffness and mass elements are available along with a spring element. The modal analyis option can be used to calculate natural frequencies and mode shapes, and it also includes response spectrum analysis, where the user inputs a response spectrum table, and the resulting displacements and stresses of the model are calculated by the program.

ANSYS-PC/THERMAL is a full-fledged heat transfer analysis program, supporting both steady-state and transient heat transfer analysis. Multiple load steps and iterations are supported allowing accurate modeling of transient thermal problems. PC/THERMAL does not support some of the more advanced thermal elements in the mainframe version. However, a nonlinear radiation link, a convection element, and 2- and 3-D solid elements are supported along with a shell element and a lumped thermal mass element.

The ANSYS-PC versions run on the IBM PC and compatible computers. The program requires 512K bytes of memory, the numeric coprocessor, and a 10M-byte hard disk. A 30- or 40M-byte hard-disk drive is recommended for larger analyses.

### 3.5.2   MSC/pal 2

The MacNeal-Schwendler Corporation, developers of the NASTRAN mainframe program, support a microcomputer statics and dynamics program called MSC/pal 2 (Ref. 5). MSC/pal 2 is not a version of NASTRAN but is a separate code written specifically for the IBM PC and compatible microcomputers and also for the Apple Macintosh. An option is provided, however, for translating MSC/pal 2 data files to NASTRAN format. MSC/pal 2 uses an in-core equation solver and thus is limited to problems of roughly 500 to 1000 DOF, depending on the type of analysis. As we mentioned earlier, in-core solvers are much faster than out-of-core solvers, and MSC/pal 2 is a good example of this fact. Of course, the trade-off is the problem size restriction.

MSC/pal 2 supports 2- and 3-D truss and beam elements, a curved beam element, quadrilateral and triangular plate elements, along with shear panel, discrete mass, spring, and damper elements, and a generalized stiffness element. The program performs static analysis and dynamic modal and transient response analysis. Solid elements and response spectrum analysis are not supported by MSC/pal 2.

MSC/pal 2 has strong interactive graphics capabilities, including deflected shapes superimposed on the original shape and stress contour plots. MSC/pal 2 is designed as a companion to larger finite element codes, allowing quick analyses of small- to medium-sized structural problems.

The program, which is written in Fortran, requires an IBM PC or compatible microcomputer, 512K bytes of RAM, graphics capability, the numeric coprocessor, and at least a 10M-byte hard disk. As mentioned earlier, a version for the Apple Macintosh is also available.

### 3.5.3   IMAGES 3D

IMAGES 3D is a microcomputer finite element program for statics and dynamics analysis, developed by Celestial Software, Inc. (Ref. 10). The program, written in compiled BASIC and assembler, allows a maximum of 400 nodes or 400 beam or truss elements or a maximum of 300 plate elements. The program supports truss, beam, plate, and spring elements and can be used for statics and both modal and response spectrum dynamic analysis.

An interesting feature of the program is a split-screen graphics format for model generation so that the model is displayed on the screen as you specify the nodal and element geometry and connectivity. IMAGES 3D also includes the capability to plot deflected shapes, although not superimposed on the original shape.

Celestial Software supplies a translator program for converting IMAGES 3D files to ANSYS and also an AISC code check postprocessor. IMAGES 3D requires an IBM PC or compatible microcomputer and the usual 512K bytes, coprocessor, graphics, and 10M-byte hard disk.

### 3.5.4   SUPERSAP

SUPERSAP from Algor Interactive Systems (Ref. 11) is derived from the SAP IV mainframe finite element program. Additional capabilities have been added such as steady-state heat transfer analysis and graphics capabilities. The program runs on the IBM PC and compatibles and also on PRIME and VAX minicomputers. Problem sizes are limited only by the computer's disk storage capacity since SUPERSAP uses an out-of-core equation solver.

SUPERSAP performs linear statics and dynamics analysis and supports all the elements listed in the description of SAP IV in the previous section. SUPERSAP supports both natural frequency analysis and response spectrum and time history analyses.

The program requires 640K bytes of RAM, the numeric coprocessor, graphics, and at least 10M bytes of hard-disk storage.

### 3.5.5   Other Microcomputer Finite Element Programs

Computers and Structures, Inc., headed by Professor Edward L. Wilson, one of the authors of SAP IV, has developed a number of microcomputer finite element programs. SAP 81 is a program for CP/M 8-bit microcomputers. SAP 80 is a similar implementation for the IBM PC (Ref. 12). These programs support beam and plate elements and are intended for static and dynamic structural analysis. The IBM PC version can support approximately 2000 to 3000 elements. An educational finite element program, called CAL-80, is also available.

Another microcomputer version of SAP IV is SAP 86 (Ref. 13). This program must be linked to a CAD system for graphics output and basically operates very much like the original batch environment of SAP IV.

FINITE/GP from COADE (Ref. 14) is a finite element program that features a Poisson equation solver for solution of a variety of field problems such as steady-state heat conduction and convection. In addition, stress analysis of plates, beams, and axisymmetric solids is also supported.

## 3.6 Some Criteria for Selecting Microcomputer Finite Element Software

Selecting the appropriate finite element package is not an easy task. There are a growing number of software firms offering finite element packages with varying degrees of capabilities and ease of use. In this section, we summarize the most important criteria that you should consider when evaluating various finite element packages.

### 3.6.1 Quality Assurance

Clearly, a program that does not produce consistently reliable and accurate results is not only worthless but also dangerous. Sample verification problems should be obtained from the software vendor. These problems should reflect all the stated capabilities of the program and should demonstrate the accuracy of the program by providing comparison of these problems to hand calculations and results from industry-standard mainframe programs such as ANSYS or NASTRAN.

For example, if the program claims to perform response spectrum analysis, a sample problem of this type should be included. The verification problems should also be of sufficient complexity to give you some confidence in the program's capabilities. All finite element vendors should have verification reports available for your inspection.

### 3.6.2 Reputation and Support

It is always useful to obtain feedback from other users of the program. The software vendor may be able to provide you with references of other users in your area. Of course, a start-up firm may not have many references. If you decide to use a finite element program from a fairly new company, pay particular attention to the issue of quality assurance discussed in Sec. 3.6.1.

An extremely important issue is technical support. Most finite element programs are fairly hard to learn. While they are getting "friendlier," you should expect some initial difficulties with the program. Prompt and knowledgeable technical support from the software vendor is critical when you first purchase the program. It can be very helpful if the software vendor offers training classes in its products.

A related issue is the overall strength of the software company. It is definitely risky to purchase a finite element program from an unproven start-up company. Finite element programs must be maintained. As they are used "in the field," errors and problems are reported by users, and the vendor then updates the program and periodically releases a new version. If your software vendor goes out of business, you are stuck with the current version. If you run into technical problems, you are on your own.

### 3.6.3 Graphics Capabilities

As we shall see in later chapters, strong graphics capability is probably the most desirable feature in a finite element program. Good plots of the finite element model are crucial to your understanding of the analysis you are performing. The graphics functions of the program should be easy to use and versatile. For example, the program should be able to plot the deflected shape of the model superimposed on the original shape as in Fig. 1.11.

The graphics functions should also include the capability to plot stress contour plots (see Chap. 6), showing the stress distribution in the model. Some programs offer this capability only in color, using different-colored regions for each stress magnitude. While this technique is helpful for viewing the plot on the screen, it poses difficulties if you have just a black-and-white printer and want to include the plot in a report. The black-and-white rendition of a color stress contour plot is hard to interpret (see Figs. 6.3a and b).

### 3.6.4 Ease of Use

Until recently, "ease of use" was a foreign concept to the developers of finite element programs. Apparently, the assumption has been that engineers are technically oriented and therefore should have no problem with obscure documentation and a terse, unforgiving software interface. After all, engineers have been using keypunch machines since the sixties. They ought to be thankful they have an interactive terminal to use! This attitude may have been acceptable in the world of mainframes, but it is inappropriate when applied to microcomputer users. A much higher level of user-friendliness is expected by microcomputer users, and that includes engineers.

As of this writing, finite element programs that are truly easy to use are a rare breed indeed. With the advent of computer-aided design (CAD) tools (see App. B), the ease of use of finite element programs should greatly improve. This is one area, however, in which you may have to compromise.

An important measure of ease of use is the program's documentation. The user manual should be clearly written and should explain each feature and command of the program. Example problems are extremely helpful in learning to use the program. A good index is invaluable in finding information quickly. The quality and presentation of the documentation should give you an indication of the overall quality of the program. Unfortunately, some of the best and most established finite element programs suffer from inadequate documentation.

The next item to evaluate is the actual operation of the program. The commands and responses of the finite element program should be easy to understand. The output of the finite element program, such as the stress and displacement results, should be readable and easy to follow (see Chap. 6 for examples). With the aid of the documentation, you should be able to successfully run an example problem without undue effort and difficulty.

It is important to be thorough when judging a program's ease of use. It is easy to be fooled initially by a slick menu system and an apparently simple command structure. When you actually run an analysis, however, you may find hidden problems, such as poor stress output, program bugs, poor recovery from user errors, and so forth. Ease of use must be carefully weighed against the overall performance of the program. You may be willing to sacrifice some ease of use for superior performance.

This is certainly the case with ANSYS-PC/LINEAR, for example. While ANSYS-PC/LINEAR offers excellent performance, its documentation is forbidding, and its commands are terse and hard to learn. On the other hand, you have the assurance of a solid software vendor with many years of experience in finite element analysis.

### 3.6.5  Performance and Capabilities

The overall performance and capabilities of the finite element package are, of course, the decisive factor. Does the program have all the element types that you will need? Does it perform the types of analyses that are required by your work? Can the program handle large enough problems to meet most of your requirements? Is the program's execution speed acceptable? These are all questions that need to be considered before selecting a finite element program.

## 3.7  Summary

While there may be no clear-cut answers as to what hardware and software to choose, there is little doubt that microcomputers offer far greater analysis capabilities than had been anticipated by the engineering profession. Engineers and finite element program developers shunned the microcomputer for several years before recognizing that it is an inexpensive but capable tool for finite element analysis.[3]

As we have emphasized throughout this chapter, the major limitation of the microcomputers is I/O speed, not computational power. With its limited memory, microcomputers are forced to read and write from disk frequently, and these operations slow down processing considerably. In addition, the 8-or 16-bit data-bus width of microcomputers contributes to slower processing. However, considering the cost of microcomputers, perhaps the reduced processing speed is worth the tremendous savings over minis and mainframes, and yes, even over engineering workstations.

In addition, the performance limitations of microcomputers will all but vanish with the introduction of machines based on the Intel 80386 microprocessor. These machines will have all the power of an engineering workstation and perhaps more.

### References

1.. Bathe, K.-J., and Edward L. Wilson: *Numerical Methods in Finite Element Analysis*, Prentice-Hall, Englewood Cliffs, N.J., 1976.
2.. Cook, R. D.: *Concepts and Applications of Finite Element Analysis*, Wiley, New York, 1981.
3. Bathe, K.-J., Edward L. Wilson, and Fred E. Peterson: *SAP IV* Report No. EERC 73-11, June 1973 National Information Service for Earthquake Engineering, 379 Davis Hall, University of California, Berkeley, Calif. 94720.
4. Swanson Analysis Systems, Johnson Road, Post Office Box 65, Houston, Pa. 15342.
5. The MacNeal-Schwendler Corporation, 815 Colorado Boulevard, Los Angeles, Calif. 90041.
6. MARC Analysis Research Corporation, 260 Sheridan Avenue, Suite 200, Palo Alto, Calif. 94306.
7. GTICES Laboratory, Georgia Institute of Technology, Atlanta, Ga. 30332.
8. System Development Corporation, Stardyne Division, 5151 Camino Ruiz, Camarillo, Calif. 93010.
9. *Mechanical Engineering Magazine* (ASME), vol. 107, no. 1, January 1985.
10. Celestial Software, Inc., 125 University Avenue, Berkeley, Calif. 94710.
11. Algor Interactive Systems, Essex House, Essex Square, Pittsburgh, Pa. 15206.
12. Computers and Structures, Inc., 1918 University Avenue, Berkeley, Calif. 94704.
13. Number Cruncher Microsystems, 1455 Hayes Street, San Francisco, Calif. 94117.
14. COADE (McGraw-Hill), 8550 Katy Freeway, Suite 122, Houston, Tex. 77024.

---

[3] One early visionary in this regard was Professor Edward Wilson, who introduced a microcomputer version of SAP in 1982.

# 4

# Modeling Techniques

In this chapter, we present guidelines and techniques for creating accurate finite element models. We primarily discuss modeling considerations and techniques that apply to statics analysis and to finite element analysis in general. Specific guidelines that relate to dynamics and heat transfer analyses are given in Chaps. 8 and 9. In the next chapter, we work through an actual example, applying the techniques presented in this chapter.

As we have emphasized in earlier chapters, the objective of a finite element analysis is to accurately represent the behavior of the physical structure being analyzed. The degree of success in achieving this objective depends largely on the modeling techniques and assumptions employed by the analyst.

There are no cookbook formulas for creating accurate finite element models. Accurate finite element modeling is an acquired skill that comes with experience and good engineering judgment. However, there are specific modeling practices that are recommended and others that should be avoided. Certain guidelines relating to the type of analysis you are performing should be followed to avoid numerical difficulties and inaccurate results. An awareness of good modeling practices and guidelines will help you create better, more efficient finite element models and enable you to "debug" problems.

The techniques and guidelines presented in this chapter have a theoretical basis in finite element numerical methods and in various engineering theories. It is beyond the scope of this book, however, to provide the theoretical background for all of the techniques and guidelines presented. References cited in Chaps. 1 and 2 (particularly Cook and Zienkiewicz) provide many of the theoretical considerations that apply to accurate finite element modeling.

## 4.1    General Modeling Considerations

In developing a finite element model, it is important to recognize that, indeed, you are making a model that is an idealization of a real structure. In real life, boundary conditions are not always as simple as "fixed" or "simply supported." There are no such things in real life as "point loads," lumped masses, or plane strain. However, these assumptions often represent a good idealization of the actual physical problem and, therefore, produce physically reasonable and conservative results. Assumptions can also be misused, leading to inaccurate results. As we shall discuss further in Chap. 6, results from finite element analysis must always be viewed with caution and critically assessed for their correspondence to actual physical conditions.

While we refer to "accurate finite element models," accuracy is a relative concept. Finite element analysis is a method of approximation. Except for the most simple beam and membrane problems which can be compared with theoretical closed-form solutions, finite element analysis does not produce exact results. With proper modeling, however, finite element analysis can give results *within a reasonable degree of accuracy*. The degree of accuracy required depends on the overall objective of the analysis and, as we shall see in Chap. 6, determines the required refinement of the finite element model.

In finite element analysis, there are usually two conflicting but desirable goals: engineering accuracy and computational speed. In general, the accuracy of a finite element model is improved by increasing the number of nodes, whereas the speed of the solution decreases with more nodes. Thus, there is a trade-off between accuracy and computational efficiency which must be carefully considered when preparing a finite element model. The controlling consideration is the required accuracy of the analysis. An inaccurate analysis is worthless, regardless of the execution speed.

An excessively complex or refined finite element model is also not desirable. As one author aptly stated, "It is a waste of time to employ methods having precision much greater than that of the input of the analysis."[1] There is not much point in refining a model to achieve a small improvement in accuracy if the input loads or boundary conditions are a rough approximation. Use of complex elements such as 21-node brick or other higher-order elements (elements with midside nodes) should be avoided unless absolutely necessary since such elements are more likely to be misused and also dramatically increase processing time.

Before embarking on a finite element analysis, it is essential to have an understanding of the physical problem. Without some initial idea of

---

[1] John M. Biggs, *Introduction to Structural Dynamics,* McGraw-Hill, New York, 1964, p. 201.

how the structure will behave under the applied loads, it is very difficult to create an accurate finite element model. If the objective is to determine the stresses in the structure, consider what regions of the structure are likely to be most highly stressed. If you are performing a heat transfer analysis, try to anticipate what regions will experience the greatest temperature gradients. In a dynamic analysis, try to visualize the first mode of vibration. As we shall see, these initial assessments are often of great benefit in determining the design of the finite element model.

The primary rule of thumb in finite element modeling is to start off with a simple model. As we discussed in Chap. 2, the great majority of finite element problems can be handled with simple beam, plate, and solid elements. A great many problems can also be solved in two dimensions. Whenever possible, simplifying assumptions such as plane stress or plane strain should be employed to reduce the size and complexity of the model. Symmetry should also be used where appropriate to simplify the problem.

An initial, simple analysis will always give you valuable information and insight with a minimal expense in labor and computer time. If additional refinement or complexity is required to achieve greater accuracy, it is far easier to implement if you have a simple model to start with. The behavior of the simple model will help you determine where additional refinement is needed. Results from your initial analysis may also indicate that the structure is overstressed and has to be redesigned, in which case there is probably nothing to be gained by creating a more refined model (unless you want more detailed results for the overstressed area).

## 4.2 Designing the Finite Element Mesh

As we mentioned in Chap. 1, the most critical part of a finite element analysis is the "discretization" of the finite element model, or, in other words, the design of the finite element mesh. This is a process that should be done on paper before sitting down at the computer.

The process of designing the finite element mesh can be broken down into several steps:

1. Define the overall geometry, loads, and supports.
2. Select the element type(s).
3. Define the nodes and elements.
4. Define the geometric and material properties.
5. Apply the loads and boundary conditions.

6. Create the model on the computer.

These steps are discussed in the following sections.

### 4.2.1   Define the Overall Geometry

The finite element model's shape and element pattern are entirely defined by the location of the nodes. Therefore, a number of factors must be considered before defining the nodes. First of all, the finite element model should closely approximate the shape of the actual structure. The first step is to draw out an outline of the structure, marking significant points such as corners, discontinuities, support points, and points of load application. An example of such a preliminary sketch is shown in Fig. 4.1.

Next, determine if you can reduce the size of the model by applying symmetry. There are four basic types of symmetry as shown in Fig. 4.2. If symmetry is used, the loads and boundary conditions must also be symmetrical.

Having completed the sketch, the next step is to establish the global coordinate system and its origin. While this step may seem trivial, the location of the origin can greatly affect the complexity of defining the nodes and elements. For symmetric problems, the origin should be along the

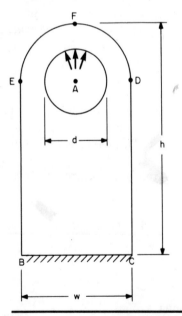

Figure 4.1   A preliminary sketch of a lifting lug. Note that the concentrated load is distributed.

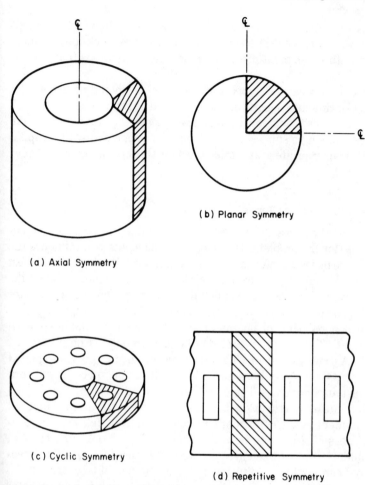

(b) Planar Symmetry

(a) Axial Symmetry

(c) Cyclic Symmetry

(d) Repetitive Symmetry

**Figure 4.2** The four types of symmetry as defined in the ANSYS program documentation (Ref. 1).

axis of symmetry. In problems involving both circular and rectangular shapes, it is often convenient to define the origin at the center of the circular portion, thus avoiding the use of a local coordinate system. For example, in the sketch of Fig. 4.1, we define the origin at point $A$ rather than at point $B$. With the origin at point $A$, we can define either a polar or Cartesian coordinate system without having to define a local origin as we did in Fig. 2.2 of Chap. 2. In fact, we could have done the same thing in Fig. 2.2 by defining point $B$ in that figure as the global origin.

The choice of coordinates is generally up to the user. However, some situations require specific coordinate choices as specified by the finite element program. For example, in axisymmetric problems, ANSYS-

PC/LINEAR requires the $X$ axis to be in the radial direction and the $Y$ axis to be in the axial direction. Therefore, it is important to check the documentation of your finite element program for specific conventions that may be used.

As we mentioned earlier, support and load points should be denoted on the sketch. Continuous supports and loads should be represented with hash marks and arrows as they would be in typical engineering drawings. Concentrated loads and single support points should be designated with a capital letter and the appropriate graphical symbol for the load or support (arrow, pin, roller, etc.).

### 4.2.2  Select the Element Types

Before defining the nodes, it is necessary to determine what type of element is appropriate for the problem. The selection of elements will influence the definition of the nodes. In most cases, your preliminary sketch should suggest what kind of elements to use. In this section, we provide some initial guidelines for selecting elements. Further details on defining elements are in later sections on node definition and creating the model on the computer.

Structures consisting of beams or trusses should be modeled with beam elements. Trusses are modeled as beam elements without moment capability. As mentioned in Chap. 2, some programs provide special truss elements, while others provide methods of specifying beam elements as truss members. The most common method is to simply specify the moments of inertia of the beam element as zero. Another method is to use moment releases. A moment release simply defines the rotational stiffness of a node to be zero. This method is only practical in small problems. Moment releases are actually more often used to specify a hinged connection at interior nodes in the model (see Sec. 4.3.1).

As we have mentioned earlier, any object whose length is much greater than its depth or width should be modeled with beam elements. In general, modeling of beam elements is fairly straightforward as long as the cross-sectional properties are properly defined and the beam is oriented properly. This is discussed further in the next section.

The choice between plate and solid elements is not always as straightforward, particularly in problems involving bending. Plate elements assume no variation in stress through the thickness of the plate. This assumption is valid provided the thickness is much less than the other dimensions. For pressure vessels and cylinders, shell or plate elements are appropriate if

$$\frac{r_o}{t} > 10 \qquad \text{(Refs. 1 and 2)}$$

where $r_o$ is the outer radius, and $t$ is the thickness. Thin wall stress approximations are reasonably accurate for radius-thickness ratios greater than 10, as shown in Fig. 4.3. Thick shell or solid, axisymmetric elements should be used in cases where $r_o/t \leq 10$.

In general, plate elements are appropriate when the thickness is no more than 10 percent of the other dimensions. This guideline should be strictly adhered to in bending problems but does not apply to pure membrane problems (see discussion of uniform stress, Chap. 2). Again, for thicker components, use thick shell or solid elements.

If your problem does not fit the criteria for beam or plate elements, the first step is to evaluate possible simplifying assumptions. Are plane strain or axisymmetry assumptions applicable? If so, you can still create a 2-D model using either plate or axisymmetric elements. See Chap. 2 for further discussion of plane strain and axisymmetry. If you intend to use plane strain or axisymmetry, you should redraw your preliminary sketch to reflect this. If these assumptions do not apply, your only recourse is a 3-D solid element model. Not all finite element programs on microcomputers provide solid elements. See Chap. 3 for information on various microcomputer finite element programs.

Finally, you may require spring or stiffness elements to model support points of the structure. If the stiffness of any part of the structure is

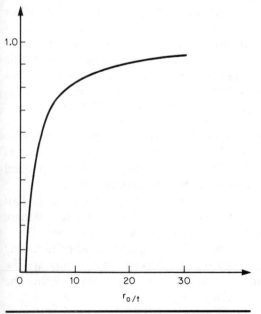

**Figure 4.3** The ratio of thin wall to thick wall stress results approaches unity as the ratio of radius to thickness increases (Ref. 1).

known, this part can be modeled with spring or stiffness elements. Stiffnesses, if known, should appear on your preliminary sketch. If other special elements are required, such as lumped mass or damping elements, these should be noted on the preliminary sketch.

While the above general guidelines should be followed, your choice of elements ultimately depends on the finite element program you are using. Above all, make sure that you adhere to the guidelines and limitations prescribed in the documentation of the finite element program. Various programs have very different element libraries and different limitations. This is particularly true in regard to solid elements.

### 4.2.3  Define the Nodes and Elements

We have arrived at the crux of the matter. At this point, we have a preliminary sketch and have determined what type of elements should be used. The next step is to determine the nodal pattern that best suits the type of element selected and also provides enough elements to give accurate results. In addition, we must configure the nodes in such a way that the elements do not violate certain geometric restrictions.

We are therefore faced with a number of considerations that depend on the types of loads and also on the type of analysis. There are a number of guidelines and rules for finite element modeling that are set forth in various finite element program manuals, conference seminar notes, and other miscellaneous sources. These are usually presented in an itemized list of "dos and don'ts." We will attempt to consolidate these rules in a similar list and then discuss them individually. The guidelines given in this section apply to finite element analysis in general. Additional guidelines specific to different types of analyses are given in later chapters.

*Rules for Finite Element Modeling*

1. In problems involving concentrated loads and/or geometric discontinuities, apply St. Venant's principle to determine minimum dimensions and areas requiring a refined mesh. (St. Venant's principle is explained in the paragraphs following this list and illustrated in Fig. 4.4.)

2. Generally, a more refined mesh is required for stress analysis than for displacement analysis. Heat transfer analysis often requires even more refinement. If necessary, perform a convergence study (see Chap. 6).

3. Place nodes at supports, at load points, and at other locations where you require information such as displacements or temperatures. For example, in a modal analysis, provide enough nodes to define the expected mode shapes (Fig. 4.5).

4. Where practical, use a uniform mesh pattern (equal node spacing). When making transitions from coarse- to fine-mesh regions, do not change the dimensions of adjacent elements by more than a factor of 2. If neces-

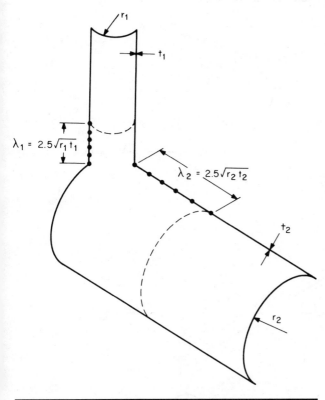

**Figure 4.4**  Attenuation lengths calculated for a nozzle-cylinder intersection. A spacing of at least six nodes is required within the dashed lines. In this problem, the regions beyond the dashed lines do not need to be included.

sary, make the transition over a series of elements to maintain this factor (Fig. 4.6).

5. When using plate or axisymmetric elements, use quadrilaterals wherever possible since they are more accurate in most cases than triangular elements. Use triangular elements only for transitions or when required by the geometry (Fig. 4.7).

6. For triangular and quadrilateral elements, the aspect ratio (length-width ratio) should be kept as close to unity (1.0) as possible. Aspect ratios of up to 5.0 are permissible but should be kept lower than 3.0, if possible (Fig. 4.8).

7. Triangular and quadrilateral elements should not have extremely acute or obtuse angles. Deviations of up to 30°from the optimum equilateral angle in triangular elements and the right angle in quad elements are permissible (Fig. 4.9).

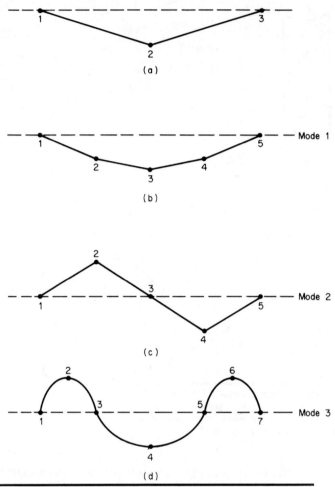

**Figure 4.5** Use enough nodes to accurately represent the physical problem. In (*a*), there are only enough nodes to crudely approximate the first mode for a simply supported beam. Five nodes are required to capture the second mode as shown in (*c*). Seven nodes are required to capture the third mode (*d*).

8. Curved surfaces may be modeled with flat elements but the subtended angle should not exceed 15°(Fig. 4.10). Plate elements should not be warped (i.e., the nodes should all be in one plane).

9. Poisson's ratio should be below 0.5. For materials approaching Poisson's ratio of 0.5, special elements are required.

10. Lengths and areas of line (beam) and area (plate, solid) elements must be nonzero.

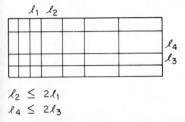

$\ell_2 \leq 2\ell_1$
$\ell_4 \leq 2\ell_3$

**Figure 4.6** Adjacent element lengths in either direction should be kept within a factor of 2.

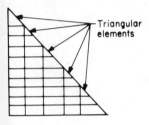

Triangular elements

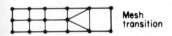

Mesh transition

**Figure 4.7** Triangular elements should be used only where geometrically necessary or in mesh transitions.

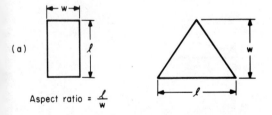

(a)

Aspect ratio = $\frac{\ell}{w}$

(b)

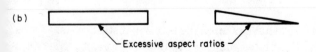

Excessive aspect ratios

**Figure 4.8** Aspect ratios ($l/w$) should be kept less than 3, if possible.

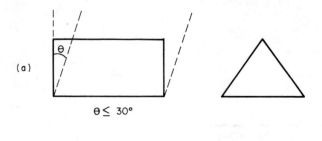

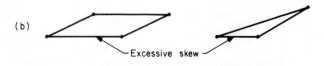

$\theta \leq 30°$

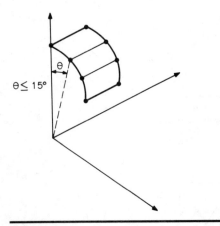

Excessive skew

**Figure 4.9** Excessively skewed elements produce poor results. Try to keep the skew angle under 30°.

$\theta \leq 15°$

**Figure 4.10** The subtended angle for flat plate elements should not exceed 15°.

11. Elements should not extend across discontinuities or thickness changes. Add additional nodes and use more small elements in these cases (Fig. 4.11).

12. Flat plate elements have no in-plane rotational stiffness (see Chap. 2). In order to model flat plates subjected to in-plane torsion, it is necessary to constrain the in-plane rotational degrees of freedom. In practice, however, flat plates must be reinforced if they are subjected to in-plane

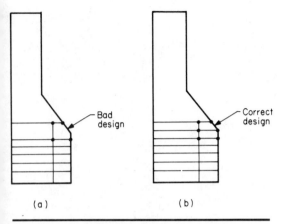

**Figure 4.11**  Do not extend elements across discontinuities. In (*a*), the corner of the discontinuity does not have a node assigned to it. The correct approach is shown in (*b*).

twisting and therefore are not accurately represented by plate elements (Fig. 4.12).

Before working with the above guidelines, the first consideration is to determine the overall dimensions of the model. In some cases, this may simply be the dimensions of the actual structure or component. In many cases, however, you are analyzing a section of the structure near applied load or discontinuity and need to determine how large this section should be. For example, a long section of pipe may have a concentrated load applied somewhere along its length. Rather than model the entire pipe, we are interested only in the area near the concentrated load. However, we have to determine how much of the pipe section should be modeled to pick up the stresses due to the concentrated load.

Referring to Rule 1, the most useful criterion for determining overall dimensions is St. Venant's principle. This principle basically states that localized loads or geometric discontinuities cause stresses and strains only in the immediate vicinity of the load or discontinuity. A good example used by Timoshenko is to visualize a clamp applied to a rubber hose (Ref. 3). The hose is deformed and stressed only in the area near the clamp.

The distance from the localized load to where the effects of the load have dissipated is called the *attenuation length*. The *ASME Boiler Code* specifies an attenuation length of $2.5 \leq \overline{rt}$ for cylinders (Ref. 5). Other sources give lengths ranging from 2 to $4 \leq \overline{rt}$ (Refs. 1 and 4). Attenuation lengths for beams on elastic foundations can also be used for other "semi-infinite" structures such as piping systems and pressure vessels. Attenuation lengths for beams on elastic foundations are given in Harvey,

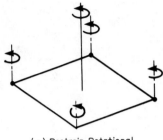

(a) Restrain Rotational
Degrees of Freedom

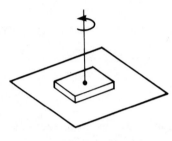

(b) Reinforced Plate

**Figure 4.12**    In-plane rotational degrees of freedom
should be restrained in flat plate problems of
this type, or thicker elements should be used.

*Pressure Component Construction* (Ref. 4) and Blake, *Practical Stress Analysis in Engineering Design* (Ref. 7). Where applicable, attenuation lengths provide a *minimum* size of the model. In most cases, other considerations such as symmetry and support points will require a larger model. The attenuation lengths for a nozzle-to-cylinder intersection are calculated in Fig. 4.4.

Saint Venant's principle is also useful in determining the number of elements required in various areas of the model. Based on this principle, only areas within the attenuation length of the applied load or discontinuity require a refined mesh. Areas outside of the attenuation length can be modeled with a coarse mesh. As a rule, at least five elements are required over the distance of the attenuation length. For example, if the attenuation length is 1 in, five elements of 0.2 in length would be the minimum requirement.

How do we determine the refinement of the mesh? The difficulty is that there are no definite rules for determining the mesh refinement. This is where your initial assessment of the model's behavior is important.

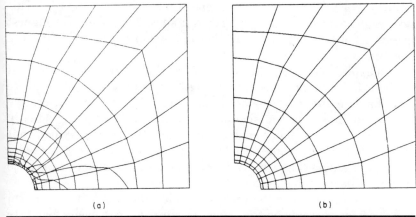

(a)                                        (b)

**Figure 4.13** Stress contours for a quarter-symmetry model of a flat plate with a hole in it and the original finite element model. The stress levels near the hole would not have been picked up with a coarser mesh.

For example, Fig. 4.13a shows the stress contours for a flat plate with a hole in it. Each contour represents an increment in stress (stress contours are discussed further in Chap. 6). Clearly, the area around the hole is much more highly stressed than outlying parts of the model. A coarse mesh would not pick up the high stresses around the hole. A fine mesh in the outlying regions would also accomplish nothing. Figure 4.13b shows the finite element model that produced the stress contour plot. Notice that the model is refined in the hole area and gradually becomes coarser.

According to Rule 2, stress analysis requires a more refined mesh than displacement analysis. In other words, if the primary objective is to determine the displacements or mode shapes of the model, a less refined mesh is needed than would be required for a stress analysis. Heat transfer analysis usually requires a more refined mesh than stress analysis. In some cases, a mesh convergence study may be required. This is discussed in Chap. 6.

In most cases, the best approach is to start with a coarse mesh. Following Rule 3, place nodes at the support points and load points. Use enough nodes to obtain the information you are looking for. It is important to remember that the nodes are your only source of information (element information is derived from the nodes). For example, use enough nodes in a modal analysis to accurately reflect the anticipated mode shapes. As shown in Fig. 4.5, an insufficient number of nodes will yield inaccurate results. For modal analysis, a suggested guideline is to provide at least two nodes per wavelength of the highest mode shape of interest. This guideline may involve some trial and error since the shape of the highest mode may not be evident. For further discussion of this guideline, see Chap. 8.

When applicable, apply St. Venant's principle as discussed above. If no specific formulas for attenuation length apply to your problem, make a reasonable estimate of the attenuation length and use at least five elements in this area. Outside of the attenuation length, gradually reduce the refinement in keeping with Rule 4. This rule states that the ratio of the dimensions of adjacent elements should not exceed a factor of 2. Radical changes in adjacent element dimensions can cause numerical inaccuracies in the analysis.

In nontransition areas, try to maintain a uniform mesh. A uniform mesh is easier to create on the computer since you can easily generate sets of nodes if the nodal spacing is uniform. In addition, results and behavior of uniform meshes are easier to interpret. There really is no purpose to nonuniform meshes except in mesh transition areas or in geometrically odd-shaped areas.

As stated in Rule 5, quadrilateral elements are generally more accurate than triangular elements. This is particularly true for solid elements. The exception to this rule involves the use of plate elements in problems of pure bending and nonlinear problems where triangular elements have been shown to give more reliable results. Clearly, there are situations that require triangular elements such as mesh transitions or geometrical limitations. In most cases, however, it is preferable to use quadrilateral elements.

The length/width or height/width ratio of quadrilateral and triangular elements is called the *aspect ratio*. According to Rule 6, this ratio should ideally be 1.0. Various types of elements have different upper limits on the aspect ratio. In general, try to keep aspect ratios below 3.0.

Rules 7 through 11 are fairly self-explanatory. These rules can be inferred from common sense. The elements in most finite element programs are based on materials with Poisson's ratio between 0.15 and 0.35. As we discussed in Chap. 1, element stresses are derived from interpolation functions, which are based on reasonably shaped elements. Excessively skewed, curved, or zero-length elements will produce unpredictable results or cause the program to abort its execution. Extending elements across discontinuities will cause numerical errors and inaccurate results.

At this point, we have determined the dimensions of our model and have an overall picture of the required mesh refinement. Nodes that identify supports and attenuation lengths should be on the sketch. The next step is to draw the mesh following the above guidelines. Each intersection of two or more lines represents a node. It is important to note that all nodes must be connected (with the exception of $K$ nodes, discussed in the next section). Interior nodes must be connected on all sides as shown in Fig. 4.14.[2]

After you have drawn out the finite element mesh, the next step is to number the nodes. You do not have to number each node, but do specify numbers for the beginning and ending nodes of uniform patterns. This is illustrated in Fig. 4.15 which shows the preliminary sketch of Fig. 4.1 ready to input into the computer. When numbering the nodes, take note of node and element numbering sequences recommended by your finite element program.

Depending on the equation solver used by the program, the node or

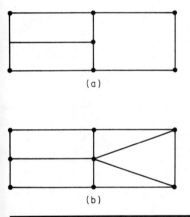

(a)

(b)

**Figure 4.14**  Interior nodes must connected as in (b). The configuration in (a) will cause the program to abort execution.

element numbering sequence can affect the size of the banded stiffness matrix or wavefront (see Chap. 3). In ANSYS-PC/LINEAR, the element numbering sequence is important. Swanson Analysis (the ANSYS vendor) recommends that element numbering proceed first across the short direction and then in the long direction of the model. In addition, "the best sequence of elements involves having the first element to use a given node as close as possible in the element sequence to the last element to use

---

[2] It should be noted, however, that some programs allow disconnected interior nodes. In this case, a "constraint equation" is required to couple the disconnected node's displacement with its adjacent nodes. Constraint equations can greatly increase the size of the bandwidth and are therefore rarely included in microcomputer programs.

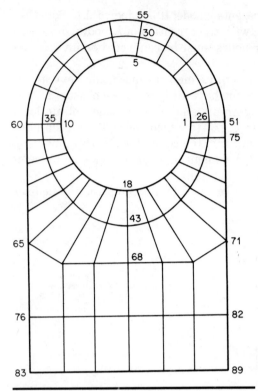

**Figure 4.15** The lifting lug of Fig. 4.1 with nodes and elements. The node numbering scheme can be inferred by the given nodes.

that node."[3] ANSYS also provides an automatic renumbering option for cases where it is inconvenient to use the ideal numbering scheme.

In other finite element programs such as MSC/pal 2 and IMAGES 3D, the node numbering sequence is important. However, these programs automatically renumber the nodes to optimize the bandwidth of the stiffness matrix. In general, try to reduce the largest difference between node numbers in an element by considering various numbering schemes before numbering the nodes.

### 4.2.4  Define the Geometric and Material Properties

The next step is to define relevant geometric and material properties. Material and geometric properties are discussed in detail in Chap. 2. If

---

[3] *ANSYS Techniques*, Swanson Analysis Systems, Inc., 1983.

your model consists of more than one material, this should be specified on your sketch. As we saw in Chap. 1, more than one material type may be defined in finite element programs. If you are performing a thermal or heat transfer analysis, bear in mind that material properties are temperature-dependent (see Chap. 9). The finite element program usually requires a reference temperature and corresponding material properties.

In static analyses, the total mass density of the structure may be negligible in comparison to the magnitude of the externally applied forces. In these situations, execution speed can be increased by setting the density to zero in the material properties definition. For dynamic analyses, mass density is required unless lumped masses are used. Specification of mass in dynamics analysis is discussed further in Chap. 8.

Geometric properties are straightforward for plate and solid elements, for which only a thickness is required. For axisymmetric 2-D solid problems, no geometric properties are required since these are determined by the dimensions of the model. Truss elements require only a cross-sectional area. Beam elements are more complicated, however. Most input errors regarding geometric properties occur in beam problems.

The major source of errors is incorrect beam orientation with respect to the specified moments of inertia. Section properties are specified with respect to *local element coordinate axes*. If your finite element model includes beam elements, it is necessary to follow the conventions for beam orientation provided by your finite element program (see Chap. 2). There are two primary methods used to specify beam element coordinate systems as shown in Fig. 4.16. One method is to specify a rotation angle for one of the axes normal to the beam axis. MSC/pal 2 uses this method. The element coordinate axes in MSC/pal 2 can be rotated using the VECTOR ORIENTATION command. ANSYS-PC/LINEAR provides an angle-orientation option or the use of $K$ nodes as described below.

The other primary method is to use a $K$ node. A $K$ node is simply a reference node used to form a plane with the beam element nodes. The plane formed by these three nodes defines the element's local coordinate axes. The $K$ node is not connected to the beam element and may be placed at an arbitrary distance away from the element but along the local axis that correctly specifies the orientation of the beam. The $K$ node is usually defined as a third node point for beam elements that are not aligned with the global axes. If the $K$ node is omitted, one of the global axes (depending on the program) is taken by default as the reference axis for the beam's local coordinate system. ANSYS (optionally), SUPERSAP, and IMAGES 3D all use $K$ nodes for defining beam orientation .

Another consideration with beam elements is shear deflection. Shear deflection can be significant in the bending of short beams. The shear area is related to the beam's cross-sectional area by the shear deflection

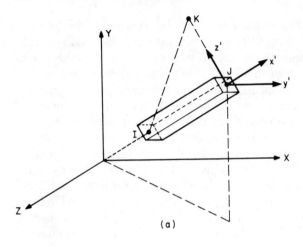

(a)

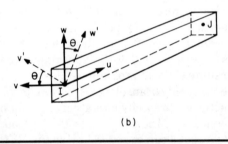

(b)

**Figure 4.16** Two methods for establishing beam orientation are shown. The $K$ node is defined as the third node and establishes the orientation of the $Z'$ axis in this example. In the second example, the orientation is defined by rotating the angle $\theta$.

constant $S$. The shear area $A_s = SA$. Table 4.1 gives values of $S$ for various common beam cross-sections. For beams whose length is substantially greater than the cross-sectional dimensions, shear deflection can be neglected.

### 4.2.5  Apply Loads and Boundary Conditions

The final step before creating the model on the computer is to determine the loads and boundary conditions. Your preliminary sketch should have the information you need. Typically, loads are input in the form of

**Table 4.1    Values of Shear Area Factor _S_ for Various Common Beam Cross-Sections**

| Cross-Section | Shear Area Factor (_S_) |
|---|---|
| Solid rectangular | 6/5 |
| Solid circular | 10/9 |
| Hollow circular (thin-walled) | 2.0 |
| Hollow square (thin-walled) | 12/5 |

SOURCE: C. R. Rogers, _ANSYS Techniques_, Swanson Analysis Systems, Inc., Houston, Pa., 1983.

concentrated forces and moments, distributed loads, pressures, temperatures, convections, or accelerations (see Chap. 2).

When defining loads and pressures, care must be taken that the correct loading direction is specified. The global and local coordinate systems that you have defined and the element coordinate system specified by the program must all be considered. In general, nodal forces and displacements are applied in the global coordinate system. In other words, if you specify a force _FY_ with a positive number, this force will be applied in the positive _Y_ direction as defined by your global coordinate system. For example, the three-member truss problem in Chap. 1 included a vertical force in the negative _Y_ direction.

Obliquely oriented forces are handled differently by various programs. When in doubt, it is best to decompose the force into its global components. In ANSYS-PC/LINEAR, oblique forces can be input by rotating the nodal coordinates in the direction of the applied force.

Concentrated loads applied to area element models should generally be distributed over two or three adjacent nodes. In this way, the load acts over a finite area rather than at a point. "Point loads" can cause unreasonably high stresses, particularly if the mesh is refined. While these stresses may be theoretically correct, point loads are physically not realistic and therefore should be used with caution.

When applying pressures, the direction depends on the conventions used by the finite element program. In MSC/pal 2, for example, pressures are applied to nodes that define a surface (three or more nodes). The sequence of the specified nodes, which must be clockwise or counterclockwise, defines the direction of the pressure according to the right-hand rule. This is illustrated in Fig. 4.17. ANSYS-PC/LINEAR specifies the directional convention for each element in its element library. In general, positive pressures are assumed to act toward the face of the element.

Distributed loads are also input according to directional conventions specified by the program. Line loads applied to beam elements act normal

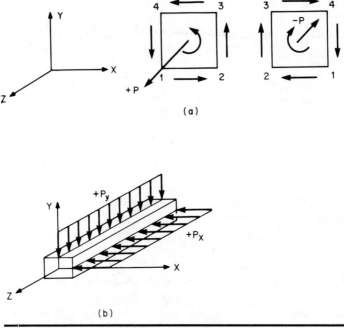

(a)

(b)

**Figure 4.17**  In (a), the sequence of specifying the nodes over which the pressure P acts determines the direction of P. This method is applied by MSC/pal 2. Note that the same approach is used to determine local element axes directions when connecting the nodes to form elements. In (b), the ANSYS-PC/LINEAR convention is shown for line loads acting on beams.

to the beam according to the beam coordinate system established by the K node or element beam coordinates. ANSYS-PC/LINEAR uses the same command as for pressure loads to specify distributed loads on beams (force per unit length).

For elements that do not have rotational degrees of freedom, force-couples may be used to apply moment loads ($M = FD$). In this case, equal and opposite forces are applied to two nodes with the magnitude F determined by the moment arm distance D (i.e., the distance between the nodes). This situation often arises in axisymmetric problems, in which the nodes have only translational degrees of freedom.

The primary types of boundary conditions are described in Chap. 2. As we saw in the truss example in Chap. 1, typical support conditions are simulated by specifying zero displacements in the appropriate directions and at the appropriate nodes. Fixed support conditions are imposed by specifying all degrees of freedom at the node to be zero. Simply supported conditions are specified by setting only the translational degrees of freedom to zero. Rollers are specified by zeroing all displacements except in the rolling direction.

Displacement constraints are also required to apply symmetry boundary conditions. The model must be restrained from displacing across the symmetric boundaries. Referring to Fig. 4.18, in quarter- or half-symmetry problems, you simply restrain the boundary nodes in the appropriate $X$, $Y$, or $Z$ direction since the boundaries are aligned with the global coordinate axes. ANSYS provides the command SYMBC which automatically specifies the symmetric boundary conditions for the specified nodes.

In problems involving cyclic symmetry, definition of the boundary conditions is complicated by the fact that usually one boundary of the model does not coincide with the global axes but is skewed at some angle (Fig. 4.19). In this case, the nodes must be constrained in the circumferential or tangential direction. Various finite element programs provide different methods for accomplishing this. The most elegant method is to rotate the nodal coordinates at the boundary so that they are aligned with the radial and tangential directions and then to set the nodal displacements to zero in the tangential direction. This can be done with the ANSYS-PC/LINEAR program.

Another method is to define spring elements in the tangential direction connected to the boundary nodes and assign these elements a large axial stiffness, thus restraining the boundary nodes (see Fig. 4.19). This

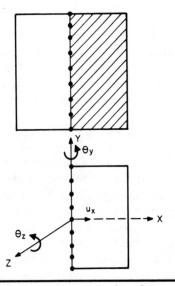

Figure 4.18 Symmetric boundary conditions require that there be no displacement across the symmetric boundary. Therefore, $u_x = \theta_y = 0$.

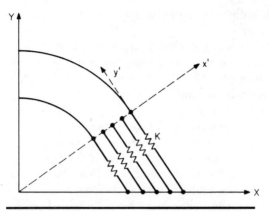

**Figure 4.19** Two methods of restraining nodes along skewed boundaries are shown. In one method, the boundary nodal coordinates are rotated, and the displacement in the $y'$ direction is set to zero. The other method is to connect the boundary nodes to nodes along the global axis by means of spring or truss elements given a large axial stiffness $K$.

is the method that must be applied with MSC/pal 2, SUPERSAP, and IMAGES 3D.

### 4.2.6 Create the Model on the Computer

Creating the finite element model on the computer has traditionally been the most tedious and time-consuming aspect of finite element analysis. However, design optimization and computer-aided design (CAD) techniques are now being applied to finite element analysis that significantly simplify the finite element design process. Further information on CAD and design optimization is included in App. B.

As of this writing, most finite element models are created using the finite element program's command processor, either interactively or by means of a batch file generated with a text editor. As we mentioned earlier, creating a model with 500 nodes would be cumbersome, indeed, if you had to define the coordinate of each node separately. Fortunately, finite element programs include commands for replicating nodes and elements. The degree of sophistication of these model-generation commands varies among different finite element programs.

The most general method of node replication is to fill in equally spaced nodes between previously defined node points. It can be safely stated that all finite element programs have this capability. Nodes can be replicated in a straight line or in a curve and, with most programs, over an area. The other common type of replication is to generate a series of nodes based on a nodal pattern. Not all programs support this type of replication. These two types of node replication are shown in Fig. 4.20.

When sitting down to the computer, you should have your preliminary sketch in hand with all the data required to fully define your finite element model. For portions of the model with uniform meshes, use replication commands to simplify the process. If your program supports pattern generation, you may be able to generate large portions of the model even if the mesh is not uniform. Some programs (ANSYS-PC/ LINEAR, for example) have commands that automatically calculate coordinates for intersections and can generate symmetrical node patterns.

Nodes do not have to be defined in order. Obviously, node replication would be difficult if this were the case. Elements, however, are defined sequentially. Once the nodes are defined, connecting them to form elements is straightforward. As with nodes, element connectivities can be replicated according to a pattern.

When connecting area elements, the sequence of nodes to be connected must be clockwise or counterclockwise. Skipping nodes is not allowed. This is also true for beam elements. Only adjacent nodes can be

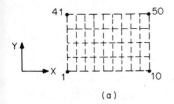

(a)

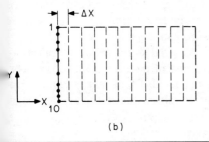

(b)

**Figure 4.20** Two types of node replication are shown. In (a), equally spaced nodes can be filled in within the dashed area defined by the four defined nodes. In (b), the nodal pattern can be replicated by the increment $\Delta X$.

connected. The order of the connected nodes is very important since most programs use the order to define the element coordinate system. The origin of the beam coordinate system is usually defined by the *first node defined in the connect command.* The direction of connectivity for area elements (clockwise or counterclockwise) defines the element coordinate axes according to the right-hand rule, similar to the sign convention for pressures as shown in Fig. 4.17.

If your finite element model involves multiple material or element types, make sure you understand how these are handled by your finite element program. For example, in ANSYS-PC/LINEAR, each material and element type is defined at the beginning of the analysis and assigned a number (MAT 1,2, ..., or TYPE 1,2, etc.). Similarly, geometric properties are defined as sets of constants, each set corresponding to an element type. The default material and element types are MAT 1 and TYPE 1. Until these types are changed, all elements defined are assumed to be of TYPE 1 and MATerial 1. The types are changed by issuing another TYPE or MAT command. See Fig. 1.9 for an example of multiple material types using ANSYS-PC/LINEAR.

Chapters 5, 7, 8, and 9 provide a number of examples of complete model input files using microcomputer finite element programs. See Fig. 1.9 for a typical, albeit extremely simple, input listing using ANSYS-PC/LINEAR.

## 4.3    Additional Modeling Topics

The discussion so far in this chapter has primarily focused on general modeling techniques and practices that are common to any analysis. In this section, we briefly cover modeling considerations that apply to more specialized applications.

### 4.3.1    Hinged Connections

In some problems, it may be necessary to include a hinged connection. A hinge can be thought of geometrically as a joint that is continuous in displacement but not in slope. In other words, the joint members can rotate independently of each other. It is useful to think of a door hinge, each side representing an element, and the hinge pin representing a node. When the door rotates, the other side of the hinge remains fixed. To model this connection in a finite element model, it is necessary to release the rotational degree of freedom of the element attached to the door or, in other words, to set the rotational stiffness of the hinge pin to zero.

Some, but not all, finite element programs have a method to release degrees of freedom. MSC/pal 2 and SUPERSAP have moment- and end-release options. In ANSYS-PC/LINEAR, however, it is necessary to use the STIF44 3-D tapered unsymmetrical beam element since this is the only element type that includes end releases. The mainframe version of ANSYS includes a coupled-degree-of-freedom option which can be used to model hinged connections. This option can be simulated in ANSYS-PC/LINEAR by using the generalized stiffness element. See *ANSYS News*, 5th issue (Ref. 6), for details.

### 4.3.2  Rigid Connections

In some problems, flexible members are joined by rigid connections that have a finite area or size. An example might be perpendicular beams connecting to a large concrete block. Since the block has area, it is not accurate to simply model the block as a node. What is required is some means to model the block as a rigid connection with its dimensions accurately represented.

Various finite element programs handle this problem differently. MSC/pal 2 uses a method called *element offsets*. In this method, the nodes of the joining elements can be attached but separated by a specified offset distance. The program then assumes that the nodes are rigidly connected over the offset distance. This is shown in Fig. 4.21. Some other programs supply rigid elements for this purpose. In ANSYS, the coupled-degree-of-freedom option is used in the mainframe version. As mentioned above, this option can be simulated in ANSYS-PC/LINEAR according to *ANSYS News*, 5th issue (Ref. 6).

### 4.3.3  Using Stiffnesses for Simulation Purposes

Often situations arise in finite element analysis for which there is no simple simulation using an element type or program command option. For example, your program may have no obvious method for modeling rigid connections or skewed boundary conditions, which we discussed

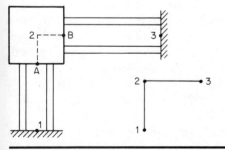

**Figure 4.21**  The element offset method used by MSC/pal 2. The nodal coordinates of node 2 are offset from the element attachment points *A* and *B*.

earlier. One of the most common methods of simulating various conditions is by specifying appropriately high or low stiffnesses to elements that represent the behavior you are trying to simulate.

For example, skewed boundary conditions can be modeled with axial spring elements given a large stiffness to rigidly constrain the connected nodes in the skewed direction (see Sec. 4.2.5). Another typical problem is coupling the displacement of adjacent nodes. This is a common application of coupled degrees of freedom. Unfortunately, most microcomputer finite element programs do not have a coupled-degree-of-freedom option. One solution is to attach the end nodes to "ground" using small spar (truss) or uniaxial spring elements in the direction in which coupling is desired. Assign a high stiffness to the elements, say 10,000,000 lb/in. In this manner, the nodes connected to the spar elements have the same axial stiffness and are therefore coupled in the axial direction.

## 4.4   Errors and Error Messages

More often than not, your first modeling attempt will contain errors. A node may have been omitted or numbered incorrectly. The elements may have been connected improperly. Or, perhaps, your mesh generation scheme did not produce the results you expected, and so forth. Some errors can be immediately detected by examining a plot of your finite element model. It should be emphasized that a plot of the finite element model should always be checked before proceeding with a complete static, dynamic, or heat transfer analysis.

Some errors, however, are not evident from the model but may turn up during execution of the analysis. The main cause of such errors is numerical errors in the stiffness and displacement matrices. Numerically deficient matrices are either *singular* or *ill-conditioned*.

A singular matrix is one for which there is no unique solution. An unconstrained structure will cause a singularity (except in modal analyses). Unconstrained joints may cause singularities. Examples are unconstrained in-plane rotational degrees of freedom in flat plate problems or two horizontally connected truss elements unconstrained in the vertical direction. Zero values for the elastic modulus or zero element dimensions will cause singularities. In many programs, singularities simply cause the program to abort. Occasionally, you may be fortunate enough to see a message such as "Zero Divide Error" or "Negative Main Diagonal Value" appear on the screen.

An ill-conditioned matrix is caused by large numerical differences in the magnitudes of the terms in the main diagonal of the stiffness matrix. Large numerical differences can be caused by unreasonable aspect ratios, excessive skewness or taper in element shapes, excessive values of Poisson's ratio, and other modeling errors. Generally, programs do not abort due to ill-conditioned matrices but, it is hoped, provide warning messages indicating the cause. In general, it is best to follow the guidelines established earlier in this chapter in order to avoid numerical errors.

## References

1. Rogers, C. R.: *ANSYS Techniques*, Swanson Analysis Systems, Inc., Houston, Pa., 1983.
2. Bednar, H.: *Pressure Vessel Design Handbook*, Van Nostrand Reinhold, New York, 1981.
3. Timoshenko, S., and J. Goodier: *Theory of Elasticity*, McGraw-Hill, New York, 1970.
4. Harvey, J. F.: *Pressure Component Construction*, Van Nostrand Reinhold, New York, 1980.
5. *ASME Boiler and Pressure Vessel Code*, Sec. III, NB-3650, 1980 edition (American Society of Mechanical Engineers, New York).
6. *ANSYS News*, 5th issue, 1985, Swanson Analysis Systems, Inc.
7. Blake, A.: *Practical Stress Analysis in Engineering Design*, Dekker, New York, 1982.

# 5

# Creating the
# Finite Element Model

In the previous four chapters, we provided a general introduction to finite element analysis and established some general guidelines for creating accurate models. Starting with this chapter, we begin concentrating on specific examples which illustrate the concepts set forth earlier. We start with a fairly simple static analysis in this chapter and use two different finite element programs to perform the analysis. We then focus on interpreting results in Chap. 6. Additional examples, including more complicated ones, are given in Chaps. 7, 8, and 9.

## 5.1  Analysis of a Lifting Lug

In this example, we analyze a steel lifting lug for static loading. Steel lifting lugs are used for lifting a wide variety of objects. In our example, let us assume that the lug is one of two lugs used for lifting a pressure vessel and is welded along its base to the sidewall of the vessel. A sketch of the lug and vessel is shown in Fig. 5.1 (also see Fig. 4.1).

According to the *American Petroleum Institute Standard 650*, lifting lugs for oil tanks must "be capable of carrying a load, applied in any reasonable manner, of twice the empty weight of the tank based on a safety factor of 4" (Ref. 1). The objective of our analysis, then, is to determine the maximum load that can be applied to the lifting lug. Note that our analysis pertains only to direct vertical loading and not to skewed or "sling" loading.

Assuming that the welded attachment of the lug to the vessel wall has been analyzed separately and meets specifications, we can consider the welded attachment as a rigid-boundary condition for our model. We can

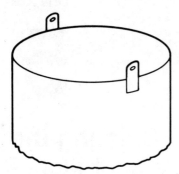

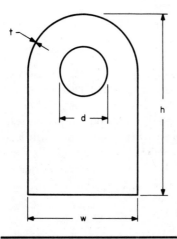

**Figure 5.1**  Sketch of a pressure vessel with two lifting lugs. The important dimensions of the lug are also indicated.

also take advantage of symmetry in this problem. Since the vertical load is applied symmetrically about the vertical axis at the top of the lug ring, we need to model only half of the lug.

Referring to Fig. 5.1, the overall dimensions of the lug are as follows:

$$h = 5 \text{ in}$$
$$w = 3 \text{ in}$$
$$d = 2 \text{ in}$$
$$t = 0.1 \text{ in}$$

The area which will be most critically stressed is the circular portion of the lug. Therefore, we need a fine mesh in the circular area and a coarser mesh in the rectangular part of the lug. Since the lug thickness is small in comparison to its other dimensions, we can employ the assumption of plane stress. Quadrilateral plate elements are a good choice for modeling the lug. A proposed model of the lug is shown in Fig. 5.2. In this model, three rows of elements are used in the circular portion. Selected nodes and elements are numbered to indicate the proposed numbering scheme.

The choice of mesh refinement is not based on specific rules in this case. The attenuation length guideline discussed in Chap. 4 does not apply to this problem. The mesh refinement is simply based on our intuitive assessment of the behavior of the lug. By using three rows across the circular portion, we can see how the stress varies through the thickness. The stress may vary considerably in the circular portion due to the concentrated load.

The rectangular portion of the lug will exhibit fairly low and uniform stresses, and therefore a coarse grid is satisfactory. In Chap. 6, we will check the accuracy of our model and discuss mesh-convergence studies

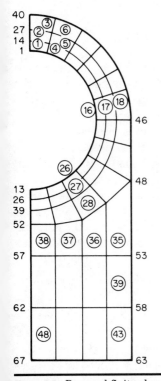

**Figure 5.2**  Proposed finite element model of lug. Element numbers are circled.

and other methods to measure the accuracy of a selected mesh refinement. As we mentioned earlier, selecting the proper mesh refinement is often a trial-and-error process based on engineering judgment and experience.

Before proceeding further, it is a good idea to determine the number of degrees of freedom in the problem. In this case, there are no rotational degrees of freedom and no $Z$-translational degrees of freedom since this is a planar membrane problem. The 11 nodes along the axis of symmetry must also be restrained in the $X$ direction to properly simulate the symmetrical boundary condition. Finally, the 5 nodes (63 to 67) at the base of the lug must be restrained in all directions. To calculate the degrees of freedom in the problem, we first calculate the total possible degrees of freedom, which is $6 \times 67 = 402$. The total degrees of freedom based on our boundary conditions are the total possible degrees of freedom minus the eliminated translational and rotational degrees of freedom ($4 \times 67$), the 11 $X$ translations along the axis of symmetry, and the translational degrees of freedom of the 5 base nodes $[(4 \times 2) + (1 \times 1)]$ (we already counted the $X$ translation of node 67):

$$402 - (4 \times 67) - 11 - [(4 \times 2) + 1] = 114$$

This is, of course, a small problem and will take only a few minutes to execute on a microcomputer.

Rigid-boundary conditions are applied along the base of the lug (nodes 63 to 67), and symmetry conditions are applied along the inside edge of the lug (the axis of symmetry). As mentioned above, rotational and translational degrees of freedom in the $Z$ direction must be set to zero.

Returning to our modeling assumptions, the load is modeled by distributing a vertical force of 50 lb across nodes 1, 2, and 3. Since we are modeling only half of the lug, this is equivalent to applying a load of 100 lb to a full model of the lug. As mentioned in Chap. 4, distributed loads are preferable to concentrated loads wherever possible. It seems reasonable that the applied lifting load would extend over the top three nodes of the inside surface.

We will use two different finite element programs to perform the lug analysis: MSC/pal 2 and ANSYS-PC/LINEAR. It is instructive to compare the methods of analysis of these two programs. In both cases, the node and element numbering scheme is the same.

## 5.2   Performing the Lug Analysis with MSC/pal 2

Before getting into the details of the lug analysis, a brief summary of MSC/pal 2's method of operation is helpful. MSC/pal 2 is divided into a series of stand-alone programs (called *modules*) that handle model generation, graphics, statics, and dynamics separately. Figure 5.3 shows the

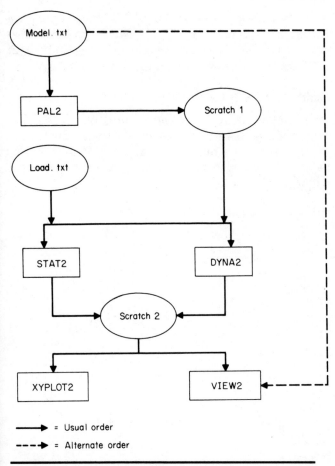

**Figure 5.3**   Main modules of MSC/pal 2.

modules that make up MSC/pal 2. Commands for generating the model are prepared in an ASCII text file [e.g., model.txt in Fig. 5.3 (see App. A for further information on text files)]. Before generating the model's stiffness matrix in the pal 2 module, it is convenient to use the VIEW2 module to view the geometry on the screen (dashed line in Fig. 5.3).

After the geometry is checked and is satisfactory, the next step is to run pal 2 and call the model text file as input. MSC/pal 2 then generates the stiffness matrix and stores it in a file (scratch 1 in Fig. 5.3) for further processing by either the STAT2 or DYNA2 modules (statics and dynamics, respectively). Applied loading is then input into STAT2 or DYNA2 by calling a second text file (load.txt in Fig. 5.3) which contains the necessary load and displacement commands. Results of the analysis in STAT2 or

DYNA2 can then be plotted or tabulated using VIEW2 for viewing the model, stress contours, and deformations, or XYPLOT2 for preparing plots or tables of output data (see Fig. 1.13 which was created using XYPLOT2). This procedure will become clear as we work through the lug analysis.

### 5.2.1  The Lug Model File for MSC/pal 2

The commands to generate the model in Fig. 5.2 are given in Fig. 5.4. The list of commands in Fig. 5.4 constitutes an ASCII text file created with a text editor (see App. A for more information on ASCII files and text editors). The origin of the global coordinate system is taken as the center of the circular part of the lug.

```
MSC/pal 2 Lug Model File

TITLE HOLE IN TAB
NODAL POINT LOCATIONS 2
1,1,90 THRU 13,1,-90
14,1.1,90 THRU 26,1.1,-90
27,1.25,90 THRU 39,1.25,-90
40,1.5,90 THRU 46,1.5,0
--BLANK LINE--
NODAL POINT LOCATIONS 1
47,1.5,-.433
48,1.5,-.866
49,1.125,-1.18
50,.75,-1.5
51,.375,-1.5
52,0,-1.5
53 1.5,-2.0
57 0,-2.0
63 1.5,-3.5
67 0,-3.5
--BLANK LINE--
NODAL POINT LOCATIONS 21
53,57,67,1,5
--BLANK LINE--
MAT 30E6,0,.733E-3,.3,30E3
QUADRILATERAL PLATE ELEMENT 1,0,.1
GENERATE CONNECTS 1 40 52 13 1
GEN CON 48 52 67 1 5
ZERO 1
TX 1 14 27 40 13 26 39 52 57 62 67
RA ALL
TZ ALL
--BLANK LINE--
END
```

Figure 5.4  Listing for finite element model in Fig. 5.5.

The first group of commands following the title defines the first 46 nodes in polar coordinates. NODAL POINT LOCATIONS 2 establishes the polar coordinate system for all following commands until a blank line is encountered. MSC/pal 2 commands can be abbreviated to their first three letters (e.g., NOD 2 would also work). The inside circumference of the lug is assigned 13 nodes, starting with node 1 at radius 1 in and rotation angle of 90°and ending with node 13 at the same radius and a rotation angle of −90°. The rotation angle is positive when measured counterclockwise from the horizontal axis of the global coordinate system. The program automatically fills in evenly spaced nodes between the starting and ending nodes using, in this case, an increment of 180°/(13 − 1) = 15°. In similar fashion, sets of nodes are generated through the thickness of the circular portion of the lug simply by incrementing the radius to 1.1, then to 1.25, and so forth. Note that node 46 is the last node to be defined in polar coordinates.

The NODAL POINT LOCATIONS 1 command sets the coordinate system to Cartesian coordinates. Nodes 47 through 52 are defined individually since the vertical and horizontal spacing between the nodes is irregular. The main tedium in finite element analysis is defining individual nodes. In large, geometrically irregular models, definition of individual nodes can become cumbersome indeed. In these situations, computer-aided design (CAD) programs are very attractive (see App. B).

Nodes 53, 57, 63, and 67 define the end points for the rectangular section of the lug. After these end-nodes are defined, the interior nodes can be filled in using the NODAL POINT LOCATIONS 21 command. This command generates blocks of nodes based on the specification of three end-nodes (the fourth node is specified implicitly by the location of the three end-nodes and the nodal increments). In our example, the three end-nodes are 53, 57, and 67, and the nodes are incremented by 1 in the horizontal direction (established by 53 and 57) and incremented by 5 in the vertical direction (established by 57 and 67).

At this point, the nodes are defined, and the next step is to define the elements. First, the material properties are defined by the MATERIAL (MAT) command. These properties are Young's modulus, the shear modulus, the material density, Poisson's ratio, and the yield stress of the material. The yield stress is optional since it is used only for reporting stress results as a percentage of yield. Notice that the shear modulus (the second field) is zero. For isotropic materials, the shear modulus is related by the elastic modulus and Poisson's ratio (see Chap. 2). Therefore, most programs, including MSC/pal 2, automatically calculate the shear modulus if it is not explicitly specified.

The next command, QUADRILATERAL PLATE TYPE (QUAD), defines the element type. The thickness is given in the third field after the command. The first two fields designate various stiffness and stress properties for the element. In our example, the number 1 in the first field indicates a plane stress model, and 0 in the second field indicates that no bending stiffness is required. Since there are no out-of-plane loads, it is reasonable to eliminate bending stiffness and thus reduce the size of the stiffness matrix.

The GENERATE CONNECTS command generates the element connectivities. Notice that all the elements are defined in two commands. Using nodes 1, 40, and 52 as end-nodes, the entire upper portion of the lug is generated with the first GENERATE command. For each element, the node numbers are incremented by 13 in the radial direction (defined by nodes 1 and 40) and by 1 in the circumferential direction (defined by nodes 40 and 52). Similarly, the lower portion of the lug is generated using nodes 48, 52, and 67. Element numbers are assigned according to the sequence in which they are generated. The numbering sequence is shown in Fig. 5.2.

Finally, the boundary conditions of symmetry and rotational and Z-direction constraints are established with the ZERO 1 command and the block of commands following it. The ZERO command removes the specified degrees of freedom from the stiffness matrix. Therefore, no reaction forces are computed for zeroed degrees of freedom. Where reaction forces are desired, the displacements are zeroed in the load input file rather than in the model input file, as we shall see shortly.

All commands following the ZERO 1 command set the specified degrees of freedom to zero until a blank line is encountered. TX stands for $X$ translation. Thus, $X$ translations are set to zero for the nodes along the axis of symmetry. RA stands for all rotations, and rotational degrees of freedom are eliminated for all nodes. Similarly, all $Z$ translations are zeroed. The vertical and horizontal degrees of freedom for the nodes at the base of the

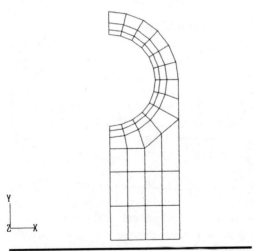

**Figure 5.5**  Finite element model of lug generated by MSC/pal 2.

lug (63 to 67) are restrained in the load file since we will want to check reaction forces.

The model input file is complete. Before generating the matrices using pal 2, the input file can be called by VIEW2, and the geometry of the model can be checked. The model is shown in Fig. 5.5. Since the model geometry is correct, the next step is to run pal 2 with the model file as input in order to generate the stiffness matrix. The output from pal 2 is minimal since pal 2 is really a building block for the actual static or dynamic analysis. MSC/pal 2 also includes a report module called ADCAP2 for producing a listing of nodal coordinates and element connectivities.

### 5.2.2   The Load Input File for MSC/pal 2

The load input file for the lug problem is shown in Fig. 5.6. The commands in this file specify the applied displacements and external loads acting on the lug. As mentioned above, there is a distinction in MSC/pal 2 between applied displacements and zeroed degrees of freedom. Applied displacements in the load file are retained in the model stiffness matrix, thus producing reaction forces. Reaction forces at the supports give a valuable check on the accuracy of the model.

```
         MSC/pal 2 Lug Load File

DISPLACEMENT APPLIED 1
ALL 0.0 63 64 65 66 67

LINE LOAD APPLIED 12
3 THRU 1 STEP 1 0,-50,0,0,0,1

SOLVE
QUIT
```

**Figure 5.6**   Load file input listing for lug model.

The DISPLACEMENTS APPLIED 1 (DISP 1) command is used to apply zero displacements in all directions to nodes 63 to 67. Since we already eliminated the rotational and $Z$-translational degrees of freedom in the model input file, we are effectively applying zero displacements in the $X$ and $Y$ directions with the DISP 1 command. It should be noted that we could have also specified the boundary conditions along the axis of symmetry at this point rather than in the model input file. We would then be able to check reaction forces along the axis of symmetry. However, we would also increase execution time.

The final step is to apply the distributed load of 50 lb. We want to distribute the total force of 50 lb over nodes 1, 2, and 3. We do this by using the LINE LOAD APPLIED 12 command. This command allows us to apply the total load over a sequence of nodes. The program automatically calculates the load per unit length and the load distribution for each node. The load is applied from node 3 to node 1 with a node increment of 1.

The first three fields following STEP 1 represent the loads in the local coordinate system. The last three fields establish the orientation of the $w$ axis of the local coordinate system. The 1 in the last field indicates that the $w$ axis is aligned with the global $Z$ axis as shown in Fig. 5.7. The direction of the $u$ axis is defined by the sequence in which the nodes are specified in the LINE LOAD command. The direction of the $v$ axis is determined by the vector product $\varepsilon\, u\, \nabla \times \varepsilon\, v\, \nabla = \varepsilon\, w\, \nabla$. In this case, the $v$ axis points toward the origin of the global coordinate system. Therefore, the load is applied in the negative $v$ direction.

The SOLVE command causes the load file and model scratch file to be processed by STAT2 in this case (for dynamics, you would use DYNA2). Analysis results can then be saved on disk, plotted, and so forth. It should be noted that MSC/pal 2 automatically generates the files on disk for storing the solution data. These files are overwritten each time you run an analysis (see App. A for more information on file handling). In Chap. 6 we will look at the results of the lug analysis.

### 5.3 Performing the Lug Analysis with ANSYS-PC/LINEAR

ANSYS-PC/LINEAR is composed of three main modules:

1. The preprocessor PREP7 for generating models, applied loads, and boundary conditions. Models can also be plotted and viewed from within PREP7.
2. ANSYS, the main number-crunching part of the system (equivalent to STAT2 and DYNA2 in MSC/pal 2).

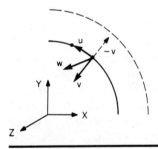

**Figure 5.7** Local coordinate system for applying distributed load in MSC/pal 2. The $u$ coordinate is determined by the sequence in which the nodes are defined in the LINE LOAD command. In this case, the $w$ axis is aligned with the global $Z$ axis. The $v$ axis is normal to $u$ such that $\varepsilon\, u\, \nabla \times \varepsilon\, v\, \nabla = \varepsilon\, w\, \nabla$.

3. The postprocessor POST for generating stress contour plots, deflected shapes, stress combinations, etc.

The lug analysis input file for PREP7 is shown in Fig. 5.8. As with MSC/pal 2, the file is created with an ASCII text editor. The commands in Fig. 5.8 could also be issued interactively within the PREP7 module. For the purposes of this book, however, we will use batch files for illustration of analyses in ANSYS-PC/LINEAR. Both the model and loading data are prepared in one file which is input to PREP7. PREP7 then generates the model stiffness matrices and stores them on a disk file for processing by ANSYS. After processing by ANSYS, POST can be used to evaluate the results of the analysis. Further information on executing files in ANSYS-PC/LINEAR is contained in App. A.

```
                    ANSYS-PC/Linear Lug Model File
                         /TITLE LUG ANALYSIS
KAN,0
ET,1,42,0,0,3              * SPECIFY STIF42 ELEMENT
EX,1,30E6                  * MATERIAL TYPE 1
R,1,0.1          * REAL CONSTANT TABLE 1 (ELEMENT THICKNESS)
CSYS,1                   * POLAR COORDINATE SYSTEM
N,1,1,90         * GENERATE NODES FOR CIRCULAR PORTION
N,13,1,-90
FILL
N,14,1.1,90
N,26,1.1,-90
FILL
NGEN,2,13,14,26,1,0.15
NGEN,2,13,27,33,1,0.25
CSYS,0                   * CARTESIAN COORDINATE SYSTEM
N,48,1.5,-.866        * GENERATE RECTANGULAR PORTION
FILL,46,48
N,50,.75,-1.5
FILL
N,52,0,-1.5
FILL
N,53,1.5,-2.0
N,57,0,-2.0
FILL
NGEN,3,5,53,57,1,0,-0.75
E,1,14,15,2               * GENERATE ELEMENTS
EGEN,3,13,1
EGEN,12,1,1,3
E,48,49,54,53
EGEN,4,1,37
EGEN,3,5,37,40
EPLOT
D,63,ALL,,,67,1           * RESTRAIN NODES AT BASE
NRSEL,X,0        * SELECT NODES ALONG AXIS OF SYMMETRY
SYMBC,0,1,ALL           APPLY SYMMETRY B.C's TO SELECTED NODES
NALL                   * RESELECT ALL NODES
P,1,2,955,,2         * APPLY PRESSURES (DISTRIBUTED LOAD)
SFWRIT
FINISH
```

Figure 5.8  ANSYS-PC/LINEAR listing for lug analysis.

Following the title line, the first step is to define the analysis type as static or dynamic (modal analysis) using the KAN command. KAN,0 indicates a static analysis. If this command is omitted, the default is static analysis.

Next, the element type (ET) is specified. The element library for ANSYS-PC/LINEAR is shown in Table 5.1. Each element type has a unique STIF number. Our choices of elements for this problem are the quadrilateral shell element STIF63 or the 2-D isoparametric stress solid STIF42. Notice in Fig. 5.8 that we have selected the STIF42 element rather than the shell element.

There are a number of good reasons for this choice. The STIF42 element is a 2-D element that can be used either as a biaxial plane element or as an axisymmetric solid element. The behavior of the element is specified by the option fields following the number 42 in the ET command. Option 3, which we have chosen, specifies a plane stress element with thickness input.

Since STIF42 is a 2-D element with only 2 DOF ($X$ and $Y$ translations), we do not have to concern ourselves with eliminating $Z$-translational or rotational degrees of freedom. The other primary advantage of the 2-D element over the shell element is that we can apply a pressure load equivalent to the distributed load we applied in the MSC/pal 2 analysis. The quadrilateral shell element accepts only pressure loads normal to its surface. We would, therefore, have to apply estimated concentrated loads at the appropriate nodes if we used the quadrilateral element.

The ANSYS-PC/LINEAR command listing in Fig. 5.8 is similar to the listing we worked through in Chap. 1 (Fig. 1.10). For material properties, only the modulus of elasticity is specified. The program default for Poisson's ratio is used (0.3), and the shear modulus is also calculated by default as discussed earlier. No material density is specified. The R (real constants)

**TABLE 5.1   Element Library for ANSYS-PC/LINEAR**

| STIF number | Name | Dimension | Degrees of freedom | Nodes |
|---|---|---|---|---|
| 1 | 2-D spar | 2 | 2 | 2 |
| 3 | 2-D elastic beam | 2 | 2 | 2 |
| 4 | 3-D elastic beam | 3 | 6 | 2 or 3 |
| 8 | 3-D spar | 3 | 3 | 2 |
| 11 | Axisym. conical shell | 2 | 3 | 2 |
| 14 | Spring | 2 or 3 | 3 | 2 |
| 21 | General mass | 2 or 3 | 6 | 1 |
| 27 | Stiff or mass matrix | 3 | 6 | 2 |
| 42 | 2-D isopar. stress solid | 2 | 2 | 4 |
| 44 | 3-D tapered unsym. beam | 3 | 6 | 3 |
| 45 | 3-D isopar. stress solid | 3 | 3 | 8 |
| 54 | 2-D taper. unsym. beam | 2 | 3 | 2 |
| 63 | Quadrilateral shell | 3 | 6 | 4 |

command specifies the element thickness of 0.1 in, which is the only geometric property required for STIF42.

Next, the coordinate system is set to polar coordinates with the CSYS command. Nodes are defined in similar fashion as in the MSC/pal 2 analysis. The FILL command simply fills evenly spaced nodes between the two previously defined nodes.

The NGEN command is used to generate additional sets of nodes based on a pattern established by specified existing nodes. The first iteration of the NGEN command creates the pattern from the existing nodes. In other words, the number of iterations must be at least two for new sets of nodes to be generated. The first NGEN command generates a nodal pattern two times (including the original pattern), incrementing the node numbers by 13, starting the pattern with node 14 and ending with node 26 in steps of 1, and incrementing the radius by 0.15. The second NGEN command creates nodes up to node 46.

We then shift to Cartesian coordinates to generate the lower portion of the model. After defining nodes 53 through 57, the NGEN command is used to create the bottom two rows of nodes, incrementing the nodes by 5 and the $Y$ coordinate by $-0.75$.

The next step is to generate the elements. The first element is defined with nodes 1, 14, 15, and 2. We then use the EGEN command to produce elements 2 and 3. As with the NGEN command, the first iteration of the EGEN command simply establishes the element pattern but does not produce additional elements. Therefore, to generate elements 2 and 3, we use 3 iterations, increment the nodes by 13, and define the pattern simply as element 1. The next EGEN command generates the circular portion of the lug based on the first three elements (12 iterations, incrementing nodes by 1, based on the pattern of elements 1 to 3). The lower portion of the lug is generated in similar fashion.

The EPLOT command plots the model on the screen. Until the model is correct, the EPLOT command should be the last command in the input file (except for the FINISH command). The subsequent commands can be added to the file after the geometry has been checked with the EPLOT command. The result of the EPLOT command is identical to Fig. 5.5 produced by MSC/pal 2 and is therefore not shown.

The remaining commands define the boundary conditions and applied loads. The D command defines all displacements to be zero for nodes 63 through 67. The NRSEL command is used to select specific nodes to be affected by subsequent commands until a new NRSEL or NALL command is issued. In this case, we use NRSEL to select nodes along the $X$ axis. We then use the SYMBC command to generate boundary conditions of symmetry for these selected nodes on the $X$ axis. The ALL field in the SYMBC command refers only to the nodes on the $X$ axis due to the previous NRSEL command. The 0,1 fields establish the boundary as a surface normal to the $X$ axis. The NALL command resets selected nodes to ALL nodes.

The P command defines the pressure acting on the surface defined by nodes 1, 2, and 3. The value of 955 is the pressure per square inch, which we have to calculate by hand. The total load is 50 lb, and the surface area per element on which this load is applied is the product of the arc length between the nodes and the thickness of the lug. Thus, the surface area is

$$\left(\frac{\pi r}{12}\right) \times t = \left(\frac{\pi}{12}\right) \times 0.1 = 0.026 \text{ in}^2$$

Since the pressure is acting on nodes 1 through 3, the total surface area is twice the above value. The pressure is, therefore, $50/(2 \times 0.026) = 955 \text{ lb/in}^2$. Clearly, this exercise is a bit more cumbersome than simply applying the LINE LOAD command in MSC/pal 2.

The analysis is complete, and the SFWRIT command saves the file to disk for processing by ANSYS. The necessary binary data files for performing the ANSYS analysis are generated automatically by PREP7. However, you must specify the text output files when you run PREP7 and ANSYS (see App. A). As mentioned earlier, we will examine the results of this analysis in the next chapter.

## 5.4  Modeling Errors

Modeling errors are caused by incorrect definitions of nodes or elements. The most common mistake is to attempt to connect elements with nodes whose coordinates have not been defined or are incorrect. Such errors are quite evident from viewing the geometry of the model. Figure 5.9 shows the lug model with the nodal coordinates of node 46 accidentally omitted. When the program attempts to connect an element to node 46, it assumes by default that node 46 is located at the origin since its coordinates have not been defined.

Frequently, modeling errors can be found in commands used to automatically generate sets of nodes or elements. It is easy to use the wrong number of iterations or to specify incorrect numbering increments. In large models, modeling errors such as the one illustrated above can be difficult to find. As we have mentioned previously, CAD programs greatly reduce these types of frustrating errors. In any case, when your plot shows an error as in Fig. 5.9, your only recourse is to carefully review your input file until you find the missing node or incorrect coordinate or element connectivity.

**Figure 5.9**  Lug model shown with missing node error.

## 5.5  Summary

We have performed the preparation phase of a simple static analysis using two different finite element programs. While the end result is the same, the approach of these two programs is somewhat different. As the reader may have noticed, each program has its strengths and weaknesses. The STIF42 plane stress biaxial element in ANSYS-PC/LINEAR offers a more "elegant" solution since we do not have to eliminate complete sets of degrees of freedom. On the other hand, the LINE LOAD command in MSC/pal 2 makes application of the load a much simpler matter than in ANSYS-PC/LINEAR. The modeling commands in MSC/pal 2 are more straightforward, and fewer lines are required to generate the model. However, the SYMBC command in ANSYS-PC/LINEAR for generating symmetric boundary conditions is very useful, particularly in larger problems.

We will continue working with these programs in the next chapter where we examine the results of our lug analysis.

## Reference

1. American Petroleum Institute, *API Standard 650*, 6th ed., April 15, 1977, Washington, D.C.

# 6

# Interpreting the Results

The reliability of the results of finite element analysis is ultimately the responsibility of the engineer, not of the finite element program. Incorrect interpretation of results can lead to serious engineering errors and potentially dangerous consequences. It is, therefore, extremely important to scrutinize and check the results of your analysis.

In this chapter, we focus on methods of checking and interpreting results. We begin by completing the lifting lug analysis started in the previous chapter. The lifting lug analysis provides a basic example of static analysis and is used to illustrate some fundamental procedures for checking results. The emphasis is on establishing a good methodology for checking results. Chapters 7, 8, and 9 provide additional examples of statics, dynamics, and heat transfer analyses, respectively.

It should be noted that more attention is devoted to interpretation of area element problems than to beam element problems. The reason for this is that area element problems are more difficult to interpret. Beam element problems are generally more straightforward and physically easier to understand. We will, however, look at a number of beam problems in Chaps. 7 and 8.

## 6.1 Graphical and Numerical Results

As we have discussed earlier, the primary results produced by finite element analysis are the nodal values of a quantity such as displacements or temperatures. Depending on the type of analysis, the finite element program calculates stresses, natural frequencies, mode shapes, or other quantities, based on the nodal results. Stresses are generally reported at the element centroid. However, most programs can also report the average stresses at the nodes.

As we shall see, this capability is useful for obtaining surface stress results in problems involving plate or solid elements.

Finite element programs generally report results in both graphical and numerical form. Graphical results are far easier to interpret than numerical results but are less detailed. Plots of displacement and stress variation give you an immediate indication of the reasonableness of your analysis and provide the best means for quickly detecting errors. As we mentioned in Chap. 3, good graphics capability should be one of the most important criteria when selecting a finite element program.

The best approach to interpreting the results of your analysis is to first inspect the graphical output to make sure that the overall physical behavior of the model is reasonable and then to look more closely at the numerical results. Following this approach, we first look at the displacement and stress contour plots for the lifting lug model of Chap. 5.

## 6.2    The Displacement Plot

The first and most revealing item to check is a plot of the nodal displacements of the model, preferably superimposed over the undeflected shape. A superimposed plot allows you to see the relationship between the undeformed and deformed shapes. A plot of the deformed shape alone is usually not as instructive since you are forced to imagine the outline of the original shape. In some cases, however, superimposed plots may be too crowded or "messy," in which case it is better to view the deformed shape separately.

Both ANSYS-PC/LINEAR and MSC/pal 2 support superimposed plots. In MSC/pal 2, the VIEW2 module (see Fig. 5.3) is used to produce the plot on the screen. VIEW2 is menu-driven, and you simply select the appropriate options to produce the plot. Using the PrtSc (print-screen) key, the plot can be output to a printer or plotter (see App. A for further information on using graphics with your microcomputer).

In ANSYS-PC/LINEAR, the plot is produced using the POST1 postprocessing module. POST1 is loaded by issuing the command POST from the DOS prompt. The following commands within POST generate the plot:

```
SET,1,1
PLDISP,1
FINISH
```

As in MSC/pal 2, the plot may be printed using the print-screen function of your computer. Again, consult App. A for further information on graphics and postprocessing.

Figure 6.1 shows the deflected shape of the lifting lug as generated by MSC/pal 2. The displacement plot immediately tells you if your results are physically reasonable. The deflected shape of the lug in Fig.

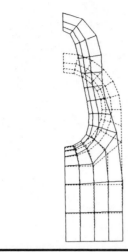

**Figure 6.1**  The deflected shape of the lifting lug model superimposed on the original shape (MSC/pal 2).

6.1 represents the behavior we would expect from the physical problem. The lug is pulled in tension at the top and is pulled inward on the sides to accommodate the vertical displacement.

Now, look at Fig. 6.2. Clearly, there is something wrong with the deformed shape of the model. If you guessed that the symmetry boundary conditions were removed, you are correct. Simply by removing the SYMBC command in ANSYS-PC/LINEAR or the TX 0 . . . command in MSC/pal 2 (see Figs. 5.4 and 5.8), we get the results in Fig. 6.2.

The problem is immediately obvious from the displacement plot. Without the $X$-translational restraints along the axis of symmetry, the lug model behaves like a cantilevered beam and deflects in the radial direction due to the applied loads. If the results of your analysis showed an error as in Fig. 6.2, the next step would be to edit your input data to correct the problem and then to rerun the analysis.

We have seen that the first and most important step after running an analysis is to examine the displacement plot. The graphical representation of the model's behavior is the most convenient and straightforward indicator of the accuracy of the analysis.

## 6.3  The Stress Contour Plot

If the displacement plot looks reasonable, the next step is to look at a stress contour plot of the model. The stress contour plot provides a

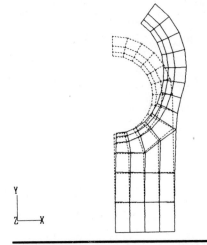

**Figure 6.2**  The lifting lug model with the symmetry boundary conditions removed. In this case, the end of the lug behaves like a cantilever beam.

graphical representation of the stress variation in the model. A stress contour plot is generated in the same way as a displacement plot. In MSC/pal 2, you use the VIEW2 module. In ANSYS-PC/LINEAR, the POST1 postprocessor is used.

Since stress is reported in components, a stress contour plot can only display one component of stress. Generally, the most useful component to plot is either the major principal stress or the Von Mises stress (see Chap. 2 for more information on stress output). Of course, you can plot all the stress components individually if you want.

Figures 6.3a and b show stress contour plots of the Von Mises stress for the lifting lug, generated by MSC/pal 2 and ANSYS-PC/LINEAR, respectively. MSC/pal 2 uses contour lines for generating contour plots. Each continuous line or contour inside the outline of the model represents a constant stress value. In this case, each contour represents a stress increment of approximately 400 lb/in$^2$. Most programs scale the contour plot increments according to the maximum and minimum stress values of the analysis. By counting contour lines starting from the outer boundaries of the model (where the stress is small or zero), it is possible to estimate the Von Mises stress value at any location on the model.

The cross-section that has the largest number of contour lines is the most highly stressed section of the model. This section, as one would expect, is located near the horizontal axis of the circular portion of the lug. Counting contour lines from the outside edge near the horizontal axis, the approximate maximum Von Mises stress is 4000 lb/in$^2$ at the inside surface of the lug.

LIFTING LUG DEFORMED SHAPE

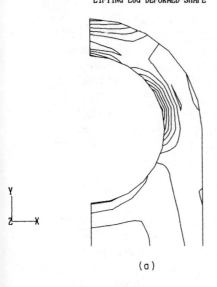

(a)

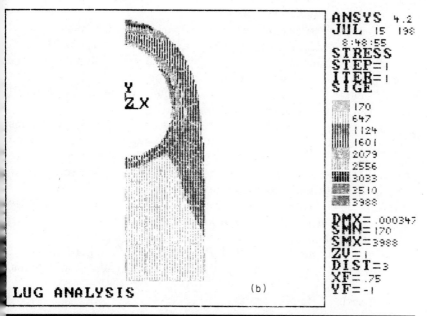

(b)

**Figure 6.3(a) and (b)**   The Von Mises stress contour plot for the critical portion of the lifting lug [(a) MSC/pal 2; (b) ANSYS-PC/LINEAR)]. Each line in Fig. 6.3a represents a constant stress increment of 400 lb/in². Counting from the outer edge near the horizontal axis of the circular portion, the maximum Von Mises stress is about 4000 lb/in² at the inside surface. Figure 6.3b is displayed in colored regions on a color terminal. In black and white, it is difficult to discern the different shades. However, the overall behavior of the lug is well represented.

The ANSYS-PC/LINEAR plot in Fig. 6.3$b$ uses shaded regions to show the stress distribution. As we discussed in Chap. 3, shaded or color contour plots are difficult to interpret in black and white. On a color monitor, however, the color contour plot is very effective. However, in most situations, it is desirable to include the stress contour plot in a report. In this case, the black-and-white line contour plot as in Fig. 6.3$a$ is preferable. Unfortunately, Revision 4.2 of ANSYS-PC/LINEAR does not support line contour plots.

The stress contour plot is an excellent graphical indicator of the behavior of the model. In addition to helping you, the analyst, understand the results, stress contour and displacement plots also provide the best and easiest method for reporting the results of your analysis to other engineers.

## 6.4    Looking at the Numbers

While the displacement and stress contour plots give you an indication of the reasonableness of your analysis and a graphical estimate of the stresses in the model, the numerical results are the true measure of the accuracy of the analysis. Your decision regarding the adequacy of the modeled structure or component is ultimately based on the numerical results of your analysis.

It is tempting to assume that the numerical results must be accurate if the graphical results are reasonable. As we mentioned earlier, numerical accuracy is a matter of degree. A coarse mesh may produce a reasonable displacement and stress plot but may not give you the desired degree of accuracy in critical sections of the model. We will look at the issue of numerical accuracy in this section.

Numerical results can be very difficult to interpret. Large problems may produce hundreds of pages of numerical output. Wading through pages and pages of data is confusing and very time-consuming. There are methods, however, to reduce the amount of data that you need to work with. Working in conjunction with your displacement and stress contour plots and making the appropriate spot checks, you can greatly simplify the interpretation of your numerical results. Again, we return to the lug problem to illustrate the important points of this section.

The entire output from ANSYS-PC/LINEAR for the lug analysis is shown in Fig. 6.4. We will refer to this listing in the following sections.

### 6.4.1    Checking External Forces

In statics analysis, most programs report the nodal displacements, the element stress components, and the external reaction forces. There may be external reaction forces at any node which has a constrained degree of freedom. Some programs also report the externally applied forces. The external reaction forces provide a good check on the accuracy of your results.

In our lug problem, the externally applied load is 50 lb. The external reaction forces are computed by the finite element program and reported as horizontal and vertical components. Therefore, the vector sum of the reaction components should be equal to the applied force of 50 lb. Since we used a distributed load or pressure, there may be a slight round-off error in the computed reactions. The reaction force components computed by ANSYS-PC/LINEAR are listed at the end of Fig. 6.4. The vector sum of these components is 49.44 lb, which represents an error of approximately 1 percent. This is acceptable and indicates that the external load was applied correctly.

If the reaction forces do not match the intended external loads, it is necessary to check your input data. It is possible that you made an error in specifying the magnitude or direction of the load or the nodes or element faces on which the load acts. Normally, errors in load direction show up in the displacement plot. Errors in magnitude, however, may not be apparent from the plot.

In the lug analysis, the relationship between the applied load and the reaction forces is quite straightforward and therefore easy to check. Problems involving pressure or thermal loads or complicated geometries may be more difficult to check. In these types of problems, try to make a gross estimate of the accuracy of the reaction loads. For example, in a pressure problem, you can multiply the total area of the model by the pressure to get a figure for the total load and compare this load to the reaction forces. In a thermal problem, you can use gross temperature differences to calculate the average thermal stress and multiply this value by the area of the model to estimate the equivalent applied load to compare to the reaction forces. In any case, it is essential to check external reaction forces as a verification of the accuracy of the applied loads.

### 6.4.2  Checking the Displacements

As we mentioned earlier, displacement results are not as sensitive to mesh refinement as stress results. A fairly coarse model will generally give acceptable displacement results. If your displacement plot looks reasonable, the numerical displacement values are probably also reasonable. Numerical checking of displacements is less important than checking of stress values. Of course, if the objective of the analysis is to determine displacements, the numbers should be checked carefully. To be on the safe side, we will take a look at the lug model displacement values.

Displacement values are usually very difficult to verify independently. After all, the primary reason for performing a finite element analysis is that you cannot get such accurate results by hand. If we could reproduce the displacements using a hand calculator and pencil and paper, we would probably be wasting our time performing a finite element analysis. The best that can be done is to compare the finite element results to a ballpark

```
*** NOTICE *** THIS IS THE ANSYS-PC/LINEAR FINITE
ELEMENT PROGRAM. NEITHER SWANSON ANALYSIS SYSTEMS, INC.
NOR THE DISTRIBUTOR SUPPLYING THIS PROGRAM ASSUME ANY
RESPONSIBILITY FOR THE VALIDITY, ACCURACY, OR APPLICABILITY
OF ANY RESULTS OBTAINED FROM THE ANSYS SYSTEM. USERS
MUST VERIFY THEIR OWN RESULTS.
*** ANSYS REV 4.2 1     SWANSON ANALYSIS CP =     16.04***
FOR SUPPORT CALL CUSTOMER SUPPORT PHONE (412) 746-3304 510-690 -8655

LUG ANALYSIS
            *** ANSYS VERSION FOR DEMONSTRATION PURPOSES ONLY ***
ELEMENT FORMATION   ELEM = 41   L.S. = 1   ITER = 1   CP = 49.43

RANGE OF ELEMENT MAXIMUM STIFFNESS IN GLOBAL COORDINATES
MAXIMUM =  0.337490E+07 AT ELEMENT                                37.
MINIMUM =  0.164858E+07 AT ELEMENT                                40.

            *** ELEMENT STIFFNESS FORMULATION TIMES ***
TYPE  NUMBER  STIF  TOTAL CP   AVE CP
  1      48     42    28.82     0.600

       TIME AT END OF ELEMENT STIFFNESS FORMULATION CP =    55.640
       MAXIMUM WAVE FRONT ALLOWED =                         100.
       EQUATION SOLUTION ELEM = 41   L.S. = 1   ITER = 1   CP = 79.75
       MAXIMUM IN-CORE WAVE FRONT =                          16.
          MATRIX SOLUTION TIMES
          READ IN ELEMENT STIFFNESSES CP =                    4.190
          NODAL COORD. TRANSFORMATION CP =                    0.000
          MATRIX TRIANGULARIZATION CP =                      13.060
       TIME AT END OF MATRIX TRIANGULARIZATION CP =          82.720

       TIME AT START OF BACK SUBSTITUTION CP =               83.540

                *** DISPLACEMENT SOLUTION ***
NODE        UX            UY
  1    0.00000E+00   0.34720E-03
  2   -0.27247E-04   0.32798E-03
  3   -0.62814E-04   0.27285E-03
  4   -0.99904E-04   0.20462E-03
  5   -0.12745E-03   0.14693E-03
  6   -0.13814E-03   0.10281E-03
  7   -0.12754E-03   0.70865E-04
  8   -0.10133E-03   0.47313E-04
  9   -0.70797E-04   0.30101E-04
 10   -0.45168E-04   0.18157E-04
 11   -0.26260E-04   0.10283E-04
 12   -0.12068E-04   0.57075E-05
 13    0.00000E+00   0.42639E-05
 14    0.00000E+00   0.34702E-03
 15   -0.12217E-04   0.32270E-03
 16   -0.40148E-04   0.25818E-03
 17   -0.83656E-04   0.18593E-03
 18   -0.12236E-03   0.13168E-03
 19   -0.14035E-03   0.98078E-04
 20   -0.13006E-03   0.77081E-04
 21   -0.99339E-04   0.58690E-04
 22   -0.65020E-04   0.39545E-04
 23   -0.38792E-04   0.23357E-04
 24   -0.21606E-04   0.11842E-04
 25   -0.95913E-05   0.52862E-05
 26    0.00000E+00   0.32184E-05
 27    0.00000E+00   0.34414E-03
 28    0.65093E-05   0.31416E-03
 29   -0.13329E-04   0.24009E-03
```

**Figure 6.4**  The complete output listing from ANSYS-PC/LINEAR for the lug analysis. The listing includes the nodal displacements, element stresses, and external reaction forces.

```
NODE        UX              UY
 30     -0.61525E-04    0.16219E-03
 31     -0.11293E-03    0.11181E-03
 32     -0.14049E-03    0.91115E-04
 33     -0.13162E-03    0.82981E-04
 34     -0.96656E-04    0.70193E-04
 35     -0.57667E-04    0.51097E-04
 36     -0.31310E-04    0.30165E-04
 37     -0.15602E-04    0.14750E-04
 38     -0.66509E-05    0.54668E-05
 39     0.00000E+00     0.26494E-05
 40     0.00000E+00     0.33735E-03
 41     0.40044E-04     0.29885E-03
 42     0.35164E-04     0.20809E-03
 43     -0.21372E-04    0.12119E-03
 44     -0.93295E-04    0.79096E-04
 45     -0.13691E-03    0.80815E-04
 46     -0.13195E-03    0.97162E-04
 47     -0.85215E-04    0.96310E-04
 48     -0.39968E-04    0.75919E-04
 49     -0.16926E-04    0.38506E-04
 50     -0.41240E-05    0.16841E-04
 51     -0.21642E-05    0.66710E-05
```

*** DISPLACEMENT SOLUTION ***

```
NODE        UX              UY
 52     0.00000E+00     0.29733E-05
 53     0.22422E-05     0.25401E-04
 54     0.23188E-05     0.22221E-04
 55     0.19700E-05     0.13609E-04
 56     0.13018E-05     0.70904E-05
 57     0.00000E+00     0.46893E-05
 58     -0.11692E-05    0.10029E-04
 59     0.11851E-05     0.94759E-05
 60     0.21081E-05     0.74705E-05
 61     0.14351E-05     0.51932E-05
 62     0.00000E+00     0.43299E-05
 63     0.00000E+00     0.00000E+00
 64     0.00000E+00     0.00000E+00
 65     0.00000E+00     0.00000E+00
 66     0.00000E+00     0.00000E+00
 67     0.00000E+00     0.00000E+00
```

```
MAXIMUMS
NODE 32 1
VALUE-0.14049E-03 0.34720E-03
EL=  1 NODES=   1   14   15    2 MAT=   1 VOL=   0.2718E-02
XC,YC= 0.1359   1.032   TEMP=   0.0
    SX,SY,SXY,SZ= -2194.1   -1165.9   25.590    0.00000E+00
    SIG1,SIG2   SIG3=-0.18071E-07   -1165.3   -2194.7
    S.I.=  2194.7     SIGE= 1901.9
EL=  2 NODES=   14   27   28   15 MAT=   1 VOL= 0.4562E-02
    XC,YC= 0.1521   1.155   TEMP=   0.0
    SX,SY,SXY,SZ= -295.42   -884.10   -336.28   0.00000E+00
    SIG1,SIG2   SIG3=-0.89249E-08 -142.86   -1036.7
    S.I.= 1036.7     SIGE= 973.13
EL=  3 NODES=   27   40   41   28 MAT=   1 VOL= 0.8897E-02
    XC,YC= 0.1779   1.352   TEMP=   0.0
    SX,SY,SXY,SZ= 2096.6   -323.66   -482.12   0.00000E+00
    SIG1,SIG2   SIG3= 2189.1   0.14315E-07 -416.17
    S.I.= 2605.2     SIGE= 2424.1
EL=  4 NODES=   2   15   16    3 MAT=   1 VOL= 0.2718E-02
    XC,YC= 0.3984   0.9618   TEMP=   0.0
    SX,SY,SXY,SZ= -1222.6   -649.63   -232.83   0.00000E+00
```

**Figure 6.4**  *(Continued)*

```
   SIG1,SIG2    SIG3=-0.97789E-08 -566.95    -1305.3
   S.I.= 1305.3      SIGE= 1133.7
EL=   5 NODES=   15   28   29   16 MAT=   1 VOL= 0.4562E-02
   XC,YC= 0.4458   1.076   TEMP=   0.0
   SX,SY,SXY,SZ= -403.02   -9.2741   -827.36   0.00000E+ 00
   SIG1,SIG2    SIG3= 644.31   0.63495E-08 -1056.6
   S.I.= 1700.9      SIGE= 1487.4
EL=   6 NODES=   28   41   42   29 MAT=   1 VOL= 0.8897E-02
   XC,YC= 0.5217   1.259   TEMP=   0.0
   SX,SY,SXY,SZ= 1035.9   301.79   -953.00   0.00000E+00
   SIG1,SIG2    SIG3= 1690.1   0.11826E-07 -352.40
   S.I.= 2042.5      SIGE= 1891.1
EL=   7 NODES=    3   16   17    4 MAT=   1 VOL= 0.2718E-02
   XC,YC= 0.6337   0.8259   TEMP=   0.0
   SX,SY,SXY,SZ= 316.58   772.27   -697.87   0.00000E+00
   SIG1,SIG2    SIG3= 1278.5   0.64439E-08 -189.70
   S.I.= 1468.2      SIGE= 1383.2
EL=   8 NODES=   16   29   30   17 MAT=   1 VOL= 0.4562E-02
   XC,YC= 0.7092   0.9242   TEMP=   0.0
   SX,SY,SXY,SZ= -236.95   1051.0   -671.99   0.00000E+00
   SIG1,SIG2    SIG3= 1337.8   0.12051E-07 -523.71
   S.I.= 1861.5      SIGE= 1662.7
EL=   9 NODES=   29   42   43   30 MAT=   1 VOL= 0.8897E-02
   XC,YC= 0.8299   1.082   TEMP=   0.0
   SX,SY,SXY,SZ= -0.17996   687.34   -474.26   0.00000E+00
   SIG1,SIG2    SIG3= 929.32   0.73537E-08 -242.16
   S.I.= 1171.5      SIGE= 1071.1
EL=   10 NODES=    4   17   18    5 MAT=   1 VOL= 0.2718E-02
   XC,YC= 0.8259   0.6337   TEMP=   0.0
   SX,SY,SXY,SZ= 960.27   2022.5   -1139.1   0.00000E+00
   SIG1,SIG2    SIG3= 2748.2   234.59   0.39930E-07
   S.I.= 2748.2      SIGE= 2638.8
EL=   11 NODES=   17   30   31   18 MAT=   1 VOL= 0.4562E-02
   XC,YC= 0.9242   0.7092   TEMP=   0.0
   SX,SY,SXY,SZ= 283.31   1466.8   -450.34   0.00000E+00
   SIG1,SIG2    SIG3= 1618.6   131.43   0.24472E-07
   S.I.= 1618.6      SIGE= 1557.1
EL=   12 NODES=   30   43   44   31 MAT=   1 VOL= 0.8897E-02
   XC,YC= 1.082   0.8299   TEMP=   0.0
   SX,SY,SXY,SZ= -177.93   296.51   153.64   0.00000E+00
   SIG1,SIG2    SIG3= 341.91   0.32802E-08 -223.33
   S.I.= 565.25      SIGE= 493.10
EL=   13 NODES=    5   18   19    6 MAT=   1 VOL= 0.2718E-02
   XC,YC= 0.9618   0.3984   TEMP=   0.0
   SX,SY,SXY,SZ= 695.74   2981.3   -1078.7   0.00000E+00
   SIG1,SIG2    SIG3= 3410.0   267.05   0.53085E-07
   S.I.= 3410.0      SIGE= 3284.6
EL=   14 NODES=   18   31   32   19 MAT=   1 VOL= 0.4562E-02
   XC,YC= 1.076   0.4458   TEMP=   0.0
   SX,SY,SXY,SZ= 481.78   1561.8   -423.09   0.00000E+00
   SIG1,SIG2    SIG3= 1707.8   335.78   0.15139E-07
   S.I.= 1707.8      SIGE= 1567.2
EL=   15 NODES=   31   44   45   32 MAT=   1 VOL= 0.8897E-02
   XC,YC= 1.259   0.5217   TEMP=   0.0
   SX,SY,SXY,SZ= 88.625   -237.00   222.05   0.00000E+00
   SIG1,SIG2    SIG3= 201.16   0.19988E-08 -349.53
   S.I.= 550.69      SIGE= 482.65
```

Figure 6.4    (*Continued*)

```
EL=   16 NODES=   6   19   20   7 MAT=   1 VOL= 0.2718E-02
   XC,YC= 1.032   0.1359   TEMP=   0.0
   SX,SY,SXY,SZ= 341.16   3003.9   -531.36   0.00000E+00
   SIG1,SIG2   SIG3= 3106.1   239.04   0.49047E-07
   S.I.= 3106.1     SIGE= 2993.7
EL=   17 NODES=   19   32   33   20 MAT=   1 VOL= 0.4562E-02
   XC,YC= 1.155   0.1521   TEMP=   0.0
   SX,SY,SXY,SZ= 408.52   1520.9   -478.22   0.00000E+00
   SIG1,SIG2   SIG3= 1698.3   231.20   0.17846E-07
   S.I.= 1698.3     SIGE= 1595.3
EL=   18 NODES=   32   45   46   33 MAT=   1 VOL= 0.8897E-02
   XC,YC= 1.352   0.1779   TEMP=   0.0
   SX,SY,SXY,SZ= 195.27   -251.04   -103.79   0.00000E+00
   SIG1,SIG2   SIG3= 218.23   0.21133E-08 -274.00
   S.I.= 492.23     SIGE= 427.19
EL=   19 NODES=   7   20   21   8 MAT=   1 VOL= 0.2718E-02
   XC,YC= 1.032   -0.1359   TEMP=   0.0
   SX,SY,SXY,SZ= 101.41   1958.6   -53.992   0.00000E+00
   SIG1,SIG2   SIG3= 1960.2   99.844   0.44246E-07
   S.I.= 1960.2     SIGE= 1912.2
EL=   20 NODES=   20   33   34   21 MAT=   1 VOL= 0.4562E-02
   XC,YC= 1.155   -0.1521   TEMP=   0.0
   SX,SY,SXY,SZ= 85.834   1308.3   -484.69   0.00000E+00
   SIG1,SIG2   SIG3= 1477.1   -0.98068E-08 -83.024
   S.I.= 1560.1     SIGE= 1520.3
EL=   21 NODES=   33   46   47   34 MAT=   1 VOL= 0.1038E-01
   XC,YC= 1.364   -0.1891   TEMP=   0.0
   SX,SY,SXY,SZ= 92.727   438.57   -356.36   0.00000E+00
   SIG1,SIG2   SIG3= 661.75   0.44501E-08 -130.45
   S.I.= 792.20     SIGE= 735.70
EL=   22 NODES=   8   21   22   9 MAT=   1 VOL= 0.2718E-02
   XC,YC= 0.9618   -0.3984   TEMP=   0.0
   SX,SY,SXY,SZ= -90.774   605.45   -21.772   0.00000E+00
   SIG1,SIG2   SIG3= 606.13   0.31244E-08 -91.455
   S.I.= 697.58     SIGE= 656.65
EL=   23 NODES=   21   34   35   22 MAT=   1 VOL= 0.4562E-02
   XC,YC= 1.076   -0.4458   TEMP=   0.0
   SX,SY,SXY,SZ= -203.77   776.69   -321.27   0.00000E+00
   SIG1,SIG2   SIG3= 872.58   0.76150E-08 -299.66
   S.I.= 1172.2     SIGE= 1054.8
EL=   24 NODES=   34   47   48   35 MAT=   1 VOL= 0.1413E-01
   XC,YC= 1.322   -0.5619   TEMP=   0.0
   SX,SY,SXY,SZ= -94.292   1122.1   -249.02   0.00000E+00
   SIG1,SIG2   SIG3= 1171.1   0.41640E-08 -143.29
   S.I.= 1314.4     SIGE= 1249.0
EL=   25 NODES=   9   22   23   10 MAT=   1 VOL= 0.2718E-02
   XC,YC= 0.8259   -0.6337   TEMP=   0.0
   SX,SY,SXY,SZ= -337.31   -228.66   -259.93   0.00000E+00
   SIG1,SIG2   SIG3= -0.18077E-07 -17.442   -548.53
   S.I.= 548.53     SIGE= 540.02
EL=   26 NODES=   22   35   36   23 MAT=   1 VOL= 0.4562E-02
   XC,YC= 0.9242   -0.7092   TEMP=   0.0
   SX,SY,SXY,SZ= -312.61   219.02   -144.90   0.00000E+00
   SIG1,SIG2   SIG3= 255.95   0.24852E-08 -349.54
   S.I.= 605.50     SIGE= 526.46
EL=   27 NODES=   35   48   49   36 MAT=   1 VOL= 0.1723E-01
   XC,YC= 1.148   -0.8895   TEMP=   0.0
```

Figure 6.4   (Continued)

```
 SX,SY,SXY,SZ= -114.07   810.40   -5.4576   0.00000E+00
 SIG1,SIG2   SIG3= 810.43   0.37816E-08 -114.10
 S.I.= 924.54       SIGE= 873.09
 STRESS EVALUATION   ELEM=   28 L.S.=   1 ITER=   1 CP=   109.90
EL=   28 NODES=   10   23   24   11 MAT=   1 VOL= 0.2718E-02
 XC,YC= 0.6337   -0.8259   TEMP=   0.0
 SX,SY,SXY,SZ= -660.16   -363.46   -408.50   0.00000E+ 00
 SIG1,SIG2   SIG3=-0.12415E-07 -77.205   -946.42
 S.I.= 946.42       SIGE= 910.27
EL=   29 NODES=   23   36   37   24 MAT=   1 VOL= 0.4562E-02
 XC,YC= 0.7092   -0.9242   TEMP=   0.0
 SX,SY,SXY,SZ= -484.45   -121.05   -160.40   0.00000E+ 00
 SIG1,SIG2   SIG3=-0.55050E-08 -60.380   -545.11
 S.I.= 545.11       SIGE= 517.57
EL=   30 NODES=   36   49   50   37 MAT=   1 VOL= 0.1608E-01
 XC,YC= 0.8460   -1.162   TEMP=   0.0
 SX,SY,SXY,SZ= -256.59   247.83   91.861   0.00000E+00
 SIG1,SIG2   SIG3= 264.04   0.25529E-08 -272.80
 S.I.= 536.84       SIGE= 464.93
EL=   31 NODES=   11   24   25   12 MAT=   1 VOL= 0.2718E-02
 XC,YC= 0.3984   -0.9618   TEMP=   0.0
 SX,SY,SXY,SZ= -977.81   -219.24   -352.67   0.00000E+ 00
 SIG1,SIG2   SIG3=-0.16391E-07 -80.613   -1116.4
 S.I.=1116.4       SIGE= 1078.4
EL=   32 NODES=   24   37   38   25 MAT=   1 VOL= 0.4562E-02
 XC,YC= 0.4458   -1.076   TEMP=   0.0
 SX,SY,SXY,SZ= -658.72   -188.98   -150.38   0.00000E+ 00
 SIG1,SIG2   SIG3=-0.49551E-08 -144.96   -702.73
 S.I.= 702.73       SIGE= 642.63
EL=   33 NODES=   37   50   51   38 MAT=   1 VOL= 0.1256E-01
 XC,YC= 0.5184   -1.322   TEMP=   0.0
 SX,SY,SXY,SZ= -353.90   -34.305   34.429   0.00000E+00
 SIG1,SIG2   SIG3=-0.44876E-08 -30.638   -357.57
 S.I.= 357.57       SIGE= 343.28
EL=   34 NODES=   12   25   26   13 MAT=   1 VOL= 0.2718E-02
 XC,YC= 0.1359   -1.032   TEMP=   0.0
 SX,SY,SXY,SZ= -1156.8   -101.94   -140.28   0.00000E+ 00
 SIG1,SIG2   SIG3=-0.17494E-07 -83.607   -1175.2
 S.I.= 1175.2       SIGE= 1135.7
EL=   35 NODES=   25   38   39   26 MAT=   1 VOL= 0.4562E-02
 XC,YC= 0.1521   -1.155   TEMP=   0.0
 SX,SY,SXY,SZ= -799.74   -169.90   -63.838   0.00000E+ 00
 SIG1,SIG2   SIG3=-0.57145E-08 -163.50   -806.14
 S.I.= 806.14       SIGE= 738.10
EL=   36 NODES=   38   51   52   39 MAT=   1 VOL= 0.9530E-02
 XC,YC= 0.1746   -1.364   TEMP=   0.0
 SX,SY,SXY,SZ= -416.11   -182.45   0.37265   0.00000E+00
 SIG1,SIG2   SIG3=-0.31297E-08 -182.45   -416.11
 S.I.= 416.11       SIGE= 361.27
EL=   37 NODES=   48   49   54   53 MAT=   1 VOL= 0.3658E-01
 XC,YC= 1.312   -1.512   TEMP=   0.0
 SX,SY,SXY,SZ= -238.63   955.63   94.067   0.00000E+00
 SIG1,SIG2   SIG3= 963.00   0.75518E-08 -246.00
 S.I.= 1209.0       SIGE= 1106.7
EL=   38 NODES=   49   50   55   54 MAT=   1 VOL= 0.2469E-01
 XC,YC= 0.9375   -1.671   TEMP=   0.0
 SX,SY,SXY,SZ= -132.73   404.78   171.52   0.00000E+00
 SIG1,SIG2   SIG3= 454.85   0.41196E-08 -182.80
```

Figure 6.4  (*Continued*)

```
  S.I. = 637.64     SIGE = 568.72
EL =    39 NODES =    50   51   56   55 MAT =    1 VOL = 0.1875E-01
  XC,YC = 0.5625   -1.750   TEMP =    0.0
  SX,SY,SXY,SZ = -28.950   75.698   146.45   0.00000E + 00
  SIG1,SIG2   SIG3 = 178.89   0.17245E-08 -132.14
  S.I. = 311.04     SIGE = 270.38
EL =    40 NODES =    51   52   57   56 MAT =    1 VOL = 0.1875E-01
  XC,YC = 0.1875   -1.750   TEMP =    0.0
  SX,SY,SXY,SZ = -59.028   -81.768   53.835   0.00000E + 00
  SIG1,SIG2   SIG3 = -0.11719E-08 -15.376   -125.42
  S.I. = 125.42     SIGE = 118.48
EL =    41 NODES =    53   54   59   58 MAT =    1 VOL = 0.2812E-01
  XC,YC = 1.312   -2.375   TEMP =    0.0
  SX,SY,SXY,SZ = 78.529   585.89   92.404   0.00000E + 00
  SIG1,SIG2   SIG3 = 602.20   62.223   0.75761E-08
  S.I. = 602.20     SIGE = 573.62
EL =    42 NODES =    54   55   60   59 MAT =    1 VOL = 0.2812E-01
  XC,YC = 0.9375   -2.375   TEMP =    0.0
  SX,SY,SXY,SZ = 99.271   407.45   170.99   0.00000E + 00
  SIG1,SIG2   SIG3 = 483.54   23.182   0.11531E-07
  S.I. = 483.54     SIGE = 472.38
EL =    43 NODES =    55   56   61   60 MAT =    1 VOL = 0.2812E-01
  XC,YC = 0.5625   -2.375   TEMP =    0.0
  SX,SY,SXY,SZ = 111.94   194.30   133.24   0.00000E + 00
  SIG1,SIG2   SIG3 = 292.58   13.661   0.71481E-08
  S.I. = 292.58     SIGE = 285.99
EL =    44 NODES =    56   57   62   61 MAT =    1 VOL = 0.2812E-01
  XC,YC = 0.1875   -2.375   TEMP =    0.0
  SX,SY,SXY,SZ = 135.18   85.687   49.195   0.00000E + 00
  SIG1,SIG2   SIG3 = 165.50   55.365   0.13745E-08
  S.I. = 165.50     SIGE = 145.92
EL =    45 NODES =    58   59   64   63 MAT =    1 VOL = 0.2812E-01
  XC,YC = 1.312   -3.125   TEMP =    0.0
  SX,SY,SXY,SZ = 25.117   397.64   8.6352   0.00000E + 00
  SIG1,SIG2   SIG3 = 397.84   24.917   0.74761E-08
  S.I. = 397.84     SIGE = 385.98
EL =    46 NODES =    59   60   65   64 MAT =    1 VOL = 0.2812E-01
  XC,YC = 0.9375   -3.125   TEMP = 0.0
  SX,SY,SXY,SZ = 71.165   360.28   56.184   0.00000E + 00
  SIG1,SIG2   SIG3 = 370.81   60.631   0.35394E-08
  S.I. = 370.81     SIGE = 344.52
EL =    47  NODES =    60   61   66   65 MAT =    1 VOL = 0.2812E-01
  XC,YC = 0.5625   -3.125   TEMP =    0.0
  SX,SY,SXY,SZ = 113.08   287.20   62.291   0.00000E + 00
  SIG1,SIG2   SIG3 = 307.19   93.088   0.25390E-08
  S.I. = 307.19     SIGE = 272.83
EL =    48 NODES =    61   62   67   66 MAT =    1 VOL = 0.2812E-01
  XC,YC = 0.1875   -3.125   TEMP =    0.0
  SX,SY,SXY,SZ = 125.87   228.22   24.321   0.00000E + 00
  SIG1,SIG2   SIG3 = 233.71   120.39   0.21349E-08
  S.I. = 233.71     SIGE = 202.43
```

Figure 6.4   (*Continued*)

| REACTION FORCES | | |
|---|---|---|
| NODE | FX | FY |
| 1 | 13.288 | |
| 13 | 6.1679 | |
| 14 | 15.465 | |
| 26 | 12.275 | |
| 27 | -23.544 | |
| 39 | 12.018 | |
| 40 | -34.817 | |
| 52 | 7.8412 | |
| 57 | -4.7693 | |
| 62 | -11.040 | |
| 63 | 1.9572 | -7.2010 |
| 64 | -0.20426 | -12.609 |
| 65 | -1.4476 | -11.945 |
| 66 | -1.5253 | -10.911 |
| 67 | -4.4586 | -5.0833 |
| TOTAL | -12.795 | -47.750 |

ELEM. STRESS CALC. TIMES

| TYPE | NUMBER | STIF | TOTAL CP | AVE CP |
|---|---|---|---|---|
| 1 | 48 | 42 | 22.98 | 0.479 |

NODAL FORCE CALC. TIMES

| TYPE | NUMBER | STIF | TOTAL CP | AVE CP |
|---|---|---|---|---|
| 1 | 48 | 42 | 2.20 | 0.046 |

PROBLEM STATISTICS

| | |
|---|---|
| NO. OF ACTIVE DEGREES OF FREEDOM = | 114 |
| R.M.S. WAVEFRONT SIZE = | 11.4 |
| TOTAL CP TIME = | 128.740 |

Figure 6.4   (*Continued*)

estimate calculated by hand. The lug analysis displacement solution from ANSYS-PC/LINEAR is shown in Fig. 6.4. The maximum displacement of $0.3472 \times 10^{-3}$ in is in the vertical direction at node 1 (see Fig. 5.2). We wish to determine if this displacement value is reasonable by performing a simple hand calculation using a simplified idealization of the lug.

The circular portion of our lug model can be thought of as a beam fixed at the horizontal axis and guided at the open end at the top. This is shown in Fig. 6.5. Clearly, this is a gross simplification of the actual situation. However, this simplified model should tell us if our results are in the ballpark.

We calculate the moment of inertia for the cross-section of the lug $(bh^3/12)$ and apply a concentrated load of 50 lb at the guided end. The displacement and stress formulas for a fixed-guided beam are given in Roark and Young, *Formulas for Stress and Strain* (Ref. 1). The displacement at the open end is given by $WL^3/12EI$ (see Fig. 6.5). This turns out to be $0.47 \times 10^{-3}$ in, which is about 35 percent higher than the actual maximum displacement at node 1. This result indicates that indeed our finite element values are reasonable. There would be cause for concern, however, if our hand calculations produced a displacement that was an order of magnitude greater, for example.

The idea here is not to try to reproduce the finite element results by hand

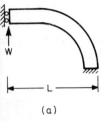

(a)

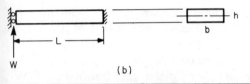

(b)

**Figure 6.5**   A simple idealization of the circular part
of the half-model of the lifting lug. Consider the
curved portion from the horizontal axis as a curved
beam, guided at the top and fixed at the other end.
A simple fixed-guided beam with the cross-section
of the circular portion of the lug is used to estimate
the accuracy of the finite element results.

but simply to see if they make sense. Obviously, the cantilever beam does
not behave exactly like the lifting lug. However, with a simple beam calculation, using the same cross-sectional properties as the lug, you can get a
"feel" for the accuracy of the results.

### 6.4.3   Checking the Stress Results

In most analyses, the stress results are the most important part of the analysis and also the most susceptible to error. Before reviewing the stress results
for the lug problem, you may wish to review the node and element numbering scheme in Fig. 5.2 and the stress contour plot in Fig. 6.3.

The stress results from ANSYS-PC/LINEAR are listed in Fig. 6.4.
Let us briefly review the meaning of the various values. First, the
element number is listed along with the four nodes that form the
element. For example, element 1 is connected by nodes 1, 14, 15, and
2. Next, the material type (there is only one type in this case) and the
volume (area × thickness) of the element are listed. The next line gives
the coordinates of the element centroid and the reference temperature,
which is not relevant to this problem. The third line gives the global
stress components. SX and SY are the tensile or compressive stresses
in the global $X$ and $Y$ directions, respectively. SXY is the shear stress
and SZ is zero for plane stress problems. SIG1, -2, and -3 are the prin-

cipal stresses. Notice that the algebraically smallest stress value is always given as SIG3. Thus, if the largest stress magnitude is represented by a compressive stress, which is negative in sign, that stress will be reported as SIG3. SI and SIGE are the stress intensity (SIG3 − SIG1) and the Von Mises or equivalent stress (see Chap. 2), respectively.

We digress here briefly to emphasize that different finite element programs use different methods for reporting stress. You must carefully study the stress output conventions of the program that you are using. Figure 6.6 shows the stress output for element 13 from both ANSYS-PC/LINEAR and MSC/pal 2.

ANSYS-PC/LINEAR, in this example, reports the stresses in coordinates parallel to the global $X$ and $Y$ axes. MSC/pal 2, on the other hand, reports the stresses in element coordinates, $U$ and $V$ (see Fig. 2.3), which are determined by the node numbering sequence. These stress coordinates are not parallel to the global coordinate axes. Ultimately, these differences in local stress output are resolved by the calculation of principal stresses and the Von Mises stress. The Von Mises stress results from both programs are virtually identical, and the principal stress results are reasonably close.

```
a) MSC/pal 2 listing for element 13
STATIC ANALYSIS SUBCASE NO. 1 ELEMENT RECOVERY
QUAD PLATE NUMBER 13, RESULTS FOR NODE 0, ELEMENT NODES: 5 18 19 6

              MEMBRANE  BEND(+T/2)  BEND(−T/2)   SUM(+T/2)   SUM(−T/2)
SIGMA U       1.6110E+02  .0000E+00   .0000E+00   1.6110E+02  1.6110E+02R
SIGMA V       3.3806E+03  .0000E+00   .0000E+00   3.3806E+03  3.3806E+03
TAU UV       −4.5805E+01  .0000E+00   .0000E+00  −4.5805E+01 −4.5805E+01
SIGMA 1       3.3812E+03  .0000E+00   .0000E+00   3.3812E+03  3.3812E+03
SIGMA 2       1.6045E+02  .0000E+00   .0000E+00   1.6045E+02  1.6045E+02
TAU MAX       1.6104E+03  .0000E+00   .0000E+00   1.6104E+03  1.6104E+03
ANGLE        −8.9185E+01  .0000E+00   .0000E+00  −8.9185E+01 −8.9185E+01
MAXIMUM STRESSES FOR QUAD ELEMENT          VON MISES CRITERION

ELEMENT  NODE    MAJOR     MINOR     SHEAR     STRESS     % YIELD
   13      0    3.381E+03  1.605E+02  1.610E+03  3.304E+03   11.0

b)ANSYS-PC/Linear listing for element 13
EL= 13 NODES= 5 18 19 6 MAT= 1 VOL= 0.2718E-02
XC,YC= 0.9618   0.3984   TEMP=   0.0
SX,SY,SXY,SZ= 695.74   2981.3   -1078.7   0.00000E+00
SIG1,SIG2,SIG3= 3410.0   267.05   0.53085E-07
S.I.= 3410.0   SIGE= 3284.6
```

**Figure 6.6** The listings from MSC/pal 2 and ANSYS-PC/LINEAR for element 13 (see Fig. 5.2). Notice that the stress values are quite different since MSC/pal 2 uses local element coordinates while ANSYS-PC/LINEAR uses global coordinates. However, the Von Mises stress from MSC/pal 2 and SIGE in ANSYS are very close, and the principal stresses are comparable since in both cases, these values are in the same coordinate system.

Of course, you might wonder why there is any difference at all in the results. The differences primarily stem from the different ways in which we applied the external load. In ANSYS-PC/LINEAR, we had to apply an estimated uniform pressure over the element faces between nodes 1, 2, and 3. In MSC/pal 2, the program automatically calculated a distributed load from our input of 50 lb. Thus, the external load distribution over the nodes is different, resulting in a slightly different stress distribution. The differences, however, are insignificant.

We now return to Fig. 6.4 and the task of interpreting the stress results of our lug analysis. As we saw from the stress contour plot, the most highly stressed area of the lug is at the inside surface near the horizontal axis of the circular portion. The element numbers in this area are 10, 13, 16, and 19 (see Fig. 5.2). From the stress listing in Fig 6.4, we see that the maximum stress occurs in element 13. The stress reported is at the centroid of element 13. This is not the stress at the surface.

In order to obtain the stress at the surface, we have to use the ANSYS-PC/LINEAR postprocessor POST1 to print out the nodal stresses. In MSC/pal 2, the standard stress output also includes the stresses at the nodes of each element and, therefore, at the surface. This is an advantage in that you do not have to use a postprocessor. The drawback, however, is that the MSC/pal 2 output is much more voluminous than in ANSYS-PC/LINEAR since there are five complete stress listings for each element, one for each node, and one at the element centroid.

Figure 6.7 shows the ANSYS-PC/LINEAR POST1 listing for the 10 highest principal and Von Mises stresses at the nodes. The maximum stress is at node 6, which is one of the nodes of element 13. The maximum Von Mises stress is 3987.66, say 4000 lb/in$^2$, to use a round figure.

The next step is to perform some hand calculations to see if the stress results make sense. First, we will check some of the elements at the bottom of the lug. The vertical stress in this area should be roughly equivalent to the total external load divided by the total cross-sectional area of the model:

$$\sigma_Y = \frac{50}{1.5 \times 0.1} = 333 \text{ lb/in}^2$$

For element 48, SY is 228 lb/in$^2$. For element 45, the value is 397 lb/in$^2$. Scanning the vertical stress values for the other elements in this area, the values range from about 100 to 400 lb/in$^2$. These results seem reasonable.

```
*****POST NODAL STRESS LISTING*****
LOAD STEP   1   ITERATION   1   SECTION= 1
TIME= 0.00000E+00 LOAD CASE= 1
```

| NODE | SIG1 | SIG2 | SIG3 | SI | SIGE |
|------|------|------|------|------|------|
| 6 | 4004.15 | 33.8373 | −0.439497 | 4004.59 | 3987.66 |
| 5 | 3782.07 | 39.9876 | −31.4519 | 3813.52 | 3778.31 |
| 40 | 3419.30 | 0.553287E−08 | −341.204 | 3760.51 | 3602.05 |
| 7 | 3068.90 | 71.6819 | −57.6339 | 3126.54 | 3063.96 |
| 41 | 2886.13 | −0.981976E−08 | −338.546 | 3224.67 | 3075.82 |
| 19 | 2436.48 | 115.607 | −4.44691 | 2440.92 | 2384.26 |
| 4 | 2412.68 | 121.449 | −90.4704 | 2503.15 | 2404.60 |
| 18 | 2321.60 | 102.867 | −23.0288 | 2344.63 | 2284.63 |
| 20 | 2008.89 | 54.6919 | −44.4490 | 2053.34 | 2006.08 |
| 17 | 1715.58 | 60.6102 | −134.667 | 1850.25 | 1765.27 |

MAXIMUMS

| NODE | 6 | 4 | 40 | 6 | 6 |
|------|------|------|------|------|------|
| VALUE | 4004.15 | 121.449 | −341.204 | 4004.59 | 3987.66 |
| POST1 | −INP | | | | |

**Figure 6.7**  The highest 10 average nodal stresses reported by the ANSYS-PC/LINEAR postprocessor POST. Nodes 5 and 6 are surface nodes near the horizontal axis of the circular part of the lug.

Checking the stress value at element 13 is somewhat more difficult. Using our fixed-guided beam idealization (see the last section, 6.4.2), we can calculate the bending stress, which is $Mc/I$ or $(WL/2)c/I$. The result of this calculation is approximately 9000 lb/in². The maximum stress from our finite element model is 4000 lb/in². While these results differ by roughly a factor of 2, we would expect a more conservative result from our grossly simplified beam idealization. The stresses in the lug are more distributed than in the beam idealization where we assume that most of the load is absorbed by the fixed end of the beam.

It is interesting to note that curved beam theory gives such conservative results as to be virtually useless. According to calculations using curved beam theory, our lifting lug is stressed to the yield point with an applied load of 100 lb! While the lifting lug problem looks fairly simple at first glance, hand calculations turn out to be quite complicated and yield extremely conservative results.

### 6.4.4  Numerical Accuracy and Mesh-Convergence Studies

All the preceding checks have indicated that our analysis is reasonable. But is it accurate enough? As you work with certain types of problems, you will be able to answer this question with some confidence simply based on previous experience. In other cases, however, it may be necessary to resort to more analytical methods to verify the accuracy of the mesh refinement. The most practical method is to perform a mesh-convergence study.

As stated earlier, the accuracy of the model will increase with more nodes and hence greater mesh refinement. There is, however, a point at which further refinement has little effect on the accuracy. At this point, the solution has converged. A mesh-convergence study simply involves analyzing a number of mesh refinements until the results converge.

Rather than experimenting with mesh refinements on full-sized models, it is usually more efficient to work with a small section of the model. Figure 6.8 shows four finite element meshes for a quarter-circle of the lifting lug. This is the part of the lug that is most critically stressed. Mesh-convergence studies should always focus on the most critically stressed portion of the model. Using MSC/pal 2, we will analyze these four meshes and then compare the results.

The four test models are quite easy to create simply by modifying the listings in Figs. 5.4 and 5.6. Figure 6.9 shows the model and load input listings for Fig. 6.8a, the very coarse model. Each model has the same node numbering sequence along the inside surface, which is our primary area of interest.

In particular, we will look at the major principal stress results for nodes 4 and 5 and the displacement of node 1. Nodes 4 and 5 are the most reliable for this convergence study since there are no external forces applied to them. Although node 6 also has no external forces applied to it, it is part of an element subjected to the external reaction forces which change in magnitude depending on the mesh refinement. While the sum of the reaction forces remains the same for each test case, the magnitude of the reaction force at each node along the base of the model changes according to the number of nodes over which the reaction forces are distributed. For example, the vertical reaction force acting on node 7 is $-14.7$ lb in the very coarse model and is 1.95 lb in the most refined model. Clearly, the stress distribution in the base elements also changes based on the distribution of the external reaction forces. Thus, the stress results at nodes 6 and 7 will not converge but will vary depending on the distribution of the reaction forces.

Nodes 1, 2, and 3 are subjected to the externally applied forces. As we mentioned in Chap. 4, concentrated nodal forces can produce artificially high stresses in highly refined models. The stresses in the elements subjected to the applied forces will keep increasing as the elements become smaller, eventually approaching the condition of a

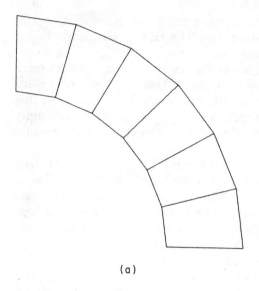

(a)

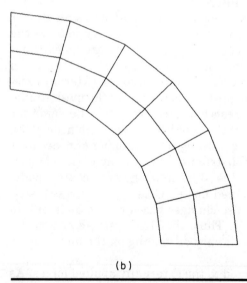

(b)

**Figure 6.8**  Four test models for a mesh-convergence study verifying the accuracy of the mesh
for the lifting lug analysis. Figures 6.8c and 6.8d
show converged results, confirming that Fig.
6.8c gives an adequate mesh refinement.

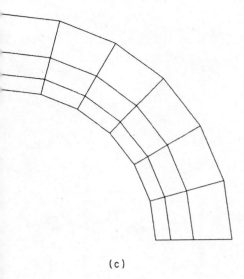

( c )

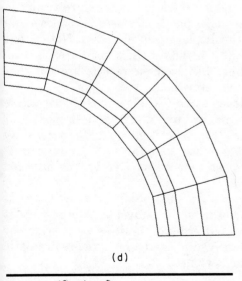

( d )

**Figure 6.8**  *(Continued)*

```
TITLE HOLE IN TAB
NODAL POINT LOCATIONS 2
1,1,90 THRU 7,1,0
8,1.5,90 THRU 14,1.5,0
--BLANK LINE--
MAT 30E6,0,.733E-3,.3,30E3
QUAD 1,0,.1
GEN CON 1 8 14 7 1
ZERO 1
TX 1 8
RA ALL
TZ ALL
END

DISP APPLIED 1
AL 0.0 7 14

LINE LOAD APPLIED 12
3 THRU 1 STEP 1 0,-50,0,0,0,1

SOLVE
QUIT
```

**Figure 6.9** The MSC/pal 2 model and load input files for the test model in Fig. 6.8a. Compare to the listings in Figs. 5.4 and 5.6.

"point load." In other words, the stresses in element 1 would converge at infinity, which does not help us much.

Nodes 4 and 5, on the other hand, are largely unaffected by external forces and will therefore give stress results that are dependent on the degree of mesh refinement, which is what we are trying to establish. Table 6.1 shows the major principal stress for nodes 4 and 5 for each test case and also the displacement at node 1. Notice that the displacement value at node 1 is almost the same for each case. As we have mentioned earlier, displacement results are not that sensitive to the degree of mesh refinement.

The principal stresses at nodes 4 and 5 are low in the very coarse model and converge between the medium- and fine-mesh models. It appears that the medium mesh (Fig. 6.8c) is adequate for accurately picking up the surface stresses in our lug analysis. By pure coincidence, of course, this is the mesh that we selected for the fullsized analysis.

It should be noted that in this simple problem, the stress variation between the very coarse mesh and the refined mesh is only about 10 percent. In problems involving discontinuities or thermal or dynamic loading, variations in results can be much more dramatic depending on the mesh refinement used.

TABLE 6.1   Stress Listing for Mesh-Convergence Study

| Node | Very coarse (Fig. 6.8a) | Coarse (Fig. 6.8b) | Medium (Fig. 6.8c) | Fine (Fig. 6.8d) |
|---|---|---|---|---|
| | Major Stress | | | |
| 4 | 2495 | 2636 | 2754 | 2768 |
| 5 | 2736 | 2864 | 3030 | 3055 |
| | Displacement ($10 \times 10^4$) ($Y$ direction) | | | |
| 1 | 1.539 | 1.516 | 1.531 | 1.537 |

## 6.5   Concluding the Lifting Lug Analysis

You may recall from Chap. 5 that our lifting lug must be able to carry a "load, applied in any reasonable manner, of twice the empty weight of the tank based on a safety factor of 4." The yield stress of the steel in this example is 36,000 $lb/in^2$. Since the maximum stress in the lug is 4000 $lb/in^2$ and our applied load was 100 lb (twice the symmetry load), the maximum load that the lug can sustain is 900 lb. Dividing by a safety factor of 4, twice the empty weight of the tank cannot exceed 225 lb. This means that the tank cannot weigh more than 112 lb for use with this lifting lug according to the standards set forth by the American Petroleum Institute.

In order to increase the load capabilities of the lug, the lug thickness could be increased and a steel with a higher yield strength could be selected. Since the lug analysis is linear and elastic, the stress results can be scaled by the increased thickness, and similarly the maximum load can be adjusted by increasing the yield strength. For example, a lug with a thickness of 0.25 in instead of 0.1 could lift a tank weighing 280 lb. Similarly, an increase in material yield strength would further increase the lifting capacity.

## 6.6   Reporting the Results

The objectives of a finite element analysis vary depending on the application. However, any engineering or design decision made on the basis of a finite element analysis must be well documented. Much of the material presented in this and the previous chapter could form the basis for a report on the lifting lug analysis.

A report of a finite element analysis should contain the following components:

1. Description of the objectives of the analysis. Describe the failure criteria or engineering requirements against which the analysis will be compared.

2. Physical description of the part to be analyzed. The overall dimensions, material, loading conditions, and description of the operation or application of the part should be included. Obviously, a sketch of the part is helpful.

3. Brief summary of the finite element program and computer system used for the analysis (this section might be omitted for an in-house report).

4. Plot of the finite element model and description of types of elements used, boundary conditions, applied loads and relevant engineering assumptions.

5. Displacement, mode shape, thermal, and/or stress contour plots. A discussion should accompany these plots, describing the behavior of the model and how it relates to the actual expected behavior of the part.

6. Table showing the stresses and displacements for critical sections of the model. Complete output is generally attached as an appendix to the report.

7. Hand calculations supporting the finite element results. A brief discussion of these calculations along with references should be included. This section might be attached as an appendix to the main body of the report.

8. Conclusions and recommendations. Describe what was learned from the analysis and what conclusions can be drawn. Summarize the results in conjunction with the failure criteria or engineering requirements. If the analysis shows an inadequate design, recommendations for design modifications would be included in this section.

The importance of thorough documentation cannot be overemphasized. First of all, documentation is required to support the design or analysis decisions resulting from the finite element analysis. Second, and of equal importance, the process of preparing the report forces you to check all aspects of your analysis. Even if your work situation does not require a formal report, it is strongly recommended that you go through the process described above as a means of checking your analysis.

## Reference

1. Roark, R. J., and W. C. Young: *Formulas for Stress and Strain*, McGraw-Hill, New York, 1975, p. 96.

# 7

# Statics Analysis

In this chapter, we present example problems in statics analysis. You may wish to review the information on statics analysis in Chap. 2 and the modeling guidelines presented in Chap. 4. The problems in this chapter are intended to provide a cross-section of typical engineering problems and, most importantly, to illustrate various modeling techniques.

## 7.1 Multiple Load Cases: Frame Problem

This problem is taken from the MSC/pal 2 example problems manual (Ref. 1). Referring to Fig. 7.1$a$, a two-story building is analyzed for the following loads:

1. Gravity load of G − 1 applied in the –$Z$ direction (dead load)
2. Design load of 20 lb/ft$^2$ on the roof and 150 lb/ft$^2$ on the second floor
3. Wind load of 20 lb/ft$^2$ acting in the positive $X$ direction on the wall defined by nodes 1, 7, 19, and 25

A 5000-lb water tank is assumed to rest on one corner of the roof (nodes 23, 24, 26, and 27). W 10 × 45 I beams are used for the columns, and W 10 × 12 I beams are used for the girders. The building is 20 ft tall. The column spacing is shown in Fig. 7.1$b$.

The frame is modeled using the MSC/pal 2 beam type 1 element. The beam type 1 element is a three-dimensional element which can have arbi-

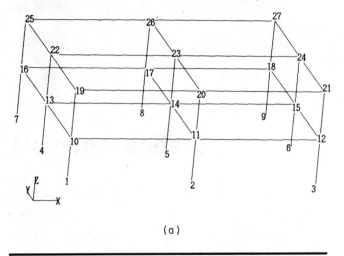

(a)

**Figure 7.1** (a) MSC/pal 2 of the two-story building model with the node numbering scheme.

trary geometric properties. MSC/pal 2 also provides rectangular and cylindrical beam elements, whose properties are specified simply by height and width and outside and inside diameters, respectively. These elements do not apply to this problem, however, since the properties of I beams are required.

In order to solve the frame problem, we could either apply all the loads simultaneously or apply separate load cases. The advantage of

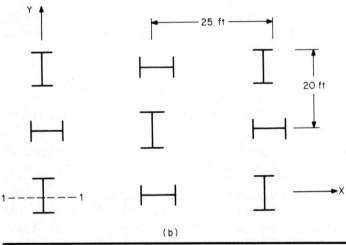

(b)

**Figure 7.1** (Continued) (b) Top view of the building model showing the orientation of the I-beam columns. Note the column spacing dimensions.

applying separate load cases is that we can evaluate the structure's response to each separate loading condition and determine which one is most critical. If we apply the loads simultaneously, we obtain the overall stress picture, but we cannot tell which loading condition produces the largest stresses.

While the application of separate load cases is often instructive, the results of each load case must still be combined to give the overall stress values. Some finite element programs provide postprocessing routines to perform load case combinations. Other programs, including MSC/pal 2, do not have this capability. In this case, you have two choices. You can either combine the stresses for the most critical elements by hand, or you can perform an additional analysis with the loads applied simultaneously. In a small problem such as this one, a reasonable approach is to first run individual load cases and then to run the analysis again with the loads applied simultaneously.

Although we are analyzing three separate load cases, the stiffness matrix has to be formulated only once since it is independent of the external loading conditions. This is an important characteristic of finite element analysis. Once the stiffness matrix has been generated from the node and element definition, it can be used repeatedly for various types of loadings. Figures 7.2a and b show the listings for generating the model and the three load cases. This problem illustrates the importance of beam orientation. Notice in Fig. 7.1b that the center and corner columns are rotated with respect to the other four columns. The major axis (axis 1–1) of the center and corner columns is parallel to the global X axis, and the moments of inertia are correctly specified in the first BEAM TYPE command (see Fig. 7.2a). For the other columns, however, it is necessary to rotate the element axes 90° in order to correctly specify the moments of inertia. This is accomplished by the VECTOR ORIENTATION command, which, in this case, aligns the major axis with the global Y axis.

The mass of the water tank is applied by means of four mass elements at the nodes listed above (see MASS commands in Fig. 7.2a). Each mass element is assigned one-quarter of the mass of the tank (1250 lb/386.4 in/sec$^2$).

The ground nodes are rigidly fixed using the DISPLACEMENTS APPLIED command (see Fig. 7.2b). Each load case is then applied and solved. Note that the units are pounds, inches, and seconds.

The displacement plots for load cases 2 and 3 are shown in Fig. 7.3a and b. When viewing the displacement plots, keep in mind that a 5000-lb water tank acts on one-quarter of the model. The element connectivities are listed along with the maximum and Von Mises stresses for each load case in Fig. 7.4. Note that the "% Yield" column is always zero since no yield stress was input in the material properties specification (MATERIAL PROPERTIES command).

```
TITLE EXAMPLE 9 — TWO STORY BUILDING
NODAL POINT LOCATIONS 1
1 0,0,0 THROUGH 19 0,0,240 STEP 9
3 600,0,0 THROUGH 21 600,0,240 STEP 9
7 0,480,0 THROUGH 25 0,480,240 STEP 9
9 600,480,0 THROUGH 27 600,480,240 STEP 9
— BLANK LINE —
NODAL POINT LOCATIONS 21
1, 3, 9, 1, 3
10, 12, 18, 1, 3
19, 21, 27, 1, 3
— BLANK LINE —
MATERIAL PROPERTIES 30E6, 0, 7.76E-4, 0.3
C ELEMENTS FOR CORNERS, CENTRAL COLUMN
BEAM TYPE 1 13.3, 1.51, 248, 53.4, 0, 0, 49.1, 13.3
GENERATE CONNECTS 1,9,27,2,9 1
C ELEMENTS FOR OTHER COLUMNS
BEAM TYPE 1 13.3, 1.51, 248, 53.4, 0, 0, 49.1, 13.3
VECTOR ORIENTATION 0,1,0
GENERATE CONNECTS 2,8,26,2,9 1
C ELEMENTS FOR GIRDERS
BEAM TYPE 1 3.54, 0.06, 53.8, 2.18, 0, 0, 10.9, 1.10
GENERATE CONNECTS 10,12,18,1,3 1
GENERATE CONNECTS 10,12,18,1,3 0
GENERATE CONNECTS 19,21,27,1,3 1
GENERATE CONNECTS 19,21,27,1,3 0
C CONCENTRATED MASS FOR WATER TANK
MASS 23 3.23
MASS 24 3.23
MASS 26 3.23
MASS 27 3.23
END DEFINITION
```

**Figure 7.2** (*a*)  Model listing for two-story building.

```
DISPLACEMENTS APPLIED 21
ALL 0 1,3,9,1,3
—BLANK LINE—
GRAVITY APPLIED 0, 0, –386.4
SOLVE
PRESSURE LOAD APPLIED 21
–.1389   19,21,27,1,3
–1.0417   10,12,18,1,3
—BLANK LINE—
SOLVE
PRESSURE LOAD APPLIED 21
.1389   1,7,25,3,9
—BLANK LINE—
SOLVE
QUIT
```

**Figure 7.2** (*Continued*) (*b*)  Load input listing for two-story building.

LOAD CASE 2 - DEFORMED SHAPE

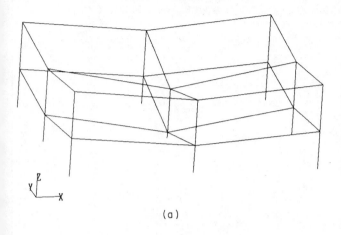

(a)

LOAD CASE 3 - DEFORMED SHAPE

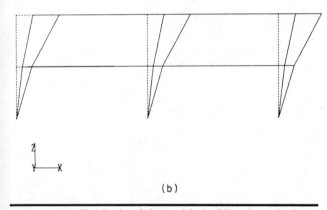

(b)

**Figure 7.3**  (a) The displaced shape of the building due to load case 2. For clarity, the undeflected shape is not included. (b) The deflected shape of the model due to load case 3, superimposed on the original shape.

It is seen from Fig. 7.4 that load case 1 produces almost negligible stresses. Load cases 2 and 3, however, produce substantial stresses, particularly in element 3, which is the lower element of the center column. The detailed stress results for element 3 are shown in Fig. 7.5. Let us look carefully at the beam stress output of MSC/pal 2.

EXAMPLE 7.1 — TWO STORY BUILDING
STATIC ANALYSIS SUBCASE NO. 1 ELEMENT RECOVERY

MAXIMUM STRESSES FOR BEAM          VON MISES CRITERION

| ELE-MENT | MAJOR | MINOR | SHEAR | STRESS | % YIELD | NODE | CONNEC-TIVITY | |
|---|---|---|---|---|---|---|---|---|
| 1 | 7.851E+01 | −2.706E+02 | 1.353E+02 | 2.706E+02 | .0 | 10 | 1 | 10 |
| 2 | 7.952E+01 | −2.717E+02 | 1.358E+02 | 2.717E+02 | .0 | 12 | 3 | 12 |
| 3 | .000E+00 | −2.354E+02 | 1.177E+02 | 2.354E+02 | .0 | 14 | 5 | 14 |
| 4 | 7.858E+01 | −2.706E+02 | 1.353E+02 | 2.706E+02 | .0 | 16 | 7 | 16 |
| 5 | .000E+00 | −3.641E+02 | 1.820E+02 | 3.641E+02 | .0 | 18 | 9 | 18 |
| 6 | 3.920E+02 | −4.696E+02 | 2.348E+02 | 4.696E+02 | .0 | 19 | 10 | 19 |
| 7 | 3.960E+02 | −4.737E+02 | 2.369E+02 | 4.737E+02 | .0 | 21 | 12 | 21 |
| 8 | .000E+00 | −1.574E+02 | 7.870E+01 | 1.574E+02 | .0 | 23 | 14 | 23 |
| 9 | 3.921E+02 | −4.698E+02 | 2.349E+02 | 4.698E+02 | .0 | 25 | 16 | 25 |
| 10 | 3.005E+02 | −5.659E+02 | 2.829E+02 | 5.659E+02 | .0 | 27 | 18 | 27 |
| 11 | .000E+00 | −1.589E+02 | 7.946E+01 | 1.589E+02 | .0 | 11 | 2 | 11 |
| 12 | 6.552E+01 | −3.020E+02 | 1.510E+02 | 3.020E+02 | .0 | 13 | 4 | 13 |
| 13 | .000E+00 | −3.964E+02 | 1.982E+02 | 3.964E+02 | .0 | 15 | 6 | 15 |
| 14 | .000E+00 | −2.512E+02 | 1.256E+02 | 2.512E+02 | .0 | 17 | 8 | 17 |
| 15 | 4.385E+01 | −1.466E+02 | 7.329E+01 | 1.466E+02 | .0 | 20 | 11 | 20 |
| 16 | 5.372E+02 | −6.381E+02 | 3.190E+02 | 6.381E+02 | .0 | 22 | 13 | 22 |
| 17 | 4.437E+02 | −7.321E+02 | 3.661E+02 | 7.321E+02 | .0 | 24 | 15 | 24 |
| 18 | .000E+00 | −2.399E+02 | 1.199E+02 | 2.399E+02 | .0 | 26 | 17 | 26 |
| 19 | 7.634E+01 | −5.696E+01 | 3.817E+01 | 7.634E+01 | .0 | 10 | 10 | 13 |
| 20 | 2.219E+01 | .000E+00 | 1.110E+01 | 2.219E+01 | .0 | 11 | 11 | 14 |
| 21 | 7.370E+01 | −5.402E+01 | 3.685E+01 | 7.370E+01 | .0 | 12 | 12 | 15 |
| 22 | 7.645E+01 | −5.707E+01 | 3.822E+01 | 7.645E+01 | .0 | 16 | 13 | 16 |
| 23 | 2.355E+01 | −4.934E−01 | 1.178E+01 | 2.355E+01 | .0 | 17 | 14 | 17 |
| 24 | 7.408E+01 | −5.446E+01 | 3.704E+01 | 7.408E+01 | .0 | 18 | 15 | 18 |
| 25 | 2.632E+01 | .000E+00 | 1.316E+01 | 2.632E+01 | .0 | 10 | 10 | 11 |
| 26 | 2.631E+01 | .000E+00 | 1.315E+01 | 2.631E+01 | .0 | 12 | 11 | 12 |
| 27 | 5.475E+01 | −9.916E+00 | 2.738E+01 | 5.475E+01 | .0 | 13 | 13 | 14 |
| 28 | 5.600E+01 | −1.117E+01 | 2.800E+01 | 5.600E+01 | .0 | 15 | 14 | 15 |
| 29 | 2.491E+01 | .000E+00 | 1.246E+01 | 2.491E+01 | .0 | 16 | 16 | 17 |
| 30 | 2.627E+01 | .000E+00 | 1.313E+01 | 2.627E+01 | .0 | 18 | 17 | 18 |
| 31 | 1.220E+02 | −1.522E+02 | 7.612E+01 | 1.522E+02 | .0 | 19 | 19 | 22 |
| 32 | 1.893E+01 | −5.546E+01 | 2.773E+01 | 5.546E+01 | .0 | 20 | 20 | 23 |
| 33 | 1.160E+02 | −1.466E+02 | 7.329E+01 | 1.466E+02 | .0 | 21 | 21 | 24 |
| 34 | 1.213E+02 | −1.515E+02 | 7.575E+01 | 1.515E+02 | .0 | 25 | 22 | 25 |
| 35 | 2.197E+01 | −5.864E+01 | 2.932E+01 | 5.864E+01 | .0 | 26 | 23 | 26 |
| 36 | 1.180E+02 | −1.486E+02 | 7.428E+01 | 1.486E+02 | .0 | 27 | 24 | 27 |
| 37 | .000E+00 | −5.616E+01 | 2.808E+01 | 5.616E+01 | .0 | 19 | 19 | 20 |
| 38 | .000E+00 | −5.602E+01 | 2.801E+01 | 5.602E+01 | .0 | 21 | 20 | 21 |
| 39 | 6.989E+01 | −1.323E+02 | 6.616E+01 | 1.323E+02 | .0 | 22 | 22 | 23 |
| 40 | 7.237E+01 | −1.348E+02 | 6.740E+01 | 1.348E+02 | .0 | 24 | 23 | 24 |
| 41 | .000E+00 | −5.324E+01 | 2.662E+01 | 5.324E+01 | .0 | 25 | 25 | 26 |
| 42 | .000E+00 | −5.595E+01 | 2.797E+01 | 5.595E+01 | .0 | 27 | 26 | 27 |

STATIC ANALYSIS SUBCASE NO. 2 ELEMENT RECOVERY

MAXIMUM STRESSES FOR BEAM          VON MISES CRITERION

| ELE-MENT | MAJOR | MINOR | SHEAR | STRESS | % YIELD | NODE | CONNEC-TIVITY | |
|---|---|---|---|---|---|---|---|---|
| 1 | .000E+00 | −1.622E+03 | 8.110E+02 | 1.622E+03 | .0 | 10 | 1 | 10 |
| 2 | .000E+00 | −1.622E+03 | 8.110E+02 | 1.622E+03 | .0 | 12 | 3 | 12 |
| 3 | .000E+00 | −6.386E+03 | 3.193E+03 | 6.386E+03 | .0 | 5 | 5 | 14 |
| 4 | .000E+00 | −1.622E+03 | 8.110E+02 | 1.622E+03 | .0 | 16 | 7 | 16 |
| 5 | .000E+00 | −1.622E+03 | 8.110E+02 | 1.622E+03 | .0 | 18 | 9 | 18 |
| 6 | .000E+00 | −2.520E+02 | 1.260E+02 | 2.520E+02 | .0 | 19 | 10 | 19 |
| 7 | .000E+00 | −2.520E+02 | 1.260E+02 | 2.520E+02 | .0 | 21 | 12 | 21 |
| 8 | .000E+00 | −7.491E+02 | 3.746E+02 | 7.491E+02 | .0 | 14 | 14 | 23 |
| 9 | .000E+00 | −2.520E+02 | 1.260E+02 | 2.520E+02 | .0 | 25 | 16 | 25 |
| 10 | .000E+00 | −2.520E+02 | 1.260E+02 | 2.520E+02 | .0 | 27 | 18 | 27 |
| 11 | .000E+00 | −3.213E+03 | 1.607E+03 | 3.213E+03 | .0 | 11 | 2 | 11 |
| 12 | .000E+00 | −3.194E+03 | 1.597E+03 | 3.194E+03 | .0 | 13 | 4 | 13 |
| 13 | .000E+00 | −3.194E+03 | 1.597E+03 | 3.194E+03 | .0 | 15 | 6 | 15 |
| 14 | .000E+00 | −3.213E+03 | 1.607E+03 | 3.213E+03 | .0 | 17 | 8 | 17 |
| 15 | .000E+00 | −4.212E+02 | 2.106E+02 | 4.212E+02 | .0 | 20 | 11 | 20 |
| 16 | .000E+00 | −3.794E+02 | 1.897E+02 | 3.794E+02 | .0 | 22 | 13 | 22 |

Figure 7.4   Stress summary for all load cases in two-story building problem.

| ELE-MENT | MAJOR | MINOR | SHEAR | STRESS | % YIELD | NODE | CONNEC-TIVITY | |
|---|---|---|---|---|---|---|---|---|
| 17 | .000E+00 | −3.794E+02 | 1.897E+02 | 3.794E+02 | .0 | 24 | 15 | 24 |
| 18 | .000E+00 | −4.212E+02 | 2.106E+02 | 4.212E+02 | .0 | 26 | 17 | 26 |
| 19 | 9.402E+01 | −8.935E+01 | 4.701E+01 | 9.402E+01 | .0 | 13 | 10 | 13 |
| 20 | 1.992E+02 | −1.882E+02 | 9.961E+01 | 1.992E+02 | .0 | 14 | 11 | 14 |
| 21 | 9.402E+01 | −8.935E+01 | 4.701E+01 | 9.402E+01 | .0 | 15 | 12 | 15 |
| 22 | 9.402E+01 | −8.935E+01 | 4.701E+01 | 9.402E+01 | .0 | 13 | 13 | 16 |
| 23 | 1.992E+02 | −1.882E+02 | 9.961E+01 | 1.992E+02 | .0 | 14 | 14 | 17 |
| 24 | 9.402E+01 | −8.935E+01 | 4.701E+01 | 9.402E+01 | .0 | 15 | 15 | 18 |
| 25 | 2.556E+01 | −2.540E+01 | 1.278E+01 | 2.556E+01 | .0 | 11 | 10 | 11 |
| 26 | 2.556E+01 | −2.540E+01 | 1.278E+01 | 2.556E+01 | .0 | 11 | 11 | 12 |
| 27 | 5.069E+01 | −5.033E+01 | 2.534E+01 | 5.069E+01 | .0 | 14 | 13 | 14 |
| 28 | 5.069E+01 | −5.033E+01 | 2.534E+01 | 5.069E+01 | .0 | 14 | 14 | 15 |
| 29 | 2.556E+01 | −2.540E+01 | 1.278E+01 | 2.556E+01 | .0 | 17 | 16 | 17 |
| 30 | 2.556E+01 | −2.540E+01 | 1.278E+01 | 2.556E+01 | .0 | 17 | 17 | 18 |
| 31 | 8.989E+01 | −9.675E+01 | 4.837E+01 | 9.675E+01 | .0 | 22 | 19 | 22 |
| 32 | 2.004E+02 | −2.169E+02 | 1.084E+02 | 2.169E+02 | .0 | 23 | 20 | 23 |
| 33 | 8.989E+01 | −9.675E+01 | 4.837E+01 | 9.675E+01 | .0 | 24 | 21 | 24 |
| 34 | 8.989E+01 | −9.675E+01 | 4.837E+01 | 9.675E+01 | .0 | 22 | 22 | 25 |
| 35 | 2.004E+02 | −2.169E+02 | 1.084E+02 | 2.169E+02 | .0 | 23 | 23 | 26 |
| 36 | 8.989E+01 | −9.675E+01 | 4.837E+01 | 9.675E+01 | .0 | 24 | 24 | 27 |
| 37 | 2.838E+01 | −2.861E+01 | 1.431E+01 | 2.861E+01 | .0 | 20 | 19 | 20 |
| 38 | 2.838E+01 | −2.861E+01 | 1.431E+01 | 2.861E+01 | .0 | 20 | 20 | 21 |
| 39 | 5.589E+01 | −5.636E+01 | 2.818E+01 | 5.636E+01 | .0 | 23 | 22 | 23 |
| 40 | 5.589E+01 | −5.636E+01 | 2.818E+01 | 5.636E+01 | .0 | 23 | 23 | 24 |
| 41 | 2.838E+01 | −2.861E+01 | 1.431E+01 | 2.861E+01 | .0 | 26 | 25 | 26 |
| 42 | 2.838E+01 | −2.861E+01 | 1.431E+01 | 2.861E+01 | .0 | 26 | 26 | 27 |

STATIC ANALYSIS SUBCASE NO. 3 ELEMENT RECOVERY

MAXIMUM STRESSES FOR BEAM          VON MISES CRITERION

| ELE-MENT | MAJOR | MINOR | SHEAR | STRESS | % YIELD | NODE | CONNEC-TIVITY | |
|---|---|---|---|---|---|---|---|---|
| 1 | 4.609E+03 | −4.603E+03 | 2.305E+03 | 4.609E+03 | .0 | 1 | 1 | 10 |
| 2 | 4.361E+03 | −4.367E+03 | 2.183E+03 | 4.367E+03 | .0 | 3 | 3 | 12 |
| 3 | 1.177E+04 | −1.177E+04 | 5.887E+03 | 1.177E+04 | .0 | 5 | 5 | 14 |
| 4 | 4.609E+03 | −4.603E+03 | 2.305E+03 | 4.609E+03 | .0 | 7 | 7 | 16 |
| 5 | 4.361E+03 | −4.367E+03 | 2.183E+03 | 4.367E+03 | .0 | 9 | 9 | 18 |
| 6 | 9.911E+02 | −9.878E+02 | 4.956E+02 | 9.911E+02 | .0 | 10 | 10 | 19 |
| 7 | 1.158E+03 | −1.161E+03 | 5.805E+02 | 1.161E+03 | .0 | 12 | 12 | 21 |
| 8 | 2.504E+03 | −2.504E+03 | 1.252E+03 | 2.504E+03 | .0 | 14 | 14 | 23 |
| 9 | 9.911E+02 | −9.878E+02 | 4.956E+02 | 9.911E+02 | .0 | 16 | 16 | 25 |
| 10 | 1.158E+03 | −1.161E+03 | 5.805E+02 | 1.161E+03 | .0 | 18 | 18 | 27 |
| 11 | 3.604E+03 | −3.604E+03 | 1.802E+03 | 3.604E+03 | .0 | 2 | 2 | 11 |
| 12 | 9.779E+03 | −9.763E+03 | 4.889E+03 | 9.779E+03 | .0 | 4 | 4 | 13 |
| 13 | 9.331E+03 | −9.346E+03 | 4.673E+03 | 9.346E+03 | .0 | 6 | 6 | 15 |
| 14 | 3.604E+03 | −3.604E+03 | 1.802E+03 | 3.604E+03 | .0 | 8 | 8 | 17 |
| 15 | 1.145E+03 | −1.145E+03 | 5.725E+02 | 1.145E+03 | .0 | 11 | 11 | 20 |
| 16 | 1.958E+03 | −1.950E+03 | 9.791E+02 | 1.958E+03 | .0 | 13 | 13 | 22 |
| 17 | 2.261E+03 | −2.269E+03 | 1.134E+03 | 2.269E+03 | .0 | 15 | 15 | 24 |
| 18 | 1.145E+03 | −1.145E+03 | 5.725E+02 | 1.145E+03 | .0 | 17 | 17 | 26 |
| 19 | 1.550E+03 | −1.555E+03 | 7.774E+02 | 1.555E+03 | .0 | 13 | 10 | 13 |
| 20 | 1.548E+03 | −1.547E+03 | 7.738E+02 | 1.548E+03 | .0 | 14 | 11 | 14 |
| 21 | 1.519E+03 | −1.514E+03 | 7.593E+02 | 1.519E+03 | .0 | 15 | 12 | 15 |
| 22 | 1.550E+03 | −1.555E+03 | 7.774E+02 | 1.555E+03 | .0 | 13 | 13 | 16 |
| 23 | 1.548E+03 | −1.547E+03 | 7.738E+02 | 1.548E+03 | .0 | 15 | 14 | 17 |
| 24 | 1.519E+03 | −1.514E+03 | 7.593E+02 | 1.519E+03 | .0 | 15 | 15 | 18 |
| 25 | 2.479E+03 | −3.012E+03 | 1.506E+03 | 3.012E+03 | .0 | 10 | 10 | 11 |
| 26 | 2.488E+03 | −2.950E+03 | 1.475E+03 | 2.950E+03 | .0 | 12 | 11 | 12 |
| 27 | 5.667E+03 | −7.549E+03 | 3.774E+03 | 7.549E+03 | .0 | 13 | 13 | 14 |
| 28 | 6.417E+03 | −6.729E+03 | 3.364E+03 | 6.729E+03 | .0 | 14 | 14 | 15 |
| 29 | 2.479E+03 | −3.012E+03 | 1.506E+03 | 3.012E+03 | .0 | 16 | 16 | 17 |
| 30 | 2.488E+03 | −2.950E+03 | 1.475E+03 | 2.950E+03 | .0 | 18 | 17 | 18 |
| 31 | 4.209E+03 | −4.222E+03 | 2.111E+03 | 4.222E+03 | .0 | 22 | 19 | 22 |
| 32 | 4.295E+03 | −4.295E+03 | 2.148E+03 | 4.295E+03 | .0 | 23 | 20 | 23 |
| 33 | 4.205E+03 | −4.193E+03 | 2.103E+03 | 4.205E+03 | .0 | 24 | 21 | 24 |
| 34 | 4.209E+03 | −4.222E+03 | 2.111E+03 | 4.222E+03 | .0 | 22 | 22 | 25 |
| 35 | 4.295E+03 | −4.295E+03 | 2.148E+03 | 4.295E+03 | .0 | 23 | 23 | 26 |
| 36 | 4.205E+03 | −4.193E+03 | 2.103E+03 | 4.205E+03 | .0 | 24 | 24 | 27 |
| 37 | 3.252E+03 | −3.594E+03 | 1.797E+03 | 3.594E+03 | .0 | 19 | 19 | 20 |
| 38 | 3.321E+03 | −3.583E+03 | 1.791E+03 | 3.583E+03 | .0 | 21 | 20 | 21 |
| 39 | 7.076E+03 | −8.002E+03 | 4.001E+03 | 8.002E+03 | .0 | 23 | 22 | 23 |
| 40 | 7.464E+03 | −7.688E+03 | 3.844E+03 | 7.688E+03 | .0 | 23 | 23 | 24 |
| 41 | 3.252E+03 | −3.594E+03 | 1.797E+03 | 3.594E+03 | .0 | 25 | 25 | 26 |
| 42 | 3.321E+03 | −3.583E+03 | 1.791E+03 | 3.583E+03 | .0 | 27 | 26 | 27 |

**Figure 7.4**  (*Continued*)

STATIC ANALYSIS SUBCASE NO. 1 ELEMENT RECOVERY

```
ELEMENT    3 BEAM      FORCE RESULTS      (NODE 5)                        (NODE 14)
AXIAL    -3.120E+03    V SHEAR  2.667E-02    V MOMENT -5.243E+00    V MOMENT -5.628E+00
TORSION   9.859E-03    W SHEAR -3.213E-03    W MOMENT  6.684E+00    W MOMENT  9.884E+00

NODE 5          NORMAL STRESS                NODE 14         NORMAL STRESS
-2.3520E+02    -2.3470E+02    -2.3419E+02    -2.3345E+02    -2.3470E+02    -2.3396E+02
-2.3509E+02    -2.3459E+02    -2.3409E+02    -2.3533E+02    -2.3459E+02    -2.3385E+02
-2.3498E+02    -2.3448E+02    -2.3398E+02    -2.3522E+02    -2.3447E+02    -2.3373E+02

           MAXIMUM STRESSES FOR BEAM                   VON MISES CRITERION
ELEMENT   MAJOR        MINOR       SHEAR       STRESS      %YIELD   NODE    CONNECTIVITY
3        .000E+00    -2.354E+02    1.177E+02    2.354E+02    .0      14       5    14
```

STATIC ANALYSIS SUBCASE NO. 2 ELEMENT RECOVERY

```
ELEMENT    3 BEAM      FORCE RESULTS      (NODE 5)                        (NODE 14)
AXIAL    -8.493E+04    V SHEAR -8.144E-15    V MOMENT -9.190E-14    V MOMENT -4.025E-14
TORSION   1.657E-17    W SHEAR  4.304E-16    W MOMENT  5.073E-13    W MOMENT -4.700E-13

NODE 5          NORMAL STRESS                NODE 14         NORMAL STRESS
-6.3857E+03    -6.3857E+03    -6.3857E+03    -6.3857E+03    -6.3857E+03    -6.3857E+03
-6.3857E+03    -6.3857E+03    -6.3857E+03    -6.3857E+03    -6.3857E+03    -6.3857E+03
-6.3857E+03    -6.3857E+03    -6.3857E+03    -6.3857E+03    -6.3857E+03    -6.3857E+03

           MAXIMUM STRESSES FOR BEAM                   VON MISES CRITERION
ELEMENT   MAJOR        MINOR       SHEAR       STRESS      %YIELD   NODE    CONNECTIVITY
3        .000E+00    -6.386E+03    3.193E+03    6.386E+03    .0       5       5    14
```

STATIC ANALYSIS SUBCASE NO. 3 ELEMENT RECOVERY

```
ELEMENT    3 BEAM      FORCE RESULTS      (NODE 5)                        (NODE 14)
AXIAL     1.490E-01    V SHEAR  4.952E-15    V MOMENT -5.781E+05    V MOMENT -1.085E+05
TORSION  -4.239E-15    W SHEAR  3.914E+03    W MOMENT -3.692E-13    W MOMENT  2.251E-13

NODE 5          NORMAL STRESS                NODE 14         NORMAL STRESS
-1.1775E+04    -1.1775E+04    -1.1775E+04    -2.2088E+03    -2.2088E+03    -2.2088E+03
 1.1204E-02     1.1204E-02     1.1204E-02     1.1204E-02     1.1204E-02     1.1204E-02
 1.1775E+04     1.1775E+04     1.1775E+04     2.2089E+03     2.2089E+03     2.2089E+03

           MAXIMUM STRESSES FOR BEAM                   VON MISES CRITERION
ELEMENT   MAJOR        MINOR       SHEAR       STRESS      %YIELD   NODE    CONNECTIVITY
3        1.177E+04   -1.177E+04    5.887E+03    1.177E+04    .0       5       5    14
```

**Figure 7.5** Detailed stress output for element 3 of two-story building model.

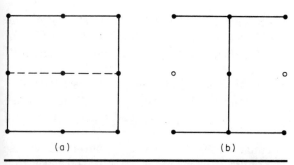

(a)                              (b)

**Figure 7.6** (a) The locations for beam stress output in MSC/pal 2. (b) Note that the two outer locations on the neutral axis of the I beam do not exist. Therefore, reported stress values at these locations should be ignored.

First, the axial and shear forces and the bending moment and torsion loads acting on the local $u$, $v$, and $w$ axes of the element (see Fig. 2.13) are reported. The bending moment is reported at each end of the beam (nodes 5 and 14). Note in load case 3 (Fig. 7.5) that the bending moment at node 5 is much larger in magnitude than the moment at node 14. This is what we would expect since node 5 is located at the base of the column and is fixed. The other loads are constant from one end of the beam to the other.

Normal (longitudinal) stresses are reported at nine locations on the beam cross-section at each end of the beam. This is illustrated in Fig. 7.6a. The top row of the stress output (Fig. 7.5) corresponds to the top three locations of the beam cross-section. The middle row corresponds to the neutral axis, and so forth. In an I beam, the stress locations at the outer ends of the major neutral axis do not exist, as shown in Fig. 7.6b. The stress values given for these locations should be ignored.

Most finite element programs, including MSC/pal 2, do not directly calculate the beam shear stresses for beam elements which have user-defined geometrical properties. This is because it is impractical to calculate the appropriate shear stress factor for arbitrary geometries. Special elements with built-in geometrical properties, such as pipe or rectangular beam elements, generally support direct shear stress calculation. It should be noted, however, that shear generally contributes a very small portion of the overall load in beam problems. Bending and axial forces are generally much more significant. In problems involving very short beams where shear may be significant, beam elements that support shear stress calculation should be used.

For the beam type 1 element, MSC/pal 2 calculates the maximum normal stresses ($\pm Mc/I \pm P/A$). The maximum tensile stress is defined as the "major stress," and the maximum compressive stress is defined as the "minor stress." Since direct shear stress is not calculated, the Von Mises stress is reported as the absolute value of the maximum normal stress. The maximum shear stress is "backed out" as one-half of the maximum normal stress.

Note that for subcases (load cases) 1 and 2, element 3 is entirely in compression. Therefore, the major stress is reported as 0. In subcase number 3, element 3 is primarily subjected to bending from the wind load.

At this point, we could manually combine the results from each load case to obtain the overall stress results. It is important to realize, however, that the maximum (major and minor) and Von Mises stresses from different load cases cannot be added algebraically since they may be derived from different locations on the beam cross-section. The normal stresses from each load case must be added at corresponding element locations.

Combining loads manually can be a laborious process. Unless the program has a postprocessor for combining loads, the best solution is to run the analysis again with the loads applied simultaneously. In this problem, all we have to do is modify the load input file as shown in Fig. 7.7 and execute the STAT2 module again (see Chap. 5). Comparing the listing in Fig. 7.7 with Fig. 7.2b, we have simply consolidated the separate load cases into a single load case.

```
DISPLACEMENTS APPLIED 21
ALL  0  1,3,9,1,3
— BLANK LINE —
GRAVITY APPLIED 0, 0, −386.4
PRESSURE LOAD APPLIED 21
−.1389  19,21,27,1,3
−1.0417  10,12,18,1,3
−1389  1,7,25,3,9
— BLANK LINE —
SOLVE
QUIT
```

**Figure 7.7** The load input file for the two-story building analysis with all load cases combined.

Since we have determined the critical element from the separate load case runs, it is necessary to request output for only element 3 in the simultaneous load case run. Results for element 3 for the combined loads are shown in Fig. 7.8.

If you are interested, you can add up the normal stresses from each load case in Fig. 7.5, using one of the three element locations in the top row for the minor (compressive) stress and one of the locations in the bottom row for the major (tensile) stress. You will get the same

```
                    EXAMPLE 9 — TWO STORY BUILDING
               STATIC ANALYSIS SUBCASE NO. 1 ELEMENT RECOVERY
  ELEMENT      3 BEAM       FORCE RESULTS            (NODE 5)              (NODE 14)
  AXIAL       -8.805E+ 04   V  SHEAR 2.667E- 02   V MOMENT -5.781E+05   V MOMENT -1.085E+05
  TORSION      9.859E- 03   W  SHEAR 3.914E+03    W MOMENT 6.684E+00    W MOMENT 9.884E+00


     NODE 5             NORMAL STRESS          NODE 14            NORMAL STRESS
  - 1.8396E+04     -1.8395E+04   -1.8395E+04   -8.8300E+03   -8.8292E+03   -8.8285E+03
  - 6.6208E+03     -6.6203E+03   -6.6198E+03   -6.6210E+03   -6.6203E+03   -6.6195E+03
    5.1542E+03      5.1547E+03    5.1552E+03   -4.4121E+03   -4.4113E+03   -4.4106E+03


       MAXIMUM STRESSES FOR BEAM              VON MISES CRITERION
  ELEMENT   MAJOR       MINOR       SHEAR     STRESS   % YIELD  NODE  CONNECTIVITY
     3     5.155E+03  -1.840E+04  9.198E+03  1.840E+04   .0      5      5      14
```

**Figure 7.8**  The combined load stress results for element 3 of the two-story building model.

totals as in Fig. 7.8. The maximum Von Mises stress is approximately 18 kip/in². We will also look at a dynamics problem involving multiple load cases in Chap. 8.

## 7.2  Pipe Junction Analysis

In this problem, contributed by Swanson Analysis, Inc. (Ref. 2), the junction of two pipes of different diameters is analyzed using ANSYS-PC/LINEAR. The objective of the analysis is to determine the stresses in the intersection due to internal pressure.

Referring to Fig. 7.9, the quarter-symmetrical model consists of 320 nodes and 277 3-D shell elements (STIF 63). The orientation of Fig. 7.9 shows the global coordinate system for the problem. Symmetry boundary conditions are imposed at the planes of symmetry, resulting in 180 imposed displacements. Thus, there is a total of 1740 active DOF. This represents a medium-sized problem on a microcomputer. The execution time for this problem is approximately 50 minutes on an IBM PC XT.

Note that the highlighted portion of the model in Fig. 7.9 consists of thicker shell elements, representing a reinforcement pad. The relevant dimensions and loading conditions are as follows:

*Smaller pipe*: Mean diameter = 11 in; thickness = 1.0 in
*Larger pipe*: Mean diameter = 21.875 in; thickness = 1.0 in
*Reinforcement pad*: thickness = 1.5 in
*Internal pressure*: 500 lb/in²

The node numbering scheme and overall dimensions of the model are shown in Fig 7.10*a* and *b*. The dimensions for the model well exceed the attenuation lengths as described in Chap. 4. A more refined mesh is used in the small pipe and in the area of the reinforcement pad. While there is a total of 320 nodes, the maximum node number is 484. As we shall see, this is because of the node generation method employed in this analysis. There is

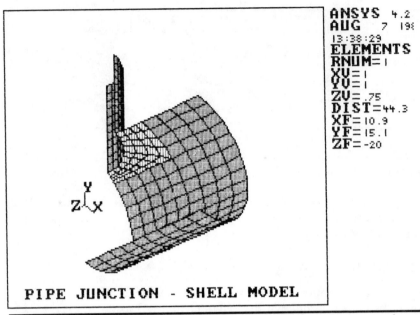

PIPE JUNCTION - SHELL MODEL

Figure 7.9   The pipe junction model. The highlighted region is a reinforcement pad.

no requirement that the node numbers must be consecutive. The listing for the analysis is shown in Fig. 7.11. Let us examine this listing in detail.

Following the title, the element type is defined as STIF63, the 3-D shell element. Two sets of real constants are defined for the shell element to allow the thickness of the reinforcement pad to be specified. When the real constant table is set to 1 (the default set), the element thickness is 1.0 in. When the real constant table is set to 2, the element thickness is 1.5 in. This will become clear when we define the elements.

The EX command defines the modulus of elasticity. Note that two adjacent commas with no separating characters denote a default field value. For example, EX,,30E6 is the same as EX,1,30E6, where the 1 is the default value for the material type number. ANSYS-PC/LINEAR uses the default value for Poisson's ratio since no value is specified. Also, note that no material density is specified.

Next, the LOCAL command establishes a local cylindrical coordinate system for defining the smaller pipe of the pipe junction. The first field following LOCAL is simply an arbitrary reference number for the coordinate system. Reference numbers for user-defined coordinate systems must be greater than 10. In this case, the local coordinate system is assigned the reference number 11.

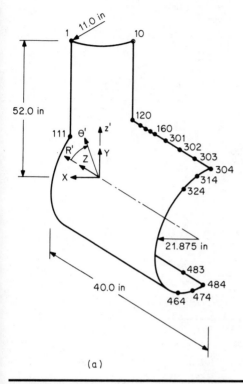

Figure 7.10 (a) The pipe model node numbering scheme and dimensions. Note the local coordinate system used to define the smaller pipe.

The next field in the LOCAL command specifies the type of coordinate system. ANSYS-PC/LINEAR identifies the Cartesian, cylindrical, spherical, and toroidal coordinate systems by 0, 1, 2, and 3, respectively. Therefore, coordinate system 1 is a cylindrical coordinate system. The following five fields use default values of 0. The first three of these fields specify the origin of the local coordinate system in global coordinates $(0, 0, 0)$. The next three fields specify any rotations with respect to the global coordinate axes. In this case, $-90$ specifies a rotation of the local $Z'$ axis so that it is parallel to the axis of the small pipe (see Fig. 7.10).

The first N command defines node 1 at local coordinates 11, 0, 52 ($R'$, $\theta'$, and $Z'$, respectively). Remember that these are local coordinates. The actual, global coordinate values for node 1 are 11, 52, and 0 ($X$, $Y$, and $Z$). Node 10 is defined next, and the FILL command fills in evenly spaced nodes between nodes 1 and 10.

The first NGEN command generates node points 111 and 120, based on

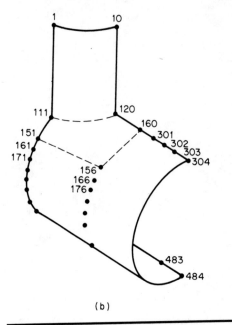

(b)

**Figure 7.10**  *(Continued)* *(b)* Nodes 160, 120, 111, 151, and 156 bound the reinforcement pad.

the pattern of nodes 1 and 10, incrementing the first node of the pattern by 9 and moving the Y coordinate -30.125 in from the location of the original pattern. Nodes 111 and 120 are now approximately at the junction of the small and large pipes. As we mentioned in Chap. 5, generation and repetition commands in ANSYS-PC/LINEAR must always count the command or pattern to be repeated or generated as one iteration. For example, NGEN,2 creates only one pattern.

The next step is to define the exact location of nodes 111 and 120 along the line of intersection of the two pipes. Since the large pipe is defined using a different coordinate system, calculation of some of the intersection coordinates is fairly difficult and would require some tedious trigonometry if ANSYS-PC/LINEAR did not provide the MOVE command.

The MOVE command locates intersection coordinates precisely. Quoting directly from the *ANSYS-PC/LINEAR User's Manual* (Ref. 3), "At an intersection the point has three coordinate values in each of two coordinate systems, one set which may be determined from the other. The MOVE command allows calculating an intersection point by specifying the two coordinate systems in which the point is located and at least three of the six coordinate values. The three most obvious values are input and the program will calculate the three more difficult values."

```
TITLE, PIPE JUNCTION—SHELL MODEL
ET,1,63
R,1,1.0
R,2,1.5
EX,,30E6
LOCAL,11,1,,,,,,-90
N,1,11,0,52
N,10,11,90,52
FILL
NGEN,2,110,1,10,9,,,-30.125
MOVE,111,1,21.875,999,0,11,11,0,999
MOVE,120,1,21.875,90,999,11,11,90,999
FILL,111,120
MOVE,112,1,21.875,999,999,11,11,10,999
RP8,1,,,,,,,10
FILL,1,111,10
RP10,1,1
CSYS,1
N,151,21.875,50,0
N,160,21.875,90,-20
N,156,21.875,50,-20
FILL,151,156
FILL,156,160
FILL,111,151,3
RP10,1,1
NGEN,15,10,151,156,1,,-10
N,304,21.875,90,-40
FILL,160,304,3,301,1
NGEN,19,10,301,304,1,,-10
E,1,2,12,11
EGEN,9,1,1
EGEN,11,10,-9
REAL,2
E,111,112,122,121
EGEN,9,1,-1
EGEN,4,10,-9
REAL,1
E,151,152,162,161
EGEN,5,1,-1
EGEN,14,10,-5
E,160,301,311,159
RP4,-1,10,10,-1
E,156,341,351,166
EGEN,14,10,-1
E,301,302,312,311
EGEN,3,1,-1
EGEN,18,10,-3
CSYS
WFRONT
WSORT,Y,-1
WFRONT
SYMBC,,1
SYMBC,,3
D,120,UY
PSF,1,1,21.875,-500.0
PSF,11,1,11,-500.0
F,314,FZ,-20879.23,,474,10
F,304,FZ,-10439.62,,484,180
F,2,FY,4751.66,,9
F,1,FY,2375.81,,10,9
SFWRIT
FINISH
```

**Figure 7.11** Pipe junction model input listing (ANSYS-PC/LINEAR).

Looking at the first MOVE command, the second and sixth fields following MOVE specify the two coordinate system reference numbers. Therefore, coordinate systems 1 (global cylindrical) and 11 (the local coordinate system) are used to calculate the intersection points. Unknown coordinate values are assigned the value 999. It is known that node 111 must have a global radial coordinate of 21.875, which is the radius of the large pipe. It is also known that the radial coordinate in the local coordinate system must be 11, which is the radius of the small pipe, and that the local angle $\theta'$ must be 0. Thus, three coordinates have been specified. The remaining coordinates are automatically calculated by the program. This is an extremely powerful command. As mentioned earlier, one of the major difficulties in these types of problems is having to calculate intersecting coordinates. The MOVE command makes it a fairly simple matter.

The MOVE command is used in similar fashion to define node 120. Then, evenly spaced nodes are filled between nodes 111 and 120. The MOVE command is used again to define node 112, and then the RP command is used to repeat the MOVE command eight times (including the first use of the repeated command) to define the other filled-in nodes. Any field from the repeated command can be incremented in the RP command. In this case, the node number (the first field in the MOVE command) is incremented by 1 with each repetition and the local coordinate $\theta'$(the eighth field in the MOVE command) is incremented by 10 each time.

Finally, the FILL command is used to fill in nodes between nodes 1 and 111, incrementing the node number by 10. This is repeated 10 times (including the first use of the FILL command), incrementing the beginning and ending nodes by 1 each time, which defines the remaining nodes of the small pipe.

The CSYS,1 command changes the coordinate system to the global cylindrical coordinate system. The next several commands generate the nodes for the large pipe. We had mentioned earlier that the node numbers are not consecutive and that the maximum node number is 484, although there are only 320 nodes. As we shall see, the irregular numbering scheme is a result of defining the reinforcement pad.

Referring to Fig. 7.9, the mesh in the reinforcement area represents a transition from the finer mesh of the small pipe to the coarser mesh in the large pipe. The reinforcement pad is bounded by nodes 111, 120, 160, 156, and 151 and extends half the length of the large pipe (20 in in the $-Z$ direction).

Recalling that the global cylindrical coordinate system is in effect, nodes 151, 160, and 156 are defined. Next, the FILL command is used to fill in evenly spaced nodes between nodes 151 and 156 and then between nodes 156 and 160.

Three nodes are filled between nodes 111 and 151. The program evenly increments the node numbers by 10 (121, 131, 141) in this case. The command is repeated 10 times (including the first FILL command) to generate the rest of the reinforcement pad, incrementing the beginning and ending nodes of the FILL command by 1.

The next NGEN command generates the rest of the first half of the large pipe, based on the node pattern of nodes 151 through 156, and incrementing the angle $\theta$ by $-10°$. Note that it is necessary to increment the node numbers by 10 since the next available node is 161. Referring to Fig. 7.10, it is seen that nodes 167 through 170 are skipped as a result, as are nodes 177 through 180, 187 through 190, and so forth. We therefore end up with a maximum node number which is greater than the actual number of nodes. The node numbering sequence is a matter of convenience and does not effect the efficiency of the solution in ANSYS-PC/LINEAR (see Chap. 3). However, the sequence in which the nodes are connected to the elements can affect the size of the stiffness matrix (see Chap. 4). As we shall see, ANSYS-PC/LINEAR provides an option to renumber the element sequence after all the elements have been defined, in order to reduce the size of the stiffness matrix.

The last node generated by the NGEN command is node 296. For convenience and consistency, node numbers 297 through 300 are skipped, and node 304 is defined at the end of the pipe. Three nodes are filled between node 160 and node 304, starting with node number 301. The final NGEN command generates the rest of the large pipe.

The elements are defined starting with the E command. Element generation is straightforward in this example. The first E command defines the first element connected by nodes 1, 2, 12, and 11. The EGEN command generates a total of nine elements (including the first element) incrementing the connecting node numbers by 1, based on the pattern of element 1 (which was the element defined by the first E command). The next EGEN command generates 11 rows of elements (including the top row), incrementing the node numbers by 10 and using the pattern established by the last nine elements defined ($-9$). At this point, the elements for the small pipe are defined.

Next, the element real constant set is set to 2 by the REAL,2 command since we are about to define the elements in the reinforcement pad. As discussed earlier, the element thickness is therefore set to 1.5 in. After the reinforcement pad elements are defined, the REAL,1 command sets the constant set back to 1. The generation of the remaining elements proceeds in similar fashion as described above for the small pipe.

Following the last EGEN command, the CSYS command activates the global Cartesian coordinate system. The WSORT command reorders the elements sorted in descending order $(-1)$ according to the $Y$ coordinate of the element centroid. As mentioned earlier, the order in which the elements are connected can affect the size of the stiffness matrix or the "wave-front" size (see Chap. 3) as it is defined in ANSYS-PC/LINEAR. The wave-front size is actually the number of simultaneous equations currently in core memory. Clearly, the fewer the equations in core memory at one time, the faster the solution will be completed.

In problems where the element definition does not proceed sequentially from one end of the model to the other, it is a good idea to reorder the elements. Along with the WSORT command, ANSYS-PC/LINEAR provides another variation in which the elements can be reordered according to node number. The WFRONT command reports the current estimated wave-front size of the model. In this problem, the wave-front size was 150 DOF before the WSORT command was issued and 132 afterward, which is a reduction of 12 percent. In terms of execution time, the reduction is approximately 7 minutes. Clearly, the reduction in wave-front size can significantly reduce the execution time for very large problems.

Returning to Fig. 7.11, the SYMBC commands impose the symmetry displacement conditions along planes normal to the global $X$ and $Z$ axes, respectively. The D command sets the $Y$ displacement of node 120 to 0 to prevent rigid-body motion. The PSF commands specify a pressure of 500 lb/in$^2$ acting on the large and small pipes, respectively. The first field following PSF specifies the coordinate systems (1 and 11, respectively). The next field specifies the surface orientation on which the pressure is to act. In this case, the orientation is normal to the radial coordinate. Next, the actual location of where the pressure is to act is defined. This location is the inside surface of the pipe, defined by the radius. Finally, the pressure value is specified.

The last step in completing the analysis is to specify the "end" or "cap" forces acting on each end of the pipe system. If we stop and consider the actual physical behavior of the pipe system, at some point the pipe is "capped," or there is a pipe elbow in the line, which causes longitudinal reaction forces to act on the pipe. To visualize this, simply imagine that we place caps on the ends of the pipe junction, defined by nodes 1 and 10, and nodes 304 and 484 (see Fig. 7.9). These caps will cause reaction forces to act on the end-nodes.

Since we will distribute the end-node reaction forces evenly, we have to calculate the reaction force per node. At the small end, there are 10 nodes. Therefore, the reaction force per node is the total surface area defined by our imaginary cap, multiplied by the pressure, and divided by 10. Due to symmetry, nodes 1 and 10 will have only half of the reaction force per node acting on them. The nodal reaction is calculated as follows:

$$F = \frac{[\pi \times (11)^2)/4] \times 500}{10} = 4751.66 \text{ lb}$$

Nodes 2 through 9 are assigned this force in the positive $Y$ direction. Nodes 1 and 10 are assigned half of this force. Similar calculations produce the forces acting in the $-Z$ direction at the large end of the pipe.

With the end forces specified, the analysis input file is complete. The EPLOT command plots the model on the screen for checking the geometry. The SFWRIT command stores the data for execution by the main ANSYS program.

As we have seen, the definition of this model is not a trivial task. A fair amount of preparation with pencil and paper is required before the listing in Fig. 7.11 is actually entered into the computer. Again, the complexity of the problem would be greatly reduced with the use of a computer-aided design (CAD) package (see App. B).

### 7.2.1. The Results of the Pipe Junction Problem

The area of main concern in this analysis is the intersection of the two pipes. The stress concentration will be highest in this area. Figure 7.12 shows a stress contour plot of the equivalent stress (Von Mises stress) at the inside surface, magnified to show the region of interest. ANSYS-PC/LINEAR Revision 4.2 provides only color stress contour plots, which are difficult to interpret in black and white. In any case, the maximum equivalent stress occurs right at the corner (node 120) and is 33,955 lb/in$^2$. The small pipe has a nominal stress of about 5000 lb/in$^2$ while the nominal stress in the large pipe ranges from approximately 9000 to 13,500 lb/in$^2$.

A quick hand calculation shows that these stresses are in agreement with values predicted from pressure vessel stress theory. For example, the nominal hoop stress (which is close in value to the equivalent stress) in the large pipe is calculated as $PR/T = 500 \times 21.875/1.0 = 10,938$ lb/in$^2$. In addition, the stress concentration factor for a circular hole in a cylinder is given as 2.5 by Harvey, *Pressure Component Construction* (Ref. 4). Therefore, the stress at the corner is predicted to be $2.5 \times 10,938 = 27,343$ lb/in$^2$. Of course, these hand-calculated results do not take into account the effects of the small pipe which causes additional bending in the large pipe. However, the results indicate

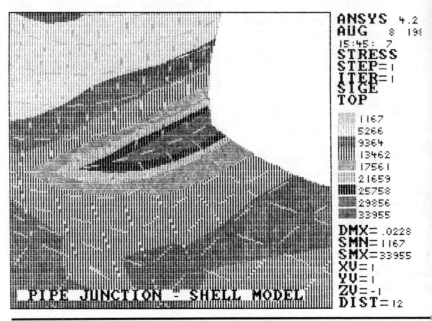

**Figure 7.12**   A blowup of the distribution of the equivalent stress at the intersection of the two pipes. The contours are displayed in color on a color graphics monitor.

the reasonableness of the analysis.

While the analysis produces good stress results in the intersection region, one modeling method used in the analysis is not strictly accurate. In an axisymmetrical analysis of a cylinder subjected to internal pressure, the end-nodes cannot actually rotate with respect to each other. In other words, the end-nodes should be coupled in the axial direction, meaning that they should displace equally in the axial direction. This boundary condition cannot be directly specified in ANSYS-PC/LINEAR since there is no option for specifying coupled degrees of freedom (see Chap. 4).

However, coupled degrees of freedom can be simulated by the use of spar elements with large stiffnesses connected to the end-nodes in the axial direction. The large stiffness in the spar element can be specified by assigning a large cross-sectional area to it. The stiffness $(EA/L)$ assigned the spar element should be four to five orders of magnitude greater than the maximum stiffness of the structure (Ref. 5). The maximum stiffness can be read from the ANSYS output file.

Figures 7.13a and b show the pipe junction equivalent stress contour plot without and with coupled end-nodes, respectively. Notice that the end of the small pipe clearly rotates in the case without the coupled end-nodes. The

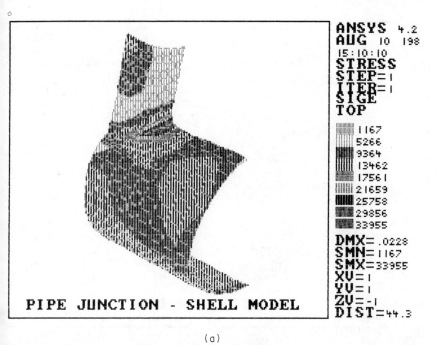

ANSYS 4.2
AUG 10 198
15:10:10
STRESS
STEP=1
ITER=1
SIGE
TOP

▓ 1167
░ 5266
▓ 9364
░ 13462
▓ 17561
░ 21659
▓ 25758
▓ 29856
▓ 33955

DMX= .0228
SMN=1167
SMX=33955
XU=1
YU=1
ZU=-1
DIST=44.3

PIPE JUNCTION - SHELL MODEL

(a)

**Figure 7.13** (a) The equivalent stress contour plot for the pipe junction. Note the rotation of the small end of the pipe.

stress distribution is more uniform in the coupled-end-node case since bending from the end rotation is eliminated. However, as we see from the stress results, the overall accuracy of the analysis is hardly affected by the use of coupled end-nodes. The conclusion, then, is that coupled end-nodes are not necessary as long as the ends are substantially removed from the region of interest.

## 7.3 Enforced Displacements and Element Offsets: Binder Clip Analysis

For a last statics analysis example, we look at the analysis of a binder clip, as shown in Fig. 7.14. The purpose of the analysis is to estimate the external force required to open the clip ½ in and to evaluate the resulting stresses in the clip. The example is contributed by The MacNeal-Schwendler Corporation and illustrates some interesting modeling and design techniques. We use MSC/pal 2 to perform the analysis.

Binder clips and other flat springs are typically manufactured from high-carbon, cold-rolled spring steel, which has an exceptionally high ultimate strength. The working stress in flat springs often exceeds

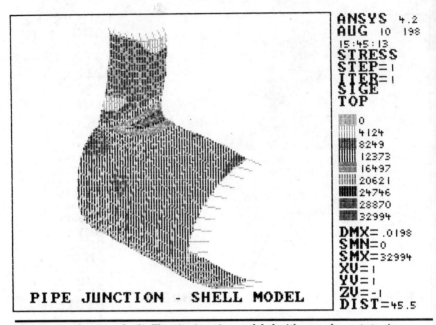

ANSYS 4.2
AUG 10 198
15:45:13
STRESS
STEP=1
ITER=1
SIGE
TOP

0
4124
8249
12373
16497
20621
24746
28870
32994

DMX= .0198
SMN=0
SMX=32994
XV=1
YV=1
ZV=-1
DIST=45.5

PIPE JUNCTION - SHELL MODEL

**Figure 7.13** (*Continued*) (*b*) The pipe junction modeled with spar elements to simulate coupled degrees of freedom in the longitudinal direction of the pipe. Note that the overall stress results are very close to those in (*a*).

100,000 lb/in$^2$ (Ref. 6). The clip shown in Fig. 7.14 is a standard 2-in-wide binder clip for use in clamping together large documents. Since the clip is axisymmetrical about its axis of rotation, it is necessary only to model one-half of the clip.

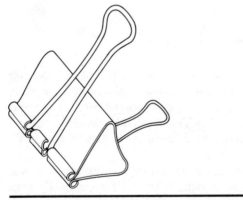

**Figure 7.14** A typical binder clip.

Quadrilateral plate elements are used to model the spring steel, and cylindrical beam elements are used to model the handle. The finite element model is shown in Fig. 7.15a. The model consists of 45 nodes, 25 plate elements, and 15 beam elements. The node numbering scheme is shown in Fig. 7.15b. The diameter of the clip handle is 0.0625 in, and the thickness of the spring steel is 0.0234 in. The approximate overall dimensions of the half-clip are 2 in × 1 in × ½ in (Y, X, and Z).

Notice the three lines offset from the clamping edge (nodes 31 through 36) in Fig. 7.15a. These lines represent offset elements used to model the curved part of the clamping edge, which holds the two ends of the clip handle in place. As described in Chap. 4 (see Fig. 4.21), offset connections are used to model rigid connections occupying a finite area.

In this case, nodes 31 through 36 are located on the flat surface of the clip. The clamping edge of the spring curls around the clip handle to form three cylindrical beams. However, the centroid of these beams is offset from the flat surface. The cylindrical beam elements are connected by the nodes along the edge, offset by the distance to the centroid of the beam. To further clarify the modeling techniques used in this analysis, we will look in detail at the model input listing, shown in Fig. 7.16.

The NODE 1 command (NODAL POINT LOCATIONS 1) is used to define most of the nodes in the model. The interior nodes of the flat plate are defined with the NODE 22 command, using nodes 13, 18, and 36 as the end-nodes, incrementing the node numbers by 1 in the direction defined by nodes 13 and 18, and by 6 in the direction defined by nodes 18 and 26. Nodes 37 through 43 are then defined to represent the round end of the clip handle.

Note that nodes 44 and 45 are practically coincident with nodes 15 and

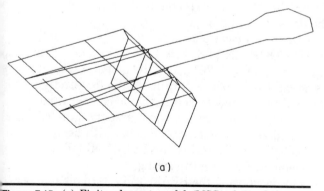

(a)

Figure 7.15 (a) Finite element model (MSC/pal 2) of the binder clip. The three lines offset from the clamping edge represent offset beam elements.

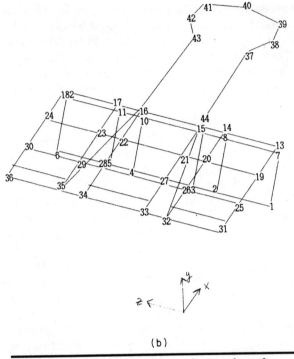

(b)

**Figure 7.15**  (*Continued*) (*b*) Node numbering scheme for
the finite element model. Nodes 31 through 36 also connect
the offset beam elements. Nodes 44 and 45 on the clip
handle are coincident with nodes 15 and 16 on the
spring.

16, respectively, separated in the Z direction by a distance equal to ½ the
diameter of the clip handle. These nodes represent the points where the clip
handle rests on the flat surface of the spring.

In order to define the nodal locations for the upper portion of the clip
handle, the LOCAL COORDINATE ANGLES command is used to
rotate the coordinate system by −26° about the global Y axis. In this
local coordinate system, the X′axis is parallel to the longitudinal axis
of the clip handle, making it easy to define the nodal coordinates.

Next, the material properties are specified, and the quadrilateral
plate element is defined as a plane stress element with bending stiffness and a thickness of 0.0234 in. The GENERATE CONNECTS command
generates the plate elements for the entire spring.

The clip handle is modeled using the BEAM TYPE 3 command, which
specifies a cylindrical beam element with an outside diameter of 0.0625 in
(the handle is solid so that the inside diameter is 0). The elements from

```
              TITLE    BINDER      CLIP
NODE            1
    1        1.094,      0,         0
    2        1.094,      0.5,       0
    3        1.094,      0.71875,   0
    4        1.094,      1.28125,   0
    5        1.094,      1.5,       0
    6        1.094,      2.0,       0
    7        1.133,      0,         0.469
    8        1.133,      0.5,       0.469
    9        1.133,      0.71875,   0.469
   10        1.133,      1.28125,   0.469
   11        1.133,      1.5,       0.469
   12        1.133,      2.0,       0.469
   13        1.055,      0,         0.547
   14        1.055,      0.5,       0.547
   15        1.055,      0.71875,   0.547
   16        1.055,      1.28125,   0.547
   17        1.055,      1.5,       0.547
   18        1.055,      2.0,       0.547
   31        0,          0,         0
   32        0,          0.5,       0
   33        0,          0.71875,   0
   34        0,          1.28125,   0
   35        0,          1.5,       0
   36        0,          2.0,       0
   44        1.055,      0.71875,   0.57825
   45        1.055,      1.28125,   0.57825
—.

NODE 22
13, 18, 36, 1, 6
—

NODE 1
37 0.0625, 0, 0.09375 THRU 43 0.0625, 0, 0.09375
—

LOCAL COORDINATE ANGLES 0, −26, 0
NODE          1
   37      2.1175,      0.75,      0
   38      2.33625,     0.609375,  0
   39      2.555,       0.640625,  0
   40      2.64875,     1.0,       0
   41      2.555,       1.359375,  0
   42      2.33625,     1.390625,  0
   43      2.1175,      1.25,      0
—

MATERIAL 30E6, 0, 0, 0.30
QUAD PLATE TYPE 1 1 0.0234
GENERATE CONNECTS 1 6 36 1 6
BEAM TYPE 3 0.0625, 0
DO CONNECT 37 TO 38 THRU 42 TO 43
CONNECT 44 TO 37
CONNECT 43 TO 45
RELEASE U V W
CONNECT 32 TO 44
RELEASE U V W
CONNECT 35 TO 45
BEAM TYPE 3 0.1719 0.125
OFFSET CONNECTION 0.0860,0,0.0860 AND 0.0860,0,0.0860
CONNECT 31 TO 32
CONNECT 35 TO 36
CONNECT 33 TO 34
OFFSET CONNECTION
BEAM 1 .01
CONNECT 44 15
CONNECT 45 16
ZERO 11
ALL OF 1 THROUGH 6 STEP 1
—

END DEFINITION
```

**Figure 7.16**  Model input listing for binder clip analysis.

node 37 through node 43 are connected, and then the elements connecting the round part of the handle to nodes 44 and 45 are defined.

Next, we connect the handle to the curved edge of the spring. The connection of the handle to the curved edge is a hinged connection. Therefore, moment releases (see Sec. 4.3.1) are applied at nodes 32 and 35. The first node specified in the CONNECT command, following a RELEASE command, is assigned the moment release.

We now define the curved portion of the clamping edge. The outside diameter of the curved part is 0.1719 in. The inside diameter is 0.125 in, which is equal to the outside diameter minus twice the spring thickness. The BEAM TYPE 3 command defines the cylindrical beam elements representing the curved edge. The OFFSET CONNECTION command specifies an offset of one-half the outside diameter of the curved edge in the $X$ and $Z$ directions, relative to the existing nodal coordinates of the connecting nodes. The OFFSET CONNECTION command remains in effect until another OFFSET CONNECTION command is issued.

The BEAM 1 command is then used to define two beams of small stiffness (small cross-sectional area) connecting nodes 44 and 45 to nodes 15 and 16. The purpose of this connection is to give the handle a small rotational stiffness to prevent an "ill-conditioned" stiffness matrix (see Chap. 4). Otherwise, the rotational stiffness of the handle is essentially zero and causes numerical problems (ill-conditioning, see Chap. 4). The beam elements have no effect on the physical accuracy of the problem since we are pushing down on the handle.

The last step is to define nodes 1 through 6 as fixed. Nodes 1 through 6 represent the axis of symmetry of the clip. The modeling phase of the analysis is complete. The PAL2 module is then executed to assemble the stiffness matrix.

The next step is to perform the static analysis using the STAT2 module. The load input file is shown in Fig. 7.17. The file simply specifies a displacement of 0.25 in at the clamping edge of the clip (nodes 31 through 36). Remember that this displacement represents half of the clip opening.

```
DISPLACEMENT APPLIED 11
TZ .25 31 36
—
SOLVE
QUIT
```

**Figure 7.17** Load input listing for binder clip analysis.

The displaced shape and Von Mises stress contour plot are shown in Figs. 7.18a and b. The contours are labeled according to the table in the figure. The highest stress occurs at the axis of symmetry of the

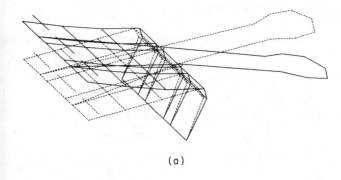

( a )

MISES STRESS
A  .0000E+00
B 1.0043E+04
C 2.0086E+04
D 3.0130E+04
E 4.0173E+04
F 5.0216E+04
G 6.0259E+04
H 7.0302E+04
I 8.0345E+04
J 9.0389E+04

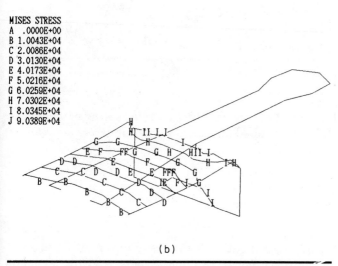

( b )

**Figure 7.18** Von Mises stress contour plot for binder clip. Note maximum stress at the axis of symmetry.

clip where the bending moment is a maximum. The maximum Von Mises stress is approximately 80,000 lb/in$^2$.

Figure 7.19 shows a partial listing of the output from the analysis. The external forces at nodes 31 through 36 represent the force per node required to open the clip ½ in. The sum of these forces is the total required external force and is approximately 15 lb. If you have a 2-in binder clip handy, you may wish to verify this result experimentally. You will find that the result is accurate within about 10 percent.

The stress results for the first three elements are shown in Fig. 7.19. Note that node 0 indicates the element centroid. These results can be verified using formulas for flat springs in Oberg, Jones, and Horton,

STATIC ANALYSIS SUBCASE NO. 1 EXTERNAL FORCES

| NODE | DIR | VALUE | NODE | DIR | VALUE | NODE | DIR | VALUE |
|------|-----|-------|------|-----|-------|------|-----|-------|
| 31 | Z T | 2.777E+00 | 32 | Z T | 1.424E+00 | 33 | Z T | 3.285E+00 |
| 34 | Z T | 3.285E+00 | 35 | Z T | 1.424E+00 | 36 | Z T | 2.777E+00 |

STATIC ANALYSIS SUBCASE NO.1 ELEMENT RECOVERY

MAXIMUM STRESSES FOR QUAD ELEMENT VON MISES CRITERION

| ELEMENT | NODE | MAJOR | MINOR | SHEAR | STRESS | % YIELD |
|---------|------|-------|-------|-------|--------|---------|
| 1 | 0 | 9.013E+04 | −9.007E+04 | 3.457E+04 | 8.164E+04 | .0 |
| 1 | 1 | 9.285E+04 | −9.439E+04 | 3.320E+04 | 8.397E+04 | .0 |
| 1 | 2 | 9.250E+04 | −9.085E+04 | 3.245E+04 | 8.225E+04 | .0 |
| 1 | 8 | 9.643E+04 | −9.479E+04 | 2.770E+04 | 8.382E+04 | .0 |
| 1 | 7 | 7.872E+04 | −8.026E+04 | 4.605E+04 | 8.679E+04 | .0 |
| 2 | 0 | 9.363E+04 | −9.219E+04 | 3.139E+04 | 8.264E+04 | .0 |
| 2 | 2 | 8.733E+04 | −8.552E+04 | 3.104E+04 | 7.784E+04 | .0 |
| 2 | 3 | 8.668E+04 | −8.561E+04 | 2.986E+04 | 7.683E+04 | .0 |
| 2 | 9 | 1.000E+05 | −9.892E+04 | 3.458E+04 | 8.857E+04 | .0 |
| 2 | 8 | 1.005E+05 | −9.872E+04 | 3.037E+04 | 8.768E+04 | .0 |
| 3 | 0 | 9.284E+04 | −9.179E+04 | 3.266E+04 | 8.259E+04 | .0 |
| 3 | 3 | 8.777E+04 | −8.673E+04 | 3.072E+04 | 7.802E+04 | .0 |
| 3 | 4 | 8.777E+04 | −8.673E+04 | 3.072E+04 | 7.802E+04 | .0 |
| 3 | 10 | 9.790E+04 | −9.686E+04 | 3.485E+04 | 8.716E+04 | .0 |
| 3 | 9 | 9.790E+04 | −9.686E+04 | 3.485E+04 | 8.716E+04 | .0 |

**Figure 7.19**   Stress output for first three elements which are along the axis of symmetry.

*Machinery's Handbook*, 20th ed. (Ref. 6). For a flat spring of thickness $t$, width $b$, length $L$, and applied force $P$, the bending stress is given by

$$S_b = \frac{6PL}{b(t^2)} = \frac{6 \times 15 \times 1.0}{2.0 \times (0.0234^2)} = 82{,}183 \text{ lb/in}^2$$

This result is in close agreement with the results from MSC/pal 2.

The binder clip analysis is a good example of using the finite element method for design work. In an actual design situation, the analysis might start off with a thicker spring, resulting in lower stresses but an excessive external force. Through iterations using varying spring thicknesses, the optimal relationship between the bending stress and the external force can be determined.

## References

1. The MacNeal-Schwendler Corporation: *MSC/pal 2 Application Manual*, Los Angeles, Calif., 1985.
2. Swanson Analysis Systems, Inc.: *Pipe Junction Example Problem*, Houston, Pa., March 5, 1985.
3. Swanson Analysis Systems, Inc.: *ANSYS-PC/LINEAR User's Manual*, Houston, Pa., June 1985, p. 4.3.6.5.

4. Harvey, J. F.: *Pressure Component Construction*, Van Nostrand/Reinhold, New York, 1980, p. 350.
5. Swanson Analysis Systems, Inc.: *ANSYS News*, 5th issue, Houston, Pa., 1985.
6. Oberg, E., F. D. Jones, and H. L. Horton: *Machinery's Handbook*, 20th ed., Industrial Press, New York, 1978, pp. 504, 516, and 547.

# 8

# Dynamics

In this chapter, we present example problems in dynamics analysis. Additional modeling guidelines relevant to dynamics are also discussed. You may wish to review the discussion of dynamics in Chap. 2 and the modeling guidelines in Chap. 4, which include some suggestions regarding modal analysis.

In general, finite element analysis of dynamics problems is more complicated than the analysis of statics problems, and far more subject to errors. It is harder to estimate the accuracy of results and much easier to make incorrect modeling assumptions. An exhaustive treatment of dynamics analysis is beyond the scope of this book. Readers with limited experience in dynamics analysis are encouraged to consult more in-depth texts on the subject (see references), in addition to the introductory material presented here.

Modal analysis (also called "mode-frequency" or "normal-modes analysis") is the most frequently used and simplest form of dynamics analysis. A modal analysis should always precede other forms of dynamic analysis in order to gain a basic understanding of the dynamic behavior of the model.

In addition to a modal analysis problem, we will also look at an example of response spectrum analysis, which can be considered an extension of modal analysis (see Chap. 2), and an example of transient response analysis. Before we proceed with the example problems, some general modeling considerations pertaining primarily to dynamics analysis are discussed.

## 8.1 Active or Master Degrees of Freedom

Dynamics problems require much more memory and CPU resources than statics problems of comparable size. Therefore, dynamics finite element programs generally provide an option to reduce the number of degrees of freedom to be processed in a dynamics analysis. This procedure is called *dynamic reduction.* The most common numerical techniques used in this procedure are called *dynamic matrix condensation* or *Guyan reduction.*

The objective of dynamic reduction is to create a subset of the total degrees of freedom in the model by eliminating degrees of freedom that do not significantly contribute to the model's dynamic behavior in the modes of interest. By including only enough degrees of freedom to accurately characterize the model's dynamic behavior, the size of large dynamics problems can be reduced substantially.

For example, the primary modes of interest in a cantilevered beam are bending modes. In this case, rotational degrees of freedom (torsion) are not necessary to characterize the bending behavior. Similarly, degrees of freedom that represent stretching modes (elongation-contraction) of the beam may also be eliminated.

In general, degrees of freedom that have no mass associated with them must be eliminated from dynamics analyses. Examples of massless degrees of freedom are the rotational degrees of freedom in quadrilateral plate elements (see Chap. 4) and degrees of freedom associated with spring or stiffness elements. Elimination of massless degrees of freedom is often performed automatically by the finite element program.

After dynamic reduction is specified, the mass and stiffness properties of the eliminated degrees of freedom are distributed among the active or "master" degrees of freedom. In ANSYS-PC/LINEAR, for example, the results of a modal analysis are in terms of "reduced-mass distributions" and "reduced eigenvectors" (mode shapes). The "reduced output" represents only the master degrees of freedom. Expanded output for all degrees of freedom can be requested for significant modes (see Sec. 8.5).

Dynamic reduction should be used with caution, however. The accuracy of the analysis decreases with increasing mode number. In general, the number of active degrees of freedom should be at least twice the number of modes of interest. The active degrees of freedom should be uniformly distributed. Large masses should always be retained as active degrees of freedom.

As mentioned above, most finite element programs perform some dynamic reduction automatically. Both ANSYS-PC/LINEAR and MSC/pal 2 have options for automatic dynamic reduction. Automatic reduction may not substantially reduce the size of the analysis. When in doubt, however, let the program perform the dynamic reduction.

The second example problem in this chapter illustrates the use of dynamic reduction.

## 8.2 Mass

In contrast to statics analyses, dynamics models must include mass. Distributed mass may be specified by including mass density in the material properties specification. Alternatively, lumped masses may be specified at various locations of the model. Lumped and distributed masses can both be specified in a single model.

As we saw in Chap. 2, finite element models with mass have a mass matrix in addition to a stiffness matrix. Finite element programs use two primary numerical methods for assembling and solving the mass matrix, resulting in two types of mass matrices. These are the *consistent mass matrix* and the *lumped mass matrix* (also called a "diagonal mass matrix"). Consistent and lumped mass matrices should not be confused with distributed and lumped mass as discussed in the last paragraph. Distributed and lumped mass simply represent two different ways of defining the mass in the structure. Consistent and lumped mass matrices represent different numerical formulations of the element mass matrix.

The theory of consistent and lumped mass matrix formulations is a topic handled by more theoretical finite element texts (Refs. 1 and 2) and is not discussed here. Essentially, the consistent mass matrix uses the same numerical formulation as the stiffness matrix and therefore includes mass terms for each degrees of freedom represented in the stiffness matrix (with the exception of some of the rotational degrees of freedom in flat plate elements). The lumped mass matrix uses only the matrix diagonal to represent mass terms and therefore includes only mass terms for the translational degrees of freedom in the model (no rotational inertia).

From the user's point of view, the distinction between consistent and lumped mass matrices is usually of little importance. Most finite element programs use consistent mass matrices by default. MSC/pal 2 provides an option to use the lumped mass formulation. ANSYS-PC/LINEAR offers the lumped mass formulation as an option with some element types.

In general, the consistent mass matrix is more accurate than the lumped mass matrix. The main reason lumped mass matrices exist is that they can be processed by the computer much more quickly than consistent mass matrices. In very large problems, this feature may be very important. However, lumped mass matrices can be inaccurate in problems with very coarse finite element meshes. In this book, the example problems all use the consistent mass matrix formulation.

## 8.3 Damping

Damping is a measure of a structure's capacity to dissipate energy. Damping is of no concern in modal analysis since, by definition, modal analysis involves undamped, free vibrations (see Chap. 2). However, damping must be considered in all other forms of dynamics analysis.

A structure is said to be critically damped when it returns to its equilibrium position without oscillation. This condition represents a very high level of damping. Good-quality scales are critically damped (i.e., when you remove the object being weighed, the scale returns to equilibrium without oscillation). Damping is primarily important in loadings of long duration such as earthquakes or the vertical free vibrations induced by a moving car. A structure's response to sudden-impact loads is not greatly affected by damping.

The damping in structures and components is generally measured as a percentage of critical damping. Typical values range from 0.1 to 10 percent of critical damping. In response spectrum analysis, the damping is built into the displacement, velocity, or acceleration values of the response spectrum. The less damping in the structure, the greater the response at a given frequency. It is therefore necessary to use response spectrum tables which correspond to the estimated damping value of the structure to be analyzed.

In transient analysis, it is necessary to specify the appropriate critical damping constant for the structure, although some programs may supply a default value of 1 percent. If discrete damping elements are used, then these must be assigned appropriate damping coefficients.

## 8.4 Modal Analysis Example: Valve Problem

A typical application in the nuclear and petrochemical industries is the modal analysis of a valve located in a piping system. The objective of the analysis is to determine the natural frequencies for the first three modes of vibration. It is generally desirable to design valve piping systems with fundamental frequencies above 33 Hz. Seismic response spectra usually exhibit maximum accelerations or velocities in the range of 0 to 15 Hz. Thus, equipment with fundamental frequencies above 33 Hz do not generally experience significant seismic excitation.

The valve analyzed in this example is a 2-in globe valve as shown in Fig. 8.1. The various components of the valve are indicated in the figure. The basic components of the valve are the valve operator, the yoke, the bonnet, and the valve body. The yoke and valve body are connected by the bonnet. The valve stem extends from the operator, through the yoke, and into the valve body.

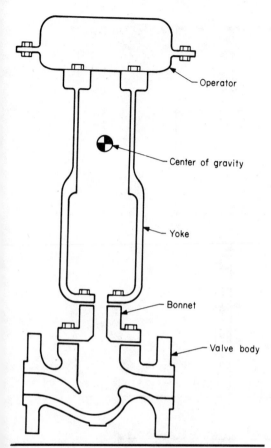

**Figure 8.1**  Typical valve with motor operator.

The stiffness of the valve assembly is primarily affected by the weight of the valve operator and the bending stiffness of the yoke legs. The other critical areas are the attachment points of the valve to the main pipe.

MSC/pal 2 is used to perform the analysis. The finite element model is shown in Fig. 8.2. The motor operator (element 18) weighs 90 lb and is modeled with a lumped mass at the center of gravity of the valve. The rest of the model consists of user-defined, three-dimensional beam elements. The model is fixed at the pipe attachment points (nodes 2 and 3).

The listing for the model input file is shown in Fig. 8.3. We will not work through the listing in detail since it is assumed at this point that the reader is fairly familiar with the commands of MSC/pal 2. Chapters 5, 6, and 7 provide more detailed information on the command

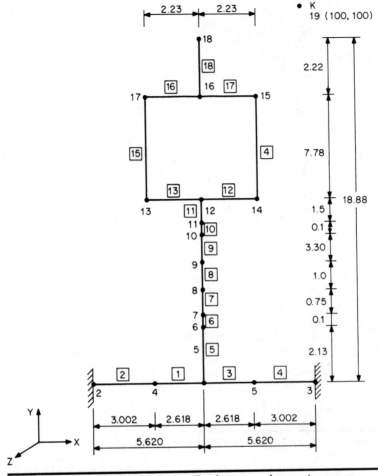

**Figure 8.2** Finite element model of valve. The element numbers are in squares.
Nodes 2 and 3 represent the attachment points to the main pipe.

syntax of this program. The beam section properties are listed following the BEAM TYPE 1 command in the following sequence: area,
torsional stiffness, moment of inertia about axis $X$–$X$, moment of inertia about axis $Y$–$Y$, and shear area. These properties are normally
provided by the valve manufacturer's design specifications.

Note the use of "rigid elements" specified by the first BEAM TYPE
1 command. These elements are assigned large section properties to
represent the valve body and the top and bottom of the yoke, which
are massive and very stiff parts of the valve. Since the cross-sectional
area is large, the material density is reduced by a factor of 10 for these

```
TITLE   VALVE ANALYSIS
NODAL POINT LOCATIONS 1
1 0,0,0
2 -5.62,0,0
3 5.62,0,0
4 -2.618,0,0
5 2.618,0,0
6 0,2.13,0
7 0,2.23,0
8 0,2.98,0
9 0,3.98,0
10 0,7.28,0
11 0,7.38,0
12 0,8.88,0
13 -2.23,8.88,0
14 2.23,8.88,0
15 2.23,16.66
16 0,16.66,0
17 -2.23,16.66,0
18 0,18.88,0
—BLANK LINE—
MATERIAL PROPERTIES 30E6,0,7.33E-5,0.3
C RIGID ELEMENTS
BEAM TYPE 1 100,1000,1000,1000,100
CONNECT 4 TO 1
CONNECT 1 TO 5
CONNECT 1 TO 6
CONNECT 17 TO 16
CONNECT 16 TO 15
CONNECT 13 TO 12
CONNECT 12 TO 14
C PIPE REDUCER ELEMENTS
MATERIAL PROPERTIES 30E6,0,7.33E-4,0.3
BEAM TYPE 1 3.166,1.8297,2.134,2.539,1.583
CONNECT 2 TO 4
CONNECT 5 TO 3
C BONNET TO VALVE-BODY BOLTING
BEAM TYPE 1 8.37,17.432,3.23,3.23,6.27
CONNECT 6 TO 7
C BONNET
BEAM TYPE 1 12.53,1000,41.95,41.95,9.39
CONNECT 7 TO 8
CONNECT 9 TO 10
CONNECT 11 TO 12
C BONNET MID-SECTION
BEAM TYPE 1 6.283,7.854,3.927,3.927,4.71
CONNECT 8 TO 9
C YOKE TO BONNET BOLTING
BEAM TYPE 1 8.37,29.186,4.864,4.864,6.27
CONNECT 10 TO 11
C YOKE
BEAM TYPE 1 3.801,0.5323,11.163,0.3129,2.55
CONNECT 14 TO 15
CONNECT 13 TO 17
C VALVE OPERATOR
BEAM TYPE 1 5.49,17.18,8.59,8.59,4.12
CONNECT 16 TO 18
C CONCENTRATED MASS FOR VALVE ACTUATOR (NODE 18, 90 LBS/G)
MASS 18 0.2329
END DEFINITION
```

Figure 8.3  Model input listing for valve analysis.

```
DISPLACEMENTS APPLIED 1
ALL 0.0 2,3
—BLANK LINE—
SOLVE
QUIT
```

**Figure 8.4**   Input listing for modal analysis of valve.

elements in order to more accurately approximate the mass contribution of these elements. Otherwise, the rigid elements would contribute unreasonably large mass to the model.

The operator weight is modeled at node 18 using the MASS command. After running the analysis through pal 2 to generate the stiffness matrix, the next step is to run the modal analysis using the DYNA2 module (see Fig. 5.3). The input file for the modal analysis is shown in Fig. 8.4. Since this is a modal analysis, there are no external forces to be defined. It is necessary to fix only the attachment points of the valve.

When the modal analysis is executed, the program asks for the number of mode shapes to calculate. We will look at the first three modes. Normally, only the first few modes are of interest.

The program reports the natural frequencies and mode shapes for the first three modes. Mode shapes are really useful only in graphical form. The actual numerical displacements of each node have no physical meaning except for their relationship to the other nodal displacements. This relationship is best seen in graphical form. The natural frequencies calculated by MSC/pal 2 for the first three modes are as follows:

*Mode 1:* 53.4 cycles per second (cps)

*Mode 2:* 108.9 cps

*Mode 3:* 637.1 cps

The mode shapes are shown in Fig. 8.5*a*, *b*, and *c*. In the first mode, the valve rotates about the $X$ axis. In the figure, the valve is moving toward us out of the page. Rotation about the $X$ axis is therefore the most flexible degree of freedom. In the second mode, the valve rotates about the $Z$ axis. The third mode is a vertical mode, with the valve moving up and down. The mode shapes correspond to the physical behavior we would expect.

Verifying the above results by hand is difficult. The only feasible approach would be to treat the valve as a cantilever beam and calculate the bending stiffness $k = EI/L$ for various portions of the valve. The stiffnesses could then be added in series $(1/k_1 + 1/k_2 \ldots = 1/K_{tot})$ to give the total estimated stiffness. Then the natural frequency formula could be applied (see Chap. 2). In any case, this sort of exercise would essentially negate the benefit of performing the finite element analy-

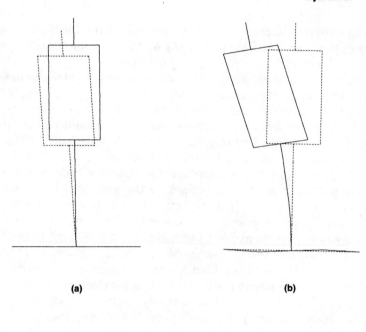

(a)                                              (b)

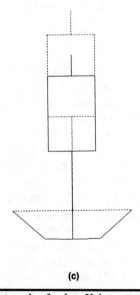

(c)

**Figure 8.5.**  (a) Plot of first mode of valve. Valve rotates out of the page about the $X$ axis.    (b) The second mode of valve analysis. Valve rotates about the $Z$ axis.  (c) The third mode. Valve moves vertically.

sis. The most practical approach is to carefully check the physical properties of the model and look carefully at the mode shapes. The mode shapes will generally reveal any major errors.

Since there are no external forces, displacements, or stresses to worry about, modal analysis is actually simpler than statics analysis. However, its simplicity can be deceiving. Since it is difficult to verify results, there is a greater tendency to accept the finite element results at face value. It is therefore very important to review your assumptions and modeling methods before accepting the results.

The two major areas to consider are the number of nodes in the model and the boundary conditions (assuming the geometry is correct). As we discussed in Chap. 4, it is important to use enough nodes to accurately define the mode shapes of interest. The commonly suggested guideline is to provide at least two nodes per wavelength of the highest mode shape of interest. The problem with this guideline is that in most actual problems, it is difficult, if not impossible, to determine the number of wavelengths in the highest mode, particularly before executing the analysis! This guideline is really useful only for very simple beam problems, which you probably would not model on a computer anyway.

The only alternative is to use common sense. In our valve example, 18 nodes were necessary to define the various components of the valve. In most real problems, the physical properties of the structure will dictate the number of nodes to use. And, in most cases, if the geometry is properly defined, the number of nodes will be sufficient to accurately characterize the first few modes.

The boundary conditions of the model should also be carefully checked. While correct boundary conditions are important in any finite element analysis, the accuracy of dynamics analyses is particularly affected by the boundary conditions. In many statics problems, local stresses in critical areas may not be greatly affected by the boundary conditions if they are far enough removed from the critical area. A good example of this situation was the pipe junction problem in Chap. 7.

In dynamics problems, however, the effect of the support conditions is critical. This is because the structure moves relative to its supports under dynamic loading. Clearly, the stiffness of the supports greatly affects the dynamic behavior of the structure. In our valve analysis, the results would change dramatically if we specified simply supported boundary conditions. The valve would be much more flexible and would exhibit lower natural frequencies.

## 8.5 Response Spectrum Analysis:
## Three-Dimensional Frame

This example of a response spectrum analysis of a three-dimensional frame is taken from the ANSYS example problems manual (Ref. 3), which accompanies the mainframe version of ANSYS. The problem is originally from a dynamics textbook by Crede (Ref. 4). The analysis is performed using ANSYS-PC/LINEAR. In addition to introducing response spectrum analysis, the problem illustrates the technique of dynamic reduction and also of load case combination. It should be noted that the actual output from this example is fairly voluminous so that it is not practical to include all of it here. Enough output is presented, however, to illustrate the general methods and principles employed in this type of analysis.

The structure is shown in Figs. 8.6a and b, and the finite element model is shown in Fig. 8.7. The frame consists of 2-in schedule 40 pipe members welded to four steel cubes. The pipes are lined with an internal damping material, and the structure is welded to a firm base. The objective of the analysis is to determine the natural frequencies and mode shapes of the structure and to evaluate the stresses and displacements when it is subjected to seismic loading.

The pipe members are modeled using the ANSYS-PC/LINEAR three-dimensional beam element STIF4 (the mainframe version used a pipe element). Consistent with the original textbook problem, lumped masses are placed at all the nodes except at the support points to repre-

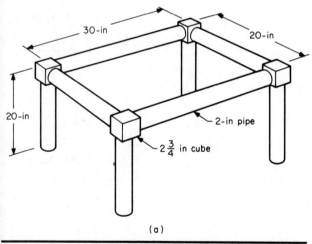

(a)

**Figure 8.6** (a) Sketch of 3-D frame. (*From C. Crede, Shock and Vibration Concepts in Engineering Design, Prentice-Hall, Englewood Cliffs, N.J., 1976. Reprinted by permission.*)

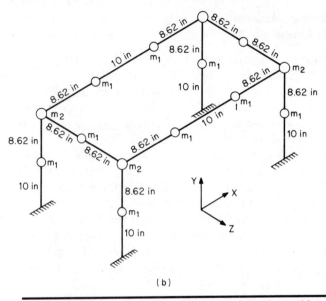

(b)

**Figure 8.6** (*Continued*) (b) Mathematical model of frame. Masses are lumped at corners and intermediate nodes (no mass at support points).

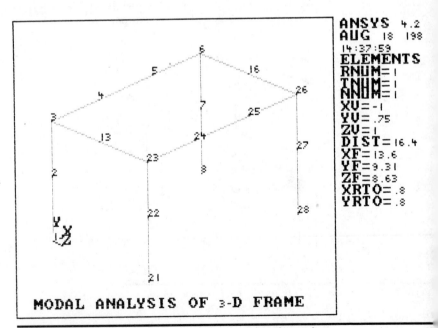

**Figure 8.7** Finite element model of 3-D frame with node numbers.

sent the weight of the pipes and the cubes. No mass is lumped at the support nodes since the pipes near the base experience insignificant vibratory motion (Ref. 4). Lumped masses are modeled using the STIF 21 three-dimensional mass element. The lumped masses are defined such that each corner includes the weight of one cube and three adjacent $8\frac{5}{8}$-in pipe members. The intermediate nodes are each assigned the weight of a 10-in length of pipe. This is a conservative approach to estimating the mass distribution in the structure. The weight and mass of each component and the lumped mass elements at the nodes are as follows:

|                    | Weight (lb) | Mass (lb-s$^2$/in) |
|--------------------|-------------|--------------------|
| Cube               | 6.0436      | 0.01566            |
| $8\frac{5}{8}$-in pipe | 1.2512  | 0.00324            |
| 10-in pipe         | 3.4517      | 0.00894            |
| Corner nodes       | 9.7972      | 0.02538            |
| Intermediate nodes | 3.4517      | 0.00894            |

The pipe weights include the internal damping material. The pipes and cubes are made from steel with a modulus of elasticity of $27.9 \times 10^6$ lb/in$^2$ and Poisson's ratio of 0.3.

The model consists of 18 nodes for a total of 108 DOF. The 4 nodes at the base are fixed so there are 84 unconstrained DOF. As discussed in Sec. 8.2, dynamic reduction can be used in dynamics analyses to further reduce the active degrees of freedom. In ANSYS-PC/LINEAR, dynamic reduction is accomplished by specifying "master" degrees of freedom.

In this problem, degrees of freedom representing longitudinal extensions of the pipe elements and rotations of the mass elements are eliminated since these degrees of freedom are insignificant in the lower modes. Figure 8.8 shows the retained 24 master DOF. The retained master degrees of freedom are those that cause bending in the structure. Degrees of freedom that would cause torsion or longitudinal strains in the pipe elements are eliminated.

In this analysis, the master degrees of freedom are specified by the analyst. They could also be selected automatically by ANSYS-PC/LINEAR. However, with automatic reduction, the user must still specify the total number of master degrees of freedom to be retained in the analysis and whether to exclude rotational degrees of freedom. This process would be better described as "semiautomatic."

The structure is subjected to a seismic disturbance in the form of velocity response spectra applied in three excitation directions corresponding to the global coordinate axes. The velocity spectrum is a table of the ground velocity

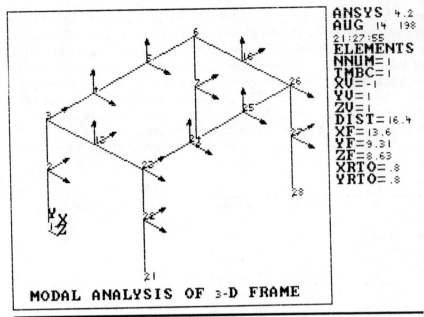

**Figure 8.8** Master degrees of freedom selected for 3-D frame. Note that the master degrees of freedom represent bending modes of the structure.

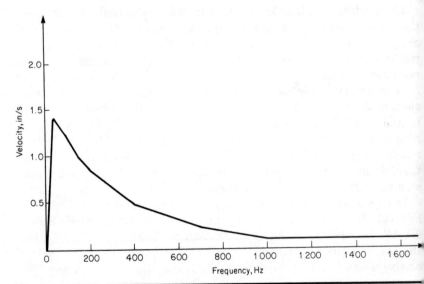

**Figure 8.9** Seismic velocity response spectrum for the $X$ and $Z$ directions (3-D frame analysis).

over a range of natural frequencies (see Chap. 2) in a particular excitation direction. The spectral values for this analysis are shown in Table 8.1. A plot of the response spectrum for the $X$ and $Z$ directions is shown in Fig. 8.9. Each response spectrum must be input as a separate load case. The results of each load case can then be combined to obtain a total solution.

Response spectrum analysis involves several steps performed by the finite element program. These are described in nonmathematical terms. For the mathematical derivation of response spectrum analysis, see Biggs, *Introduction to Structural Dynamics* (Ref. 5) or other dynamics texts on numerical analysis.

First, the natural frequencies and mode shapes of the structure are calculated as they would be in a modal analysis. (It is therefore not necessary to perform a modal analysis prior to a response spectrum analysis.) Next, the modal participation factors (also called mass participation factors) are calculated for each mode. As mentioned in Chap. 2, the modal participation factor is essentially the product of the modal vector, mass matrix, and load-direction vectors, and measures the participation of the mass of the structure in that particular mode.

The corresponding spectral velocity for each mode is extracted from the response spectrum. As an example, let us assume that the calculated natural frequency of the first mode is 40 cps. From Table 8.1, the spectral velocity for the first mode in the $X$ or $Z$ direction would be 1.4 in/s. The mode coefficient is then calculated as the product of the spectral velocity and the modal participation factor divided by the natural frequency (in radians) for that mode. The mode coefficient is a measure of the maximum amplitude of the mode.

The mode with the largest mode coefficient is the most significant mode for the particular excitation direction. This mode is assigned a mode coefficient ratio of 1.0. The mode coefficient ratio for each remaining mode in the excitation direction is the ratio of its mode coefficient to the largest mode coefficient. ANSYS-PC/LINEAR treats modes with mode coefficient ratios

**TABLE 8.1** Response Spectra Values for 3-D Frame Problem

| $X$ and $Z$ directions | | $Y$ direction | |
|---|---|---|---|
| Frequency (cps) | Velocity (in/s) | Frequency (cps) | Velocity (in/s) |
| 40.0 | 1.40 | 30.0 | 7.00 |
| 100.0 | 1.24 | 70.0 | 3.25 |
| 150.0 | 1.00 | 100.0 | 0.44 |
| 200.0 | 0.85 | 200.0 | 0.22 |
| 400.0 | 0.47 | 300.0 | 0.15 |
| 700.0 | 0.22 | 400.0 | 0.12 |
| 1000.0 | 0.10 | 500.0 | 0.10 |
| 2000.0 | 0.10 | 2000.0 | 0.10 |

greater than 1/1000 as significant modes. If requested by the user, ANSYS-PC/LINEAR calculates the stresses in the structure for the significant modes.

The above process is then repeated for the other excitation directions using separate load cases. To clarify this rather confusing process, we

```
/TITLE, MODAL ANALYSIS OF 3-D FRAME KAN,2
ET,1,4
ET,2,21,,,2
KAY,2,3
KAY,3,6
EX,1,27.9E6
R,1,1.075,0.666,0.666,2.375,2.375
R,2,0.00894
R,3,0.02538
N,1
N,2,,10
N,3,,18.625
N,4,8.625,18.625
N,5,18.625,18.625
N,6,27.25,18.625
N,7,27.25,10
N,8,27.25
NGEN,3,10,1,8,1,,,8.625
E,1,2
TYPE,2
REAL,2
E,2
EGEN,6,1,1,2
TYPE,1
REAL,1
E,7,8
E,3,13
TYPE,2
REAL,2
E,13
TYPE,1
REAL,1
E,13,23
EGEN,2,3,14,16
EGEN,2,20,1,13
TYPE,2
REAL,3
EMODIF,4
EMODIF,10
EMODIF,23
EMODIF,29
M,2,UX,7,5,UZ
M,22,UX,27,5,UZ
M,3,UX
M,4,UY,5,1,UZ
M,24,UY,25,1,UZ
M,13,UX,16,3,UY
M,23,UX,,,UZ
M,26,UZ
ITER,1,1
SED,1
FREQ,40,100,150,200,400,700,1000,2000
SV,,1.40,1.24,1.00,0.85,0.47,0.22,0.1,0.1
D,1,ALL,,,8,7
D,21,ALL,,,28,7
/VIEW,,,-0.8,1,1
EPLOT
SFWRITE
FINISH
```

**Figure 8.10**  Input listing for 3-D frame analysis (ANSYS-PC/LINEAR).

look at the input listing in Fig. 8.10 and then examine some of the output of the analysis.

Referring to Fig. 8.10, two element types (STIF4 and 21) are defined. The STIF21 mass element is defined as a 3-D mass without rotational inertia by the third field following 21. The first KAY command specifies that the first three modes are to be expanded. This occurs, however, only if the mode is significant, as described above. The second KAY command specifies that the reduced mode shapes for the first six modes are to be printed.

The R commands define three sets of real constants, the first for the beam element (schedule 40 pipe) and the other two for the intermediate and corner mass elements, respectively. Next, the nodes and elements are defined. The EMODIF commands set the previously defined corner nodes to real constant table 3 (the mass of the corner elements).

The M commands specify the master degrees of freedom. As we mentioned earlier, this could be done automatically using the TOTAL command and requesting a total of 24 DOF to be selected and rotational degrees of freedom to be excluded.

The ITER command requests a full stress printout for the significant modes. The SED command specifies the seismic excitation direction as the $X$ direction (SED,0,1,0 would be the $Y$ direction, SED,0,0,1 would be $Z$). The FREQ and SV commands are used to input the response spectrum table for the $X$ direction. The displacements for the ground nodes are zeroed with the D commands.

PREP7 is used to generate the model, and then ANSYS is executed to perform the analysis. Some of the output for the $X$ direction load case is shown in Fig. 8.11. Figure 8.12 shows the first mode shape.

The natural frequencies are listed in Fig. 8.11, followed by the reduced-mass distribution. The reduced-mass distribution table shows how the mass is redistributed among the master degrees of freedom. The total mass acting in each direction is also given.

Of particular interest in Fig. 8.11 is the section entitled RESPONSE CALCULATION SUMMARY. Note that the modal participation factor and the mode coefficient are maximum for mode 1. The column SV gives the spectral velocity for each mode. You can verify the spectral velocity for mode 1 by reading the value for 116.2 cps on the plot in Fig. 8.9.

Looking at the M.C. RATIO column, modes 2, 11, and 12 are considered significant. However, none of these modes has significant mass participation. Therefore, the stresses for these modes are insignificant. Since we requested expanded output only for the first three modes, stresses are not calculated for modes 11 and 12.

The REDUCED EIGENVECTOR FOR MODE 1 data give the relative amplitudes for each master degree of freedom. As noted in the modal analysis example, these numbers are relative values and have no physical meaning in terms of actual displacement.

The expanded-mode shape for mode 1 is shown next. The expanded-mode values are actual displacements based on the response spectrum input. Note that the numbers bear no resemblance to the reduced eigenvector values. However, the ratios of the numbers in either table are the same. For example, try dividing the maximum nodal amplitude UX by the UY value (node 13 by node 4) in each table. The ratio is the same.

Finally, the stresses for the first mode are listed for each element. These are the stresses for the STIF4 beam element. SDIR is the axial stress, and SBZ and SBY are the bending stresses about the major and minor axes. SIG1 and SIG3 are the maximum and minimum stress in the beam, respectively (similar to MSC/pal 2 output in the beam example of Chap. 7). Stresses for mode 2 are shown in abbreviated form in Fig. 8.11$b$ (SXI = SDIR).

At this point, the solution for one excitation direction is complete. However, the $Y$ and $Z$ response spectra must also be evaluated as separate load cases. The results can then be combined using the square root of the sum of the squares (SRSS) method. In other words, the significant modes from the other load cases are calculated, and the stresses in the elements resulting from each load case are combined using the SRSS method:

$$S_{comb} = \sqrt{S_1^2 + S_2^2 + S_3^2}$$

This is the most common method of evaluating multidirectional loading.

Unfortunately, the combining of loads in ANSYS-PC/LINEAR is not as straightforward as it is in the mainframe version of ANSYS. First of all, the load cases (response spectra) must be input in separate analysis runs. The ANSYS output file for each load case must be renamed before executing the next load case so that the output file is not overwritten. Finally, a fairly involved series of commands using the ANSYS-PC/LINEAR postprocessor computes the combined stresses.

The execution of multiple load cases is best accomplished using ANSYS-PC/LINEAR interactively. An excellent feature of ANSYS-PC/LINEAR is the ability to resume a previous analysis. After the first load case is completed, we can go back into PREP7 and type RESUME.

MODAL ANALYSIS OF 3-D FRAME
ANSYS VERSION FOR DEMONSTRATION PURPOSES ONLY
CENTROID, MASS, AND MASS MOMENTS OF INERTIA

CALCULATIONS ASSUME ELEMENT MASS AT ELEMENT CENTROID
TOTAL MASS =   0.19092

| CENTROID | MOM. OF INERTIA ABOUT ORIGIN | MOM. OF INERTIA ABOUT CENTROID |
|---|---|---|
| XC = 13.625 | IXX =  84.47 | IXX = 15.03 |
| YC = 17.010 | IYY =  92.22 | IYY = 42.57 |
| ZC =  8.6250 | IZZ = 122.5 | IZZ = 31.86 |
|  | IXY = −44.25 | IXY = −0.1088E−13 |
|  | IYZ = −28.01 | IYZ = −0.1135E−13 |
|  | IZX = −22.44 | IZX = −0.7503E−14 |

MASS SUMMARY BY ELEMENT TYPE

| TYPE | MASS |
|---|---|
| 2 | 0.190920 |

RANGE OF ELEMENT MAXIMUM STIFFNESS IN GLOBAL COORDINATES
MAXIMUM= 0.861746E+07   AT ELEMENT   30.
MINIMUM= 0.743256E+07   AT ELEMENT   32.

ELEMENT STIFFNESS FORMULATION TIMES

| TYPE | NUMBER | STIF | TOTAL CP | AVE CP |
|---|---|---|---|---|
| 1 | 18 | 4 | 1.69 | 0.094 |
| 2 | 14 | 21 | 0.06 | 0.004 |

TIME AT END OF ELEMENT STIFFNESS FORMULATION   CP=   32.020
MAXIMUM WAVE FRONT ALLOWED =   400.
EQUATION SOLUTION ELEM=   17 L.S.=   1 ITER=   1   CP=   46.69
MAXIMUM IN-CORE WAVE FRONT =   35.
MATRIX SOLUTION TIMES
READ IN ELEMENT STIFFNESSES   CP=   3.100
NODAL COORD. TRANSFORMATION   CP=   0.000
MATRIX TRIANGULARIZATION   CP=   21.740
TIME AT END OF MATRIX TRIANGULARIZATION   CP= 69.150
TIME AT START OF EIGENVALUE EXTRACTION   CP=   70.470
NUMBER OF MODES AVAILABLE FROM REDUCED MATRICES =   24.
EIGENVALUE EXTRACTION TIME   CP=   44.220

EIGENVALUE (NATURAL FREQUENCY) SOLUTION

| MODE | FREQUENCY (CYCLES/TIME) |
|---|---|
| 1 | 116.240219 |
| 2 | 122.209470 |
| 3 | 143.819652 |
| 4 | 227.202585 |
| 5 | 421.925007 |
| 6 | 450.197096 |
| 7 | 482.256108 |
| 8 | 603.477902 |
| 9 | 806.105200 |
| 10 | 836.600742 |
| 11 | 943.026886 |
| 12 | 996.413699 |
| 13 | 1028.05199 |
| 14 | 1030.24675 |
| 15 | 1087.24270 |
| 16 | 1122.51911 |
| 17 | 1131.23876 |

Figure 8.11   (a) Partial listing from output for load case 1 (response spectrum in the X direction).

| MODE | FREQUENCY (CYCLES/TIME) |
|---|---|
| 18 | 1139.64469 |
| 19 | 1174.77562 |
| 20 | 1212.82952 |
| 21 | 1316.54442 |
| 22 | 1342.59330 |
| 23 | 1364.41500 |
| 24 | 1469.11345 |

REDUCED MASS DISTRIBUTION

| ROW | NODE | DIR | VALUE |
|---|---|---|---|
| 1 | 2 | UX | 0.87301E-02 |
| 2 | 13 | UY | 0.84917E-02 |
| 3 | 2 | UZ | 0.11758E-01 |
| 4 | 24 | UZ | 0.81311E-02 |
| 5 | 24 | UY | 0.86576E-02 |
| 6 | 25 | UY | 0.11555E-01 |
| 7 | 3 | UX | 0.63130E-01 |
| 8 | 23 | UZ | 0.56289E-01 |
| 9 | 27 | UZ | 0.90496E-02 |
| 10 | 4 | UY | 0.86654E-02 |
| 11 | 4 | UZ | 0.11142E-01 |
| 12 | 27 | UX | 0.14517E-01 |
| 13 | 16 | UY | 0.80002E-02 |
| 14 | 5 | UZ | 0.76692E-02 |
| 15 | 16 | UX | 0.18719E-01 |
| 16 | 5 | UY | 0.11641E-01 |
| 17 | 26 | UZ | 0.56133E-01 |
| 18 | 22 | UZ | 0.91600E-02 |
| 19 | 7 | UX | 0.14684E-01 |
| 20 | 7 | UZ | 0.12160E-01 |
| 21 | 13 | UX | 0.10392E-01 |
| 22 | 23 | UX | 0.63138E-01 |
| 23 | 25 | UZ | 0.11928E-01 |
| 24 | 22 | UX | 0.87474E-02 |

MASS(X,Y,Z) =    0.2021    0.5701E-01    0.1934

RESPONSE SPECTRUM CALCULATION SUMMARY

| MODE | FREQUENCY | SV | PARTIC. FACTOR | MODE COEF. | M.C. RATIO | EQUIV. MASS |
|---|---|---|---|---|---|---|
| 1 | 116.2 | 1.1448 | 0.4348 | 0.6815E-03 | 1.000000 | 0.3280E-01 |
| 2 | 122.2 | 1.1448 | -0.6258E-03 | -0.9086E-06 | 0.001333 | 0.2252E-01 |
| 3 | 143.8 | 1.0226 | 0.4083E-03 | 0.4620E-06 | 0.000678 | 0.3967E-01 |
| 4 | 227.2 | 0.7622 | -0.1865E-03 | -0.9956E-07 | 0.000146 | 0.3915E-01 |
| 5 | 421.9 | 0.4372 | -0.1622E-03 | -0.2675E-07 | 0.000039 | 0.8947E-02 |
| 6 | 450.2 | 0.4004 | -0.1504E-03 | -0.2129E-07 | 0.000031 | 0.9000E-02 |
| 7 | 482.3 | 0.3647 | -0.1435E-05 | -0.1727E-09 | 0.000000 | 0.9009E-02 |
| 8 | 603.5 | 0.2690 | 0.1262E-03 | 0.8952E-08 | 0.000013 | 0.1080E-01 |
| 9 | 806.1 | 0.1610 | 0.2809E-04 | 0.8933E-09 | 0.000001 | 0.9116E-02 |
| 10 | 836.6 | 0.1483 | 0.2042E-02 | 0.5763E-07 | 0.000085 | 0.9228E-02 |
| 11 | 943.0 | 0.1138 | -0.4997E-01 | -0.9601E-06 | 0.001409 | 0.9144E-02 |
| 12 | 996.4 | 0.1008 | -0.6759E-01 | 0.1088E-05 | 0.001597 | 0.9518E-02 |
| 13 | 1028. | 0.1000 | 0.1824E-01 | 0.2824E-06 | 0.000414 | 0.9450E-02 |
| 14 | 1030. | 0.1000 | 0.5606E-03 | 0.8660E-08 | 0.000013 | 0.9291E-02 |
| 15 | 1087. | 0.1000 | 0.7379E-04 | 0.1080E-08 | 0.000002 | 0.9264E-02 |
| 16 | 1123. | 0.1000 | 0.9160E-03 | 0.1299E-07 | 0.000019 | 0.9082E-02 |
| 17 | 1131. | 0.1000 | 0.1995E-02 | 0.2807E-07 | 0.000041 | 0.9296E-02 |
| 18 | 1140. | 0.1000 | -0.4609E-03 | -0.6437E-08 | 0.000009 | 0.9592E-02 |
| 19 | 1175. | 0.1000 | -0.3071E-01 | -0.4161E-06 | 0.000611 | 0.9951E-02 |
| 20 | 1213. | 0.1000 | -0.1255E-02 | -0.1647E-07 | 0.000024 | 0.9470E-02 |
| 21 | 1317. | 0.1000 | -0.1861E-02 | -0.2250E-07 | 0.000033 | 0.9919E-02 |
| 22 | 1343. | 0.1000 | 0.2632E-01 | 0.3120E-06 | 0.000458 | 0.9504E-02 |
| 23 | 1364. | 0.1000 | 0.2485E-01 | 0.2899E-06 | 0.000425 | 0.9411E-02 |
| 24 | 1469. | 0.1000 | 0.1528E-01 | 0.1656E-06 | 0.000243 | 0.9771E-02 |

Figure 8.11a  (Continued)

SIGNIFICANCE FACTOR FOR EXPANDED MODES =   0.10000E−02

EIGENVECTOR (MODE SHAPE) SOLUTION

REDUCED EIGENVECTOR FOR MODE 1 FREQUENCY = 116.2402 (CYCLES/TIME)

| NODE | UX | UY | UZ | ROTX | ROTY | ROTZ |
|---|---|---|---|---|---|---|
| 2 | 1.1463 | | −0.65087E−03 | | | |
| 3 | 2.4861 | | | | | |
| 4 | | −0.20415 | −0.10135E−01 | | | |
| 5 | | 0.20402 | 0.53243E−02 | | | |
| 7 | 1.1462 | | −0.15523E−02 | | | |
| 13 | 2.5197 | 0.18101E−01 | | | | |
| 16 | 2.5195 | 0.18090E−01 | | | | |
| 22 | 1.1465 | | −0.10609E−02 | | | |
| 23 | 2.4866 | | −0.20954E−02 | | | |
| 24 | | −0.20412 | 0.57340E−02 | | | |
| 25 | | 0.20413 | −0.10533E−01 | | | |
| 26 | | | −0.24727E−02 | | | |
| 27 | 1.1464 | | −0.11402E−02 | | | |

MAXIMUMS

| NODE | 13 | 4 | 25 | 0 | 0 | 0 |
|---|---|---|---|---|---|---|
| VALUE | 2.5197 | −0.20415 | −0.10533E−01 | 0.00000E+00 | 0.00000E+00 | 0.00000E+00 |

EXPANDED MODE SHAPE FOR MODE 1 LOAD STEP 1
FREQUENCY =   116.240 (CYCLES/TIME)

| NODE | UX | UY | UZ | ROTX | ROTY | ROTZ |
|---|---|---|---|---|---|---|
| 1 | 0.00000E+00 | 0.00000E+00 | 0.00000E+00 | 0.00000E+00 | 0.00000E+00 | 0.00000E+00 |
| 2 | 0.78117E−03 | 0.64721E−05 | −0.44356E−06 | −0.62081E−07 | 0.13623E−05 | −0.12157E−03 |
| 3 | 0.16943E−02c | 0.12054E−04 | −0.93712E−06 | −0.55194E−07 | 0.25373E−05 | −0.66880E−04 |
| 4 | 0.16875E−02 | −0.13913E−03 | −0.69067E−05 | −0.48735E−07 | −0.58080E−06 | 0.18896E−04 |
| 5 | 0.16796E−02 | 0.13904E−03 | 0.36285E−05 | −0.41246E−07 | −0.11866E−05 | 0.18414E−04 |
| 6 | 0.16728E−02 | −0.11317E−04 | −0.30690E−05 | −0.34786E−07 | 0.45247E−05 | −0.65211E−04 |
| 7 | 0.78112E−3 | −0.60762E−05 | −0.10579E−05 | −0.25193E−06 | 0.24294E−05 | −0.12001E−03 |
| 8 | 0.00000E+00 | 0.00000E+00 | 0.00000E+00 | 0.00000E+00 | 0.00000E+00 | 0.00000E+00 |
| 13 | 0.17172E−02 | 0.12336E−04 | −0.11825E−05 | 0.15765E−07 | 0.13559E−05 | −0.66885E−04 |
| 16 | 0.17170E−02 | −0.12328E−04 | −0.23771E−05 | 0.40743E−07 | 0.58937E−08 | −0.65216E−04 |
| 21 | 0.00000E+00 | 0.00000E+00 | 0.00000E+00 | 0.00000E+00 | 0.00000E+00 | 0.00000E+00 |
| 22 | 0.78133E−03 | 0.64913E−05 | −0.72297E−06 | −0.11058E−06 | −0.13299E−05 | −0.12160E−03 |
| 23 | 0.16946E−02 | 0.12090E−04 | −0.14280E−05 | −0.20363E−07 | −0.24769E−05 | −0.66890E−04 |
| 24 | 0.16878E−02 | −0.13911E−03 | 0.39077E−05 | −0.63149E−07 | 0.63634E−06 | 0.18900E−04 |
| 25 | 0.16799E−02 | 0.13911E−03 | −0.71779E−05 | −0.11276E−06 | 0.12975E−05 | 0.18420E−04 |
| 26 | 0.16731E−02 | −0.11238E−04 | −0.16852E−05 | −0.15554E−06 | −0.44240E−05 | −0.65221E−04 |
| 27 | 0.78128E−03 | −0.60340E−05 | −0.77702E−06 | −0.97016E−07 | −0.23753E−05 | −0.12004E−03 |
| 28 | 0.00000E+00 | 0.00000E+00 | 0.00000E+00 | 0.00000E+00 | 0.00000E+00 | 0.00000E+00 |

MAXIMUMS

| NODE | 13 | 4 | 25 | 7 | 6 | 22 |
|---|---|---|---|---|---|---|
| VALUE | 0.17172E−02 | −0.13913E−03 | −0.71779E−05 | −0.25193E−06 | 0.45247E−05 | −0.12160E−03 |

STRESS EVALUATION   ELEM =    1 L.S. = 1 ITER =    1 CP =     162.08
EL = 1 NODES = 1   2 MAT = 1
TCENT,TTOPZ,TBOTY = 0.0  0.0   0.0 QZ,QY = 0.00000E+00 0.00000E+00

| END | SDIR | SBZ | SBY | SIG1 | SIG3 |
|---|---|---|---|---|---|
| I | 18.057 | 0.47039 | −747.31 | 765.84 | −729.72 |
| J | 18.057 | −0.59024E−01 | −58.258 | 76.374 | −40.259 |

**Figure 8.11a**   *(Continued)*

```
EL =    3 NODES =    2    3 MAT = 1
TCENT,TTOPZ,TBOTY = 0.0   0.0   0.0 QZ,QY = 0.00000E+00 0.00000E+00
```

| END | SDIR | SBZ | SBY | SIG1 | SIG3 |
|---|---|---|---|---|---|
| I | 18.057 | -0.59024E-01 | -58.258 | 76.374 | -40.259 |
| J | 18.057 | 0.61155E-02 | 478.44 | 496.50 | -460.39 |

```
EL =    5 NODES =    3    4 MAT = 1
TCENT,TTOPZ,TBOTY = 0.0   0.0   0.0 QZ,QY = 0.00000E+00 0.00000E+00
```

| END | SDIR | SBZ | SBY | SIG1 | SIG3 |
|---|---|---|---|---|---|
| I | -22.035 | -18.573 | 478.45 | 474.99 | -519.06 |
| J | -22.035 | -5.3827 | 180.53 | 163.88 | -207.95 |

```
EL =    7 NODES =    4    5 MAT = 1
TCENT,TTOPZ,TBOTY = 0.0   0.0   0.0 QZ,QY = 0.00000E+00 0.00000E+00
```

| END | SDIR | SBZ | SBY | SIG1 | SIG3 |
|---|---|---|---|---|---|
| I | -22.035 | -5.3827 | 180.53 | 163.88 | -207.95 |
| J | -22.035 | 1.3683 | -183.73 | 163.06 | -207.13 |

```
EL =    9 NODES =    5    6 MAT = 1
TCENT,TTOPZ,TBOTY = 0.0   0.0   0.0 QZ,QY = 0.00000E+00 0.00000E+00
```

| END | SDIR | SBZ | SBY | SIG1 | SIG3 |
|---|---|---|---|---|---|
| I | -22.035 | 1.3683 | -183.73 | 163.06 | -207.13 |
| J | -22.035 | 42.510 | -458.72 | 479.20 | -523.27 |

```
EL =   11 NODES =    6    7 MAT = 1
TCENT,TTOPZ,TBOTY = 0.0   0.0   0.0 QZ,QY = 0.00000E+00 0.00000E+00
```

| END | SDIR | SBZ | SBY | SIG1 | SIG3 |
|---|---|---|---|---|---|
| I | -16.953 | -2.9041 | -458.71 | 444.66 | -478.56 |
| J | -16.953 | 1.2359 | 37.689 | 21.972 | -55.877 |

```
EL =   13 NODES =    7    8 MAT = 1
TCENT,TTOPZ,TBOTY = 0.0   0.0   0.0 QZ,QY = 0.00000E+00 0.00000E+00
```

| END | SDIR | SBZ | SBY | SIG1 | SIG3 |
|---|---|---|---|---|---|
| I | -16.953 | 1.2359 | 37.689 | 21.972 | -55.877 |
| J | -16.953 | 0.43352 | 757.54 | 741.02 | -774.93 |

```
EL =   14 NODES =    3   13 MAT = 1
TCENT,TTOPZ,TBOTY = 0.0   0.0   0.0 QZ,QY = 0.00000E+00 0.00000E+00
```

| END | SDIR | SBZ | SBY | SIG1 | SIG3 |
|---|---|---|---|---|---|
| I | -0.79391 | 22.045 | 0.25201E-01 | 21.276 | -22.864 |
| J | -0.79391 | -41.434 | -0.57035 | 41.210 | -42.798 |

```
EL =   16 NODES =   13   23 MAT = 1
TCENT,TTOPZ,TBOTY = 0.0   0.0   0.0 QZ,QY = 0.00000E+00 0.00000E+00
```

| END | SDIR | SBZ | SBY | SIG1 | SIG3 |
|---|---|---|---|---|---|
| I | -0.79391 | -41.434 | -0.57035 | 41.210 | -42.798 |
| J | -0.79391 | 22.301 | 0.84791 | 22.355 | -23.943 |

```
EL =   17 NODES =    6   16 MAT = 1
TCENT,TTOPZ,TBOTY = 0.0   0.0   0.0 QZ,QY = 0.00000E+00 0.00000E+00
```

| END | SDIR | SBZ | SBY | SIG1 | SIG3 |
|---|---|---|---|---|---|
| I | 2.2382 | 48.701 | -2.9232 | 53.863 | -49.386 |
| J | 2.2382 | -83.418 | 2.3429 | 87.999 | -83.522 |

```
EL =   19 NODES =   16   26 MAT = 1
TCENT,TTOPZ,TBOTY = 0.0   0.0   0.0 QZ,QY = 0.00000E+00 0.00000E+00
```

| END | SDIR | SBZ | SBY | SIG1 | SIG3 |
|---|---|---|---|---|---|
| I | 2.2382 | -83.418 | 2.3429 | 87.999 | -83.522 |
| J | 2.2382 | 49.384 | -0.83496 | 52.457 | -47.981 |

Figure 8.11a   (Continued)

```
EL=    20 NODES=   21   22 MAT= 1
TCENT,TTOPZ,TBOTY= 0.0   0.0   0.0 QZ,QY= 0.00000E+00 0.00000E+00

   END          SDIR           SBZ          SBY        SIG1        SIG3
    I           18.111        0.70441     -747.46    766.28    -730.06
    J           18.111        0.28350E-01  -58.264    76.403    -40.181
EL=    22 NODES=   22   23 MAT= 1
TCENT,TTOPZ,TBOTY= 0.0   0.0   0.0 QZ,QY= 0.00000E+00 0.00000E+00

   END          SDIR           SBZ          SBY        SIG1          SIG3
    I           18.111        0.28350E-01  -58.264    76.403    -40.181
    J           18.111       -0.72149     478.55    497.39    -461.16
EL=    24 NODES=   23   24 MAT= 1
TCENT,TTOPZ,TBOTY= 0.0   0.0   0.0 QZ,QY= 0.00000E+00 0.00000E+00

   END          SDIR           SBZ          SBY        SIG1          SIG3
    I          -22.006       18.911     478.54    475.44    -519.46
    J          -22.006        5.0065    180.55    163.55    -207.56
EL=    26 NODES=   24   25 MAT= 1
TCENT,TTOPZ,TBOTY= 0.0   0.0   0.0 QZ,QY= 0.00000E+00 0.00000E+00

   END          SDIR           SBZ          SBY        SIG1          SIG3
    I          -22.006        5.0065    180.55    163.55    -207.56
    J          -22.006       -0.62561   -183.72    162.34    -206.36
EL=    28 NODES=   25   26 MAT= 1
TCENT,TTOPZ,TBOTY= 0.0   0.0   0.0 QZ,QY= 0.00000E+00 0.00000E+00

   END          SDIR           SBZ          SBY        SIG1          SIG3
    I          -22.006       -0.62561   -183.72    162.34    -206.36
    J          -22.006      -43.331     -458.86    480.18    -524.20
EL=    30 NODES=   26   27 MAT= 1
TCENT,TTOPZ,TBOTY=  0.0   0.0   0.0 QZ,QY= 0.00000E+00 0.00000E+00

   END          SDIR           SBZ          SBY        SIG1          SIG3
    I          -16.835        0.70854   -458.88    442.75    -476.42
    J          -16.835       -0.25891     37.736    21.160    -54.830

EL=    32 NODES=   27   28 MAT= 1
TCENT,TTOPZ,TBOTY=  0.0   0.0   0.0 QZ,QY= 0.00000E+00 0.00000E+00

   END          SDIR           SBZ          SBY        SIG1          SIG3
    I          -16.835       -0.25891     37.736    21.160    -54.830
    J          -16.835        0.90177    757.67    741.74    -775.41

            REACTION FORCES     FREQ.= 116.24   MODE=   1

   NODE     FX        FY         FZ          MX         MY         MZ
    1     -38.645  -19.411   0.29692E-01  0.26381   -1.9472    419.12
    8     -40.372   18.224  -0.44999E-01  0.24313   -3.4724    424.86
   21     -38.653  -19.469   0.37916E-01  0.39506    1.9009    419.21
   28     -40.377   18.097   0.65096E-01  0.50575    3.3951    424.93
  TOTAL  -158.05    -2.5591  0.87705E-01  1.4078    -0.12364   1688.1

                 ELEM. STRESS CALC. TIMES

   TYPE          NUMBER           STIF      TOTAL CP    AVE CP
    1              18                4         4.94      0.274

                 NODAL FORCE CALC. TIMES

   TYPE          NUMBER           STIF      TOTAL CP    AVE CP
    1              18                4         0.95      0.053
```

**Figure 8.11***a*  (*Continued*)

```
                POST1 ELEMENT STRESS LISTING
ITERATION=  2  SECTION=  1
FREQ=  122.21  LOAD CASE=  1


   ELEM          SXI            SBZI            SBYI
    1         -0.44746E-01    1.0602         0.26469E-02
    3         -0.44746E-01    0.14178E-01    0.14732E-03
    5          0.67838E-02    0.12757       -0.34794E-02
    7          0.67838E-02   -0.94697E-01    0.13006E-02
    9          0.67838E-02   -0.94472E-01    0.20515E-02
   11         -0.44745E-01   -0.73892       -0.28920E-02
   13         -0.44745E-01    0.14129E-01    0.89378E-03
   14         -0.32121E-01   -0.11390       -0.73911
   16         -0.32121E-01    0.45671E-02   -0.41459E-02
   17         -0.32182E-01    0.11272       -0.73893
   19         -0.32182E-01   -0.32154E-02   -0.42067E-02
   20          0.46277E-01    1.0506        -0.49659E-03
   22          0.46277E-01    0.33510E-01    0.26853E-03
   24         -0.55212E-02    0.10792        0.11181E-02
   26         -0.55212E-02   -0.81413E-01   -0.12364E-02
   28         -0.55212E-02   -0.81565E-01   -0.57532E-03
   30          0.46309E-01   -0.75845        0.22653E-02
   32          0.46309E-01    0.33513E-01    0.36553E-03
```

**Figure 8.11** (*Continued*) (*b*) Stress for mode 2, load case 1 (abbreviated listing from ANSYS postprocessor).

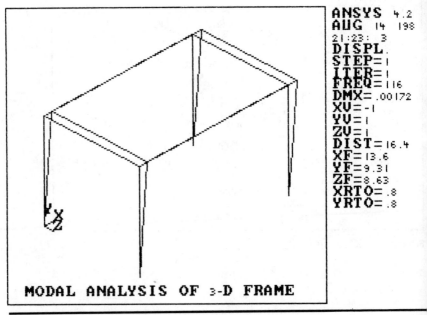

**Figure 8.12** Mode shape for first mode, load case 1.

This command will load the results of the previous session with PREP7, which in this case is represented by the command set used in Fig. 8.10. We can then issue a new SED command with the appropriate excitation direction, enter a new response spectra table, and then issue the SFWRIT command. This will modify the input file used by ANSYS for executing the analysis.

Before executing the next load case, it is necessary to rename the output file FILE12.DAT to a different file name. We will call it LD1DAT (no file extension is included). We can then execute ANSYS for the next load case and then rename the new FILE12.DAT file LD2DAT, for example, and go back to PREP7 to enter the third load case excitation direction and response spectra table. Finally, we execute the third load case and rename FILE12.DAT to LD3DAT.

Figure 8.13 shows the response spectrum calculation summary for load cases 2 and 3. In the $Y$ direction, the most significant mode is mode 6. Note, however, that the velocity is only 0.109 in/s at this frequency, an order of magnitude less than the velocity for the most significant mode in the $X$ and $Z$ directions. The modal participation factor is also small. Based on the low stresses for mode shape 1 in the $X$ direction, it can be assumed that stresses in the $Y$ direction are negligible.

The second mode in the $Z$ direction is the most significant mode. The stresses in this mode are larger than the stresses in mode 1 of the $X$ direction. These stresses are shown in abbreviated form in Fig. 8-14. As in Fig 8-11$b$, SXI is the axial stress, and SBZI and SBYI are bending stresses.

The final step is to combine the load cases to obtain the combined element stresses. This is accomplished by the commands in Fig. 8.15. We will not examine these commands in detail, but we will briefly summarize the function of the command set. The objective is to combine by the SRSS method the stresses for mode shapes 1 and 2 of load case 1 ($X$ direction) with the stresses for mode shape 2 of load case 3 ($Z$ direction). Recalling that we renamed the ANSYS output files LD1DAT, LD2DAT, etc., the stresses from each output file are read in as separate load cases into the ANSYS postprocessor using the NFILE and STRESS commands.

The file name LCASE,2 stores the stresses from the second mode of load case 1; LCASE,3 stores the stresses from the second mode of load case 3; and LCASE,4 stores the combined stresses computed by the LCSRSS command. The PRSTRS commands print the stresses for each load case. The combined stress results are shown in Fig. 8.16. To verify these results, try combining the axial stress in element 1 from Fig. 8-11, Fig. 8-11$b$, and Fig. 8-14, using the SRSS method. You will obtain the result for element 1 in Fig. 8.15.

Load Case 2: Y Excitation Direction

RESPONSE SPECTRUM CALCULATION SUMMARY

| MODE | FREQUENCY | SV | PARTIC.FACTOR | MODE COEF. | M.C. RATIO | EQUIV. MASS |
|---|---|---|---|---|---|---|
| 1 | 116.2 | 0.3785 | 0.7040E-02 | 0.3649E-05 | 0.489676 | 0.3280E-01 |
| 2 | 122.2 | 0.3600 | 0.6208E-02 | 0.2911E-05 | 0.390697 | 0.2252E-01 |
| 3 | 143.8 | 0.3059 | 0.6375E-04 | 0.2158E-07 | 0.002897 | 0.3967E-01 |
| 4 | 227.2 | 0.1950 | -0.1982E-03 | -0.2707E-07 | 0.003634 | 0.3915E-01 |
| 5 | 421.9 | 0.1149 | -0.2347E-02 | -0.1017E-06 | 0.013648 | 0.8947E-02 |
| 6 | 450.2 | 0.1090 | -0.1934 | -0.7451E-05 | 1.000000 | 0.9000E-02 |
| 7 | 482.3 | 0.1030 | 0.3449E-04 | 0.1172E-08 | 0.000157 | 0.9009E-02 |
| 8 | 603.5 | 0.1000 | -0.3123E-02 | -0.8235E-07 | 0.011052 | 0.1080E-01 |
| 9 | 806.1 | 0.1000 | -0.1038 | -0.2049E-05 | 0.274953 | 0.9116E-02 |
| 10 | 836.6 | 0.1000 | 0.1509E-04 | 0.2871E-09 | 0.000039 | 0.9228E-02 |
| 11 | 943.0 | 0.1000 | 0.1336E-02 | 0.2255E-07 | 0.003027 | 0.9144E-02 |
| 12 | 996.4 | 0.1000 | -0.1175E-01 | -0.1877E-06 | 0.025190 | 0.9518E-02 |
| 13 | 1028. | 0.1000 | -0.3604E-01 | -0.5579E-06 | 0.074883 | 0.9450E-02 |
| 14 | 1030. | 0.1000 | -0.8092E-03 | -0.1250E-07 | 0.001678 | 0.9291E-02 |
| 15 | 1087. | 0.1000 | -0.4413E-03 | -0.6461E-08 | 0.000867 | 0.9264E-02 |
| 16 | 1123. | 0.1000 | -0.4348E-01 | -0.6165E-06 | 0.082745 | 0.9082E-02 |
| 17 | 1131. | 0.1000 | -0.2902E-03 | -0.4083E-08 | 0.000548 | 0.9296E-02 |
| 18 | 1140. | 0.1000 | 0.8220E-02 | 0.1148E-06 | 0.015406 | 0.9592E-02 |
| 19 | 1175. | 0.1000 | 0.6132E-02 | 0.8307E-07 | 0.011149 | 0.9951E-02 |
| 20 | 1213. | 0.1000 | -0.7022E-01 | -0.9215E-06 | 0.123675 | 0.9470E-02 |
| 21 | 1317. | 0.1000 | -0.8446E-04 | -0.1021E-08 | 0.000137 | 0.9919E-02 |
| 22 | 1343. | 0.1000 | -0.8270E-04 | -0.9804E-09 | 0.000132 | 0.9504E-02 |
| 23 | 1364. | 0.1000 | -0.1386E-03 | -0.1617E-08 | 0.000217 | 0.9411E-02 |
| 24 | 1469. | 0.1000 | -0.1659E-02 | -0.1797E-07 | 0.002412 | 0.9771E-02 |

SIGNIFICANCE FACTOR FOR EXPANDED MODES =   0.10000E-02

Load Case 3: Z Excitation Direction

RESPONSE SPECTRUM CALCULATION SUMMARY

| MODE | FREQUENCY | SV | PARTIC.FACTOR | MODE COEF. | M.C. RATIO | EQUIV. MASS |
|---|---|---|---|---|---|---|
| 1 | 116.2 | 1.1448 | -0.2413E-03 | -0.3782E-06 | 0.000603 | 0.3280E-01 |
| 2 | 122.2 | 1.1148 | -0.4319 | -0.6271E-03 | 1.000000 | 0.2252E-01 |
| 3 | 143.8 | 1.0226 | 0.1794E-03 | 0.2030E-06 | 0.000324 | 0.3967E-01 |
| 4 | 227.2 | 0.7622 | 0.1941E-03 | 0.1036E-06 | 0.000165 | 0.3915E-01 |
| 5 | 421.9 | 0.4372 | -0.2411E-03 | -0.3977E-07 | 0.000063 | 0.8947E-02 |
| 6 | 450.2 | 0.4004 | -0.3102E-04 | -0.4390E-08 | 0.000007 | 0.9000E-02 |
| 7 | 482.3 | 0.3647 | 0.4303E-02 | 0.5178E-06 | 0.000826 | 0.9009E-02 |
| 8 | 603.5 | 0.2690 | 0.3132E-01 | 0.2223E-05 | 0.003544 | 0.1080E-01 |
| 9 | 806.1 | 0.1610 | -0.4513E-03 | -0.1435E-07 | 0.000023 | 0.9116E-02 |
| 10 | 836.6 | 0.1483 | 0.2289E-05 | 0.6461E-10 | 0.000000 | 0.9228E-02 |
| 11 | 943.0 | 0.1138 | -0.1751E-03 | -0.3365E-08 | 0.000005 | 0.9144E-02 |
| 12 | 996.4 | 0.1008 | 0.8141E-03 | 0.1311E-07 | 0.000021 | 0.9518E-02 |
| 13 | 1028. | 0.1000 | 0.2179E-02 | 0.3374E-07 | 0.000054 | 0.9450E-02 |
| 14 | 1030. | 0.1000 | 0.1672E-02 | 0.2582E-07 | 0.000041 | 0.9291E-02 |
| 15 | 1087. | 0.1000 | -0.2272E-01 | -0.3326E-06 | 0.000530 | 0.9264E-02 |
| 16 | 1123. | 0.1000 | -0.9760E-02 | -0.1384E-06 | 0.000221 | 0.9082E-02 |
| 17 | 1131. | 0.1000 | 0.3327E-02 | 0.4681E-07 | 0.000075 | 0.9296E-02 |
| 18 | 1140. | 0.1000 | -0.8750E-01 | -0.1222E-05 | 0.001949 | 0.9592E-02 |
| 19 | 1175. | 0.1000 | 0.1457E-02 | 0.1974E-07 | 0.000031 | 0.9951E-02 |
| 20 | 1213. | 0.1000 | -0.6657E-02 | -0.8735E-07 | 0.000139 | 0.9470E-02 |
| 21 | 1317. | 0.1000 | 0.2681E-03 | 0.3241E-08 | 0.000005 | 0.9919E-02 |
| 22 | 1343. | 0.1000 | 0.7726E-04 | 0.9159E-09 | 0.000001 | 0.9504E-02 |
| 23 | 1364. | 0.1000 | -0.7713E-04 | -0.8997E-09 | 0.000001 | 0.9411E-02 |
| 24 | 1469. | 0.1000 | -0.7781E-04 | -0.8429E-09 | 0.000001 | 0.9771E-02 |

SIGNIFICANCE FACTOR FOR EXPANDED MODES =   0.10000E-02

Figure 8.13  Response spectrum calculation summary for load cases 2 and 3 (Y- and Z-response spectra, respectively).

```
         POST1 ELEMENT STRESS LISTING
ITERATION = 2 SECTION =  1   FREQ =     122.21
         LOAD CASE =  3    ELEM
       SXI        SBXI        SBYI
 1   -30.881     731.68       1.8267
 3   -30.881       9.7844     0.10167
 5     4.6817     88.040     -2.4013
 7     4.6817    -65.354      0.89757
 9     4.6817    -65.198      1.4158
11   -30.880    -509.95      -1.9959
13   -30.880       9.7512     0.61683
14   -22.168     -78.605   -510.09
16   -22.168       3.1519    -2.8612
17   -22.210      77.793   -509.96
19   -22.210      -2.2190    -2.9032
20    31.937     725.03      -0.34271
22    31.937      23.126      0.18532
24    -3.8104     74.482      0.77163
26    -3.8104    -56.186      0.85331
28    -3.8104    -56.291     -0.39705
30    31.959     523.44       1.5634
32    31.959      23.129      0.25227
```

Figure 8.14  Stresses for mode 2, load case 3.

```
LCLIM,4
NFILE,LD1DAT
STRESS,SXI,4,13
STRESS,SBZI,4,14
STRESS,SBYI,4,15
SET,1,1
ERSEL,STIF,4
LCASE,2
STRESS,SXI,4,13
STRESS,SBXI,4,14
STRESS,SBYI,4,15
SET,1,2
NFILE,LD3DAT
Y
LCASE,3
STRESS,SXI,4,13
STRESS,SBXI,4,14
STRESS,SBYI,4,15
SET,1,2
LCFACT,1,1
LCSRSS,4,1,2,3
LCASE,1
PRSTRS
LCASE,2
PRSTRS
LCASE,3
PRSTRS
LCASE,4
PRSTRS FINISH
```

Figure 8.15  Listing for combining stresses. The LCASE commands do not represent the actual analysis load cases but are storage areas in the postprocessor for performing separate calculations. The LCSRSS command performs the actual stress combination and stores results on LCASE,4.

```
      POST1 ELEMENT STRESS LISTING
CALCULATED LOAD CASE = 4
ELEM    SXI        SBZI       SBYI
 1    35.773     731.68     747.31
 3    35.773       9.7846    58.258
 5    22.526      89.978    478.46
 7    22.526      65.575    180.53
 9    22.526      65.213    183.73
11    35.228     509.96     458.71
13    35.228       9.8292    37.694
14    22.182      81.638    510.09
16    22.182      41.554      2.9175
17    22.322      91.780    509.97
19    22.322      83.447      3.7307
20    36.715     725.04     747.46
22    36.715      23.126     58.264
24    22.334      76.845    478.54
26    22.334      56.409    180.55
28    22.334      56.294    183.73
30    36.122     523.44     458.88
32    36.122      23.130     37.737
```

Figure 8.16  Combined stress results. Load case 4 represents a separate storage area in the ANSYS postprocessor.

## 8.6 Transient Response Analysis

As a final example, we will look at a transient response analysis of the valve that we analyzed in the first example of this chapter. Before we begin, we discuss several important modeling guidelines associated with transient analysis.

As we saw in Chap. 2, transient response analysis involves the calculation of a structure's response to time-varying forces, accelerations, or displacements. The time-varying loads are input in the form of a time history as in Fig. 1.13. The response of the structure depends primarily on its natural frequencies, damping characteristics, and the frequency content of the time-varying load.

The primary responsibility of the analyst is to specify the appropriate time intervals over which the response of the structure is to be calculated and the duration of the calculation. In order to correctly specify these parameters, it is necessary to know the natural frequencies of the structure. For this reason, the first step in performing a transient response analysis is to perform a modal analysis.

After the natural frequencies have been determined, the next step is to determine the number of modes to be included in the analysis. Usually, only the first few modes are absolutely neccessary to pick up the structure's response. However, if the excitation input (the time history) includes high-frequency loading, modes that cover the loading-frequency range should be included.

In our valve example, we will use the first two modes for the analysis. From Sec. 8.4, the frequencies for the first two modes are 53.4 and 108.9 cps, respectively. The objective of this analysis is to determine the displacement of the motor operator when the valve is subjected to a acceleration time history of 0.1 second.

The time history is shown in tabular and graphical form in Figs. 8.17 and 8.18, respectively. The units in the tabular form are in percentage of the acceleration of gravity (% G). In the plot, the units have been converted to inches per second squared (in/s$^2$). Based on the information we have, the parameters for the analysis can be determined. There are two main parameters required for transient response analysis:

1. *Duration of analysis.* The minimum length of the duration should be $1/f_1$, where $f_1$ is the frequency of the lowest mode of interest (usually, the first mode). This ensures that all modes will oscillate at least once. Thus, the minimum duration for this analysis should be $1/53.4 = 0.02$ second. We will run the analysis for 0.1 second.

2. *Solution time increment.* The solution increment should not exceed $\frac{1}{2}f_h$, where $f_h$ is the highest mode of interest. In this case, the time increment should be $1/(2 \times 108.9) = 0.005$ second. While the solution time increment should be 0.005 second, we may not wish to have the program output

```
EXCITATION, ACCELERATION TIME HISTORY (PERCENT OF GRAVITY)
0.00,0.015      0.01, 0.005     0.02,0.0853     0.03,−0.043     0.04,0.235
0.045,−.056     0.05,0.112      0.055,0.165     0.0595,0.049    0.065,0.101
0.070,0.234     0.080,−0.146    0.089,−0.036    0.096,0.036     0.10,0.15


SOLVE
QUIT
```

**Figure 8.17**  Acceleration time history table. The first field represents the time increment. The second field represents accelerations in percent of the acceleration of gravity (% G).

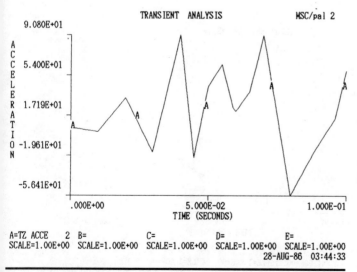

**Figure 8.18**  The acceleration time history in units of in/s$^2$.  Note that the curve $A$ is described in the lower left corner as TZ ACCE2, which means translational acceleration in the $Z$ direction, node 2.

```
TIME RANGE  0.1  0.001  2
ACCELERATIONS APPLIED   11
TZ     386.4    2 through 3
RA       0      2 through 3
TY       0      2 through 3
TX       0      2 through 3


USE FIRST 2 MODES
DAMPING PERCENTAGES
1.5 PERCENT IN MODE 1,2

GET
TIMEHIST
```

**Figure 8.19** Input listing for transient response analysis.

the results at the same interval. For example, we can have the solution output at an interval of 0.01 second and have 2 solutions executed per interval, which is the same as a solution time increment of 0.005 second.

In our example, a duration of 0.1 second and a time increment of 0.005 second result in 20 solution increments. Since this is a small problem, we

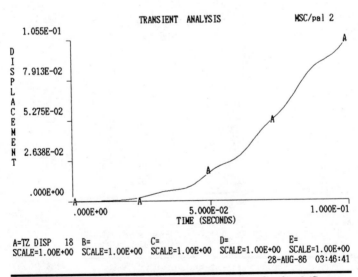

**Figure 8.20** Plot of displacement in the $Z$ direction of node 18 (See lower left corner of plot for description of curve $A$).

can increase the accuracy by decreasing the time increment and thus increasing the number of solutions.

Figure 8.19 shows the input listing for the transient analysis of the valve. A time range of 0.1 second and a solution increment of 0.0005 second (0.001-second solution output and two solutions per output interval) are specified. Since the acceleration time history is in terms of percentage of the acceleration of gravity (Fig. 8.17), the acceleration of gravity is input as a boundary condition at the base of the valve at nodes 2 and 3. The acceleration is zero for the other degrees of freedom. A damping value of 1.5 percent for the valve and pipe system is assumed. The file TIMEHIST.TXT (Fig. 8.17) is called by the GET command. The GET command is convenient for calling separate time history files.

Note that imposed accelerations and imposed displacements are mutually exclusive. In the modal analysis of the valve, we used zero displacements at nodes 2 and 3 to constrain the model. In this transient run, the accelerations are the imposed boundary conditions. At time = 0, the accelerations are zero, which is equivalent to applied zero displacements. The transient analysis calculates the natural frequencies at time = 0, producing the same results as our modal analysis.

The results of the analysis are shown in graphical form in Fig. 8.20. The displacement of node 18 (the motor operator) in the $Z$ direction is approximately 0.1 in after 0.1 second.

Many interesting problems can be solved with transient response analysis. Time histories can also be in terms of force or displacement. Output can be in terms of stresses or reaction forces. For example, transient analysis is very useful in the field of automated machinery and robotics. Let us assume a robot arm has rotated 30° in 3 seconds. This displacement can be expressed as a displacement time history. Then, the reaction forces or displacements due to vibrations of the arm after it comes to rest can be calculated by means of a transient response analysis. By varying the geometrical and material properties of the arm (and thus its stiffness and natural frequencies), an optimal design can be determined. Many other problems involving shock and vibration can also be solved by transient response analysis.

## References

1. Cook, R. D.: *Concepts and Applications of Finite Element Analysis*, Wiley, New York, 1981.
2. Bathe, Klaus-Jürgen, and Edward L. Wilson: *Numerical Methods in Finite Element Analysis*, Prentice-Hall, Englewood Cliffs, N.J., 1976.
3. Swanson Analysis Systems, Inc.: *ANSYS Engineering Analysis System Examples Manual* (for ANSYS Revision 4.2), Houston, Pa., July 1, 1985.
4. Crede, C.: *Shock and Vibration Concepts in Engineering Design*, Prentice-Hall, Englewood Cliffs, N.J., 1965, pp. 26–27.
5. Biggs, J. M.: *Introduction to Structural Dynamics*, McGraw-Hill, New York, 1964.

Chapter

# 9

# Heat Transfer Analysis

In previous chapters, we focused on problems involving structural and mechanical loads such as accelerations and applied forces or pressures. Displacements, forces, or stresses were the unknowns. In this chapter, we turn to the topic of heat tranfer analysis in which the unknowns are temperatures. The objective in heat transfer analysis is to determine the temperature distribution of the structure or component. Once the nodal temperatures are known, the problem can be further analyzed for displacements and stresses using principles of statics analysis. You may wish to review the material on heat transfer analysis in Chap. 2.

Like dynamics, heat transfer analysis is a complex subject, and we provide a very basic introduction here. Readers with limited experience in heat transfer analysis are encouraged to consult some of the more comprehensive texts listed in the references. The example problems in this chapter are solved using ANSYS-PC/THERMAL, the companion program to ANSYS-PC/LINEAR.

Of the three types of finite element analysis covered in this book, heat transfer analysis is the most sensitive to modeling errors. The modeling techniques set forth in Chap. 4 should be strictly followed when performing heat transfer analysis, particularly the guidelines on element aspect ratios and distortion angles. Elements with excessive aspect ratios or skew angles will give inaccurate temperature results.

Mesh refinement can also be very critical in heat transfer analyses. In general, the same mesh-refinement guidelines that apply to structural analysis apply to heat transfer problems. A refined mesh should be used near discontinuities and surfaces exposed to large thermal gradients. A gradual transition to a coarser mesh is appropriate in areas removed from the thermal loading.

In Chap. 6, we discussed a procedure for performing convergence studies. The same approach is recommended for heat transfer problems requiring a high degree of accuracy, such as problems involving severe thermal transients. We will discuss convergence further in the section on transient analysis.

## 9.1  Overview of ANSYS-PC/THERMAL

ANSYS-PC/THERMAL is a companion program of ANSYS-PC/LINEAR and, in many respects, is very similar. As we mentioned in Chap. 2, the ANSYS-PC programs are subsets of the ANSYS mainframe program which includes statics, dynamics, and heat transfer modules. Therefore, the command structures of ANSYS-PC/THERMAL and ANSYS-PC/LINEAR are essentially identical. The main difference is the element library. Table 9.1 shows the element library for ANSYS-PC/THERMAL.

Notice that the number of degrees of freedom is not listed. This is because there is only 1 DOF per node in heat transfer analysis, namely, the temperature. Therefore, the eight-noded thermal solid element has 8 DOF. The four-noded STIF55 element has 4 DOF, and so forth.

Most of the elements in Table 9.1 have equivalent structural elements in ANSYS-PC/LINEAR, as shown in Table 9.2. This makes it possible to use the same finite element model in both programs. You can first perform the thermal analysis in ANSYS-PC/THERMAL and then use the results in a statics analysis with ANSYS-PC/LINEAR. You simply change the element type when you perform the statics analysis. Those thermal elements which have no equivalent can be defined as "null elements" in the statics analysis. We will look at this procedure in more detail later in this chapter.

**TABLE 9.1**  Element Library for ANSYS-PC/THERMAL

| STIF Number | Name | Dimension | Nodes |
|:---:|:---|:---:|:---:|
| 31 | Radiation link | 2 or 3 | 2 |
| 32 | 2-D conducting bar | 2 | 2 |
| 33 | 3-D conducting bar | 3 | 2 |
| 34 | Convection link | 2 or 3 | 2 |
| 55 | 2-D isopar. thermal Solid | 2 | 4 |
| 57 | Isopar. quad. thermal Shell | 3 | 4 |
| 70 | Isopar. thermal solid | 3 | 8 |
| 71 | Lumped thermal mass | 2 or 3 | 1 |

**Table 9.2   ANSYS-PC/LINEAR Elements that Correspond to ANSYS-PC/THERMAL Elements**

| ANSYS-PC/LINEAR Element | ANSYS-PC/THERMAL Element |
|---|---|
| 2-D spar (STIF1) | 2-D conducting bar (STIF32) |
| 3-D spar (STIF8) | 3-D conducting bar (STIF33) |
| 2-D solid (STIF42) | 2-D thermal solid (STIF55) |
| Quad. shell (STIF63) | Quad. thermal shell (STIF57) |
| 3-D solid (STIF70) | 3-D thermal solid (STIF70) |
| Generalized mass (STIF21) | Lumped thermal mass (STIF71) |

ANSYS-PC/THERMAL consists of four modules:

1. The preprocessor PREP7 for generating models, applied loads, and boundary conditions (Models can also be plotted and viewed from within PREP7.)

2. THERMAL, the main number-crunching part of the system (equivalent to ANSYS in ANSYS-PC/LINEAR; see Chap. 5)

3. The postprocessor POST1 for plotting contour plots, printing results, etc.

4. The special postprocessor POST26 for plotting graphs of time-dependent results and other data relationships

The first three modules are equivalent to the ANSYS-PC/LINEAR modules. POST26 is an additional module in ANSYS-PC/THERMAL and is not available in Revision 4.2 of ANSYS-PC/LINEAR.

An important feature in ANSYS-PC/THERMAL is multiple-load-step capability. As we saw in Chap. 8, multiple load cases cannot be executed in a single analysis in ANSYS-PC/LINEAR. In ANSYS-PC/THERMAL, however, multiple load steps may be executed in a single analysis. For example, you can execute separate steady-state and transient load steps in a single analysis. We will look at an example of multiple load steps later in the chapter.

ANSYS-PC/THERMAL also provides automatic steady-state convergence checking and transient time step optimization for problems requiring iterative solutions. The following types of analysis require an iterative solution:

1. Steady-state analyses that include nonlinear elements (STIF31, 34, and 71)

2. Steady-state analyses that include temperature-dependent material properties, heat-generation rates, or convection boundary conditions

3. All transient thermal analyses

"Automatic convergence checking" means that the steady-state solution is terminated when it has converged, regardless of the number of iterations specified. By default, ANSYS-PC/THERMAL defines convergence to exist when consecutive iterations produce a temperature difference of less than 1°. This criterion can be changed by the user.

Transient time step optimization is an automatic numerical procedure which minimizes the number of iterations required to compute the thermal response over the defined load step time period. A discussion of the mathematics behind this procedure can be found in Swanson Analysis Systems, Inc., *ANSYS-PC/THERMAL User's Manual* (Ref. 1). We will look at an example of transient time step optimization in the section on transient analysis.

It should also be noted that ANSYS-PC/THERMAL can be used for other Laplace or Poisson field equation problems by substituting the appropriate equation variables into the corresponding heat transfer equation variables in ANSYS-PC/THERMAL. See Chap. 2 for further information.

## 9.2  General Considerations in Heat Transfer Analysis

In this section, we look at some of the general differences between structural and heat transfer analysis.

### 9.2.1  Matrices and Boundary Conditions

As we saw in Chap. 2, the matrices for heat transfer analysis are the conductivity and specific heat matrices. These are analogous to the stiffness and mass matrices, respectively. In problems that do not involve time-dependent temperature changes, the solution involves only the conductivity matrix (analogous to statics analysis). In time-dependent thermal problems, the specific heat matrix is also required (similar to dynamics analysis).

While imposed displacements, pressures, and forces are the typical boundary conditions in structural and mechanical problems, temperatures, convections, and heat flows are the boundary conditions in heat transfer analysis. Thermal boundary conditions are specified at nodes and element faces in the same manner as structural boundary conditions.

The most common types of boundary conditions in heat transfer analysis are temperatures and convections. Temperatures are simply specified at the appropriate nodes. Convections are specified in terms of the convection heat transfer coefficient, which has units of heat flow/

area-time-temperature, e.g., Btu/in$^2$-s-°F. Convections can be applied either to element faces or to individual nodes.

The applicable convection heat transfer coefficients must be calculated before beginning the heat transfer analysis. There are a great many analytically and empirically derived equations for calculating convection heat transfer coefficients for all sorts of geometries and physical loading conditions; from fluid flow in pipes to air flow on cooling fins. Most introductory heat transfer texts provide many of these equations (Ref. 2).

### 9.2.2 Material Properties

The material properties definition is dependent on the type of elements used in the problem. The most general heat transfer material properties are the density (DENS), the thermal conductivity (KXX, KYY, and KZZ), and the specific heat (C) (the terms in parentheses are the ANSYS-PC/THERMAL commands for these quantities). For isothermal problems, KYY and KZZ are not specified and default to KXX. Radiation elements require the emissivity to be specified. The convection link element requires a convection coefficient to be specified.

Material properties may be input as a function of temperature in both ANSYS-PC/THERMAL and ANSYS-PC/LINEAR. The input is of the form

$$\text{Property(T)} = C0 + C1(T) + C2(T)^2 + C3(T)^3 + \cdots$$

where the property can be any material property such as the thermal conductivity, the coefficient of thermal expansion, or even the modulus of elasticity. For constant material properties, only the value C0 is input. For example, EX,1,30E6 is a constant material property. If the property equation is linear, then only two constants (C0 and C1) need to be defined. For example, ALPX,1,8E − 6,0.0003 means that the coefficient of thermal expansion for material type 1 is evaluated according to the equation ALPX $= 8 \times 10^{-6} + 0.0003(T)$.

Temperature-dependent material properties may also be specified in the form of a temperature table using the MPTEMP and MPDATA commands. The temperatures and corresponding property values are specified in ascending order using MPTEMP for temperature and MPDATA for the material property.

The importance of using temperature-dependent material properties depends on the temperature range of the problem and also the type of material. In steels, for example, the thermal conductivity increases approximately 4 to 6 percent for each increase of 100°F. If the temper-

ature range of the problem is only 100 to 200°F, it is probably acceptable to use constant material properties (depending on the desired
degree of accuracy). If however, the temperature range is 400 or 500°F,
temperature-dependent effects are quite significant.

## 9.3  Steady-State Analysis

As we discussed in Chap. 2, the objective of steady-state analysis is to
determine the temperature distribution in a component or structure
when it has reached thermal equilibrium with the environmental thermal conditions. When the steady-state condition has been reached, the
temperature distribution remains constant unless the environmental
conditions are changed.

The simplest form of heat transfer analysis is the steady-state conduction problem. The tutorial problem in the *ANSYS-PC/THERMAL
User's Manual* (Ref. 1) is a simple example of a steady-state conduction problem. Figure 9.1 shows the physical problem and the finite
element model. The thick-walled cylinder has an internal temperature
of 100°F, while the outside temperature is 70°F. By taking an axisymmetric slice of the cylinder and applying the appropriate temperatures
at the inside and outside surfaces, the temperature distribution through
the thickness of the wall can be determined.

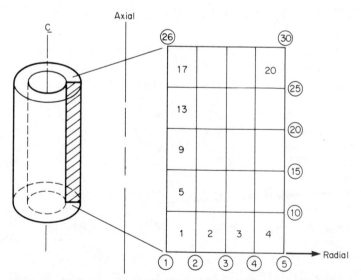

**Figure 9.1**  Finite element model of thick-walled cylinder using axisymmetric elements. *[Swanson Analysis Systems, Inc., ANSYS-PC/THERMAL
User's Manual (for ANSYS Revision 4.2) Houston, Pa., March 1, 1986.]*

```
/TITLE, THICK WALL CYLINDER
ET,1,55,,,1
KXX,1,3
N,1,3
N,5,11
FILL
NGEN,6,5,1,5,1,,4
E,1,2,7,6
EGEN,4,1,1
EGEN,5,5,-4
NT,1,TEMP,100,,26,5
NT,5,TEMP,70,,30,5
ITER,1,1
AFWRIT
FINISH
```

**Figure 9.2**  ANSYS-PC/THERMAL input listing for thick-walled cylinder problem.

Figure 9.2 shows the input listing for the thermal analysis. First, the STIF55 thermal solid element is specified. The 1 in the last field of the ET command specifies the axisymmetric option. Next, the thermal conductivity of the material is specified arbitrarily as 3 Btu/s-in-°F. It is important to pay particular attention to units in heat transfer analyses. Most texts give heat transfer coefficients in terms of British thermal units, hours, and feet. In most problems, you will want to use British thermal units, seconds, and inches.

The next several commands define the nodes and elements. These commands should look familiar to you if you have worked through the ANSYS-PC/LINEAR example problems in previous chapters. If not, you may wish to review Chap. 5, which describes the ANSYS commands in detail. The model consists of 30 nodes and 20 elements.

The temperatures at the inside and outside surfaces are defined with the NT commands. The NT commands specify the boundary conditions of the problem. Since 12 temperatures are specified, there are 18 active DOF in the problem. As we discussed earlier, the specified temperatures are equivalent to imposed displacements in structural analysis. The ITER command requests a printout of the temperature solution.

The input file is executed in PREP7 to generate the conductivity matrix. The analysis is then performed using the THERMAL module. Figure 9.3 shows the output from the analysis. The "load summary" confirms that 12 temperatures were specified. The temperature solution shows the nodal temperatures at steady state. The heat flow rates (British thermal units per second) at the inside and outside surface nodes are also listed. The heat flow rates are analogous to reaction forces in structural analysis. Note that the heat flow rates are positive at the inside surface and negative at the outside surface. The direction of heat flow is positive to negative.

```
THICK WALL CYLINDER
**ANSYS VERSION FOR DEMONSTRATION PURPOSES ONLY**
NUMBER OF REAL CONSTANT SETS =  0
NUMBER OF ELEMENTS =  20
MAXIMUM MODE NUMBER =  30

LOAD SUMMARY—      12 TEMPERATURES      0 HEAT FLOWS      0 CONVECTIONS

RANGE OF ELEMENT MAXIMUM CONDUCTIVITY IN GLOBAL COORDINATES
MAXIMUM=  0.252500E+02    AT ELEMENT    20.
MINUMUM=  0.102500E+02    AT ELEMENT    17.
***ELEMENT STIFFNESS FORMULATION TIMES
   TYPE   NUMBER   STIF   TOTAL CP   AVE CP
     1      20      55     4.62      0.231
TIME AT END OF ELEMENT STIFFNESS FORMULATION CP=        49.550
MAXIMUM WAVE FRONT ALLOWED =   400.
MAXIMUM IN-CORE WAVE FRONT =    5.
    MATRIX SOLUTION TIMES
    READ IN ELEMENT STIFFNESSES    CP=    1.040
    NODAL COORD. TRANSFORMATION    CP=      0.000
    MATRIX TRIANGULARIZATION    CP=    1.870
TIME AT END OF MATRIX TRIANGULARIZATION CP=  56.250
    TIME AT START OF BACK SUBSTITUTION   CP=  56.910
LOAD STEP=  1    ITERATION=  1    CUM. ITER.=  1

*****TEMPERATURE SOLUTION        TIME=   0.00000E+00
LOAD STEP=  1 ITERATION=  1    CUM. ITER.=  1

NODE TEMP     NODE TEMP     NODE TEMP     NODE TEMP     NODE TEMP
 1   100.000   2   88.312    3   80.519    4   74.675    5   70.000
 6   100.000   7   88.312    3   80.519    9   74.675   10   70.000
11   100.000  12   88.312   13   80.519   14   74.675   15   70.000
16   100.000  17   88.312   18   80.519   19   74.675   20   70.000
21   100.000  22   88.312   23   80.519   24   74.675   25   70.000
26   100.000  27   88.312   28   80.519   29   74.675   30   70.000
MAXIMUM TEMPERATURE=100.00   AT   NODE    26
MINIMUM TEMPERATURE = 70.000   AT   NODE    30
*****ELEMENT HEAT FLOW RATES*****     TIME=   0.000000E+00
LOAD STEP=    1   ITER.=    1      CUM.ITER.=      1
*****HEAT FLOW RATES INTO NODES*****    TIME    =0.00000E+00
LOAD STEP=    1   ITER.=      1      CUM. ITER.=      1
NODE        HEAT

 1          140.26
 5         -140.26
 6          280.52
10         -280.52
11          280.52
15         -280.52
16          280.52
20         -280.52
21          280.52
25         -280.52
26          140.26
30         -140.26

TOTAL  -0.14211E-11
***ELEM. HT. FLOW CALC. TIMES
TYPE  NUMBER  STIF  TOTAL CP  AVE CP
  1      20     55    1.04    0.052
```

**Figure 9.3**  Temperature solution output from thick-walled cylinder problem.

```
***NODAL HT. FLOW CALC. TIMES
TYPE   NUMBER   STIF   TOTAL CP   AVE CP
1        20       55     0.59       0.029
***LOAD STEP   1   ITER   1   COMPLETED.   TIME =      0.000000E + 00
TIME INC =      0.000000E + 00    CUM. ITER. =      1
***PROBLEM STATISTICS
NO. OF ACTIVE DEGREES OF FREEDOM =   18
R.M.S. WAVEFRONT SIZE =   4.3
TOTAL CP TIME =   73.000
```

**Figure 9.3** *(Continued)*

The temperature contour plot for the cylinder wall is shown in Fig. 9.4. As in ANSYS-PC/LINEAR, the contours are in color and are intended to be viewed on a color graphics monitor. We include the plot primarily to illustrate the normal procedure for interpreting results.

## 9.4  Thermal Stress Analysis

If the temperature distribution is the desired result of the analysis, the solution using ANSYS-PC/THERMAL in the above example would be all that is required. However, in many cases, the ultimate objective is to determine the thermal stresses in the model. If this is the case, the next step is to use the temperature solution from ANSYS-PC/THERMAL in a thermal stress analysis using ANSYS-PC/LINEAR.

The procedure for performing the thermal stress analysis is best illustrated using the cylinder wall example solved in the previous section.

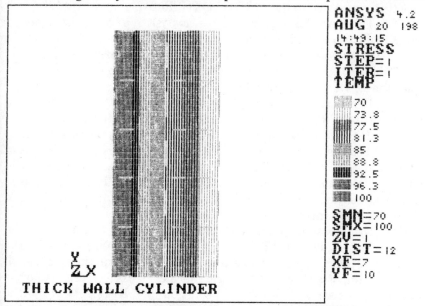

**Figure 9.4**  Steady-state temperature contour plot for thick-walled cylinder. The inside surface is at 100°F, and the outside surface is at 70°F.

```
RESUME
KAN,0
ET,1,42,,,1
TREF,70
EX,1,30E6
ALPX 1,8.55E-6
KTEMP,-1
TREAD, 1,1
D,1,UY,0.0,,5
D,26,UY,0.0,,30
SFWRIT
FINISH
```

**Figure 9.5** Commands for performing thermal stress analysis of thick-walled cylinder.

When ANSYS-PC/THERMAL performs a thermal analysis, the nodal temperature results are stored in a file called FILE4.DAT. If we use the exact same finite element model in ANSYS-PC/LINEAR, we can simply have ANSYS-PC/LINEAR read FILE4.DAT as input for the thermal stress analysis.

The PREP7 commands required to perform the thermal stress analysis for the thick-walled cylinder are shown in Fig. 9.5. These commands either could be entered interactively in PREP7 or could be submitted as a batch input file to PREP7 (see App. A). Note that we are now using the PREP7 module in ANSYS-PC/LINEAR rather than in ANSYS-PC/THERMAL. This can be somewhat confusing if you have both programs installed in the same hard disk (see App. A).

As we discussed in Chap. 8, ANSYS allows continuation of an existing analysis by issuing the RESUME command. In this case, the model geometry that we created in the ANSYS-PC/THERMAL analysis is loaded into PREP7. The KAN,0 command sets the analysis type to statics analysis. PREP7 will respond with a warning that the thermal element STIF55 cannot be used in a statics analysis. We therefore change the element type to STIF42 (see Table 9.2) by entering a new ET command. The 1 in the last field indicates the axisymmetric option for the element.

Next, the material properties are specified. Note that the reference temperature (TREF) and corresponding coefficient of thermal expansion (ALPX) are required for a thermal stress analysis. The KTEMP TREAD command reads the first load step and first iteration from command sets FILE4.DAT as the input file for the temperatures. The FILE4. Note that any load step from a thermal analysis can be used for the stress analysis. The load step and iteration number can be read from the temperature output listing (see Fig. 9.3).

Next we impose displacement constraints on the end-nodes in the axial direction. The SFWRIT command prepares the input file for the ANSYS stress run. We then execute ANSYS to perform the stress analysis. It is important to note that the thermal stress analysis will overwrite the existing temperature solution (FILE12.DAT) from the ANSYS-PC/THERMAL run. It is therefore a good idea to rename the previous FILE12.DAT file or to copy it to another directory.

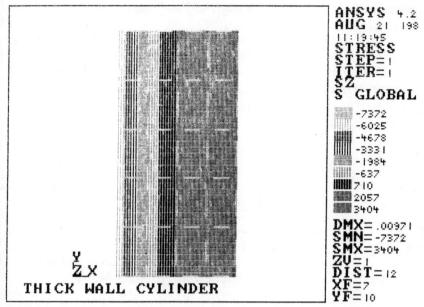

**Figure 9.6** Stress contour plot of thick-walled cylinder. Maximum hoop stress is -7372 lb/in$^2$ at inside surface.

The stress contour plot for the hoop stress SZ in the cylinder wall is shown in Fig. 9.6. Note that the warmer, inner portion of the wall is in compression, while the cooler outer region is in tension. The warmer material wants to expand, but it is prevented from doing so by the cooler material. It is therefore held in a state of compression. The cooler material wants to contract, but it is held in tension by the warmer material. A good description of the thermal behavior of pressure vessels can be found in Harvey, *Pressure Component Construction* (Ref. 3).

## 9.5    Transient Analysis

The objective of transient heat transfer analysis is to determine the temperature distribution in the structure or component when it is subjected to time-varying thermal loads. A typical transient problem is described in Sec. 2.7.3 and illustrated in Fig. 2.17. In this section, we discuss modeling techniques pertaining to transient analysis and then present an example problem.

### 9.5.1    Selecting the Time Step for the Analysis

As in transient dynamics analysis, the user must select the appropriate time interval (time step) for performing the analysis. In ANSYS-PC/THERMAL, the time step is actually expressed in terms of the duration of the thermal transient and the number of iterations to be performed. For example, if the duration of the transient is 10 seconds and 10 iterations are specified, the time step is 1 second.

The criterion that determines the appropriate time step in heat transfer analysis is the conduction length in the direction of the heat flow of the smallest element in the model. The time step is calculated by the following equation (see Refs. 1 and 2):

$$\text{Time step} \geq \frac{\delta^2}{4\alpha} \tag{9.1}$$

where $\delta$ = the conduction length (in)
$\alpha$ = the thermal diffusivity of the material (in$^2$/s)

To clarify the use of this equation, consider the finite element mesh in Fig. 9.7a. The heat flow is in the $X$ direction. The minimum element length is 0.1 in in the $X$ direction. The thermal diffusivity of the material is 0.007 in$^2$/s (typical value for steel). Applying Eq. (9.1),

$$\text{Time step} \geq \frac{0.1^2}{4 \times 0.007} = 0.357 \text{ s}$$

Now, let us assume that a thermal time history of 15 seconds is to be input in the analysis. Then the number of iterations required is 15/0.357 = 42 iterations. Note that you may specify a time step larger than that obtained by Eq. (9.1). However, the accuracy of the analysis will decrease with increasing time step size. In general, it is good practice to specify a time step close to that obtained from Eq. (9.1). Time step values less than those calculated by Eq. (9.1) may cause inaccurate temperature fluctuations in the analysis results. We will discuss a method for determining the optimal mesh refinement in the next section.

As we mentioned earlier, the user can select automatic time step optimization, regardless of the number of iterations specified. The optimization option is strongly recommended because in most problems, it substantially reduces the number of iterations that are executed and, therefore, reduces the computer processing time.

### 9.5.2  Determining the Mesh Refinement

We mentioned earlier that the degree of mesh refinement can be critical in heat transfer analyses involving severe thermal transients. To minimize computer processing time, it is desirable to use the largest possible time step while still retaining the required accuracy of the analysis. As we saw in the last section, the time step is related to the element conduction length and hence the mesh refinement. By running a series of test cases with varying mesh refinements, the optimal mesh refinement and corresponding time step can be determined.

The procedure is essentially the same as the one we used in Chap. 6 to determine the appropriate mesh refinement for the lifting lug problem. In thermal problems, we apply the appropriate thermal transient to a small test model, varying the number of elements through the thickness. When the nodal temperature values converge, the optimal mesh refinement has been found.

For example, consider the element meshes in Fig 9.7. Assume that these are axisymmetric slices of a cylinder exposed to fluid convection on the inside surface. The first mesh has five evenly spaced elements. The second mesh has six elements, and the third has seven. The time steps calculated from Eq. (9.1) are (in round figures) 0.4, 0.1, and 0.03 second, respectively. A transient step change in the fluid temperature of 400 to 100°F is applied to each mesh. The analysis is performed for each test case using time steps ranging from 0.4 to 0.05 second. Table 9.3 shows the results. The temperature $T$ is calculated at node 1 on the surface. In the table we see that the six-element finite element mesh with a time step of 0.1 second gives converged results. This configuration would, therefore, be appropriate for the actual problem. Of course, the same transient and convection coefficient would have to be applied in the actual problem.

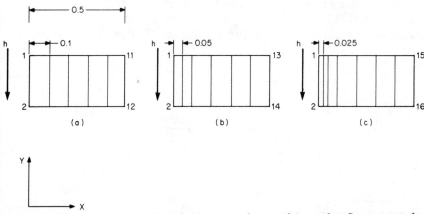

**Figure 9.7**  Three possible mesh configurations to be tested in mesh-refinement study. The inside surface defined by nodes 1 and 2 is subjected to convection $h$ and thermal transient.

Table 9.3    Mesh-Refinement Study

| Number of elements | Time step | $T$ at 0.8 s | $T$ at 0.4 s |
|---|---|---|---|
| 5 | 0.4 | 184.5 | 220.4 |
| 6 | 0.4 | 174.4 | 215.3 |
| 6 | 0.2 | 165.3 | 210.2 |
| 6 | 0.1 | 159.5 | 204.2 |
| 7 | 0.05 | 158.0 | 203.7 |

### 9.5.3    Transient Analysis Example Problem

A classic heat transfer problem involves the transient analysis of a cooling fin. For example, air-cooled engines typically use fins to conduct heat away from the engine. There are, of course, many other applications of cooling fins. This example problem of a radiator fin is taken from the sample problems in the *ANSYS-PC/THERMAL User's Manual* (Ref. 1).

The radiator fin is shown in Fig. 9.8. The thick portion of the fin is called the *root*. The inside surface of the root (opposite the end with the fin) is heated to 247°F. The convection coefficient is 0.036 Btu/in²-s-°F on the inside surface and 0.15 Btu/in²-s-°F on the outside surfaces. The root is made from steel, and the fin is made from aluminum.

The analysis is performed in two load steps. First, the temperature distribution at steady state is determined by a steady-state analysis. The results of this analysis are automatically used as the initial conditions for the transient load step, in which the inside of the fin is heated to 247°F. This is an important characteristic of multiple load steps. The conditions at the end of the previous load step are used at the beginning of the next load step.

The finite element model shown in Fig. 9.9 consists of 3-D solid elements (STIF70) representing the root of the fin, and STIF57 thermal shell elements representing the fin itself. The root requires the

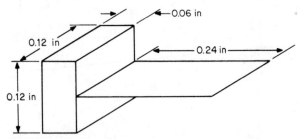

**Figure 9.8**   Dimensions of a radiator fin. *[Swanson Analysis Systems, Inc., ANSYS-PC/THERMAL User's Manual (for ANSYS Revision 4.2), Houston, Pa., March 1, 1986.]*

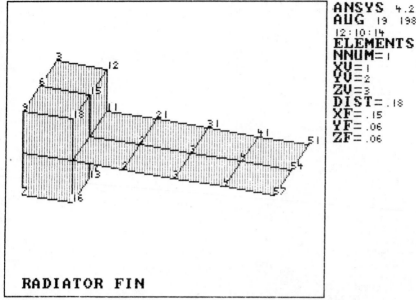

Figure 9.9 Finite element model of a radiator fin with some node numbers shown.

3-D elements in order to obtain the temperature distribution in the direction parallel to the fin and also in the transverse direction. The shell element is used for the fin since only the in-plane temperature distribution is required. The origin is located at the lower inside corner of the root (directly below node 3). The coordinates of node 3 are 0, 0.12, and 0.

Figure 9.10 shows the input listing for the problem. Material properties are specified for steel (type 1) and aluminum (type 2). The real constant table specifies the thickness of the shell elements as 0.0755 in. The nodes and elements are specified as usual (see Chap. 5 for a detailed explanation of ANSYS modeling commands).

Next the CVSF commands specify the convection coefficients at the inside and outside surfaces of the root for the steady-state analysis. The specification of convections is almost identical to the specification of pressures in ANSYS-PC/LINEAR (see Chap. 7, pipe junction problem). The bulk temperature for the steady-state load step is 75°F.

The ESEL command selects element type 2, the fin elements, and the EC commands define the convection coefficients on both sides of the fin (faces 1 and 2). Note that commands following an ESEL command apply only to the elements specified in the ESEL command. For example, the ALL designation in the EC command applies only to type 2 elements as specified by the previous ESEL command. A reset

```
/TITLE, RADIATOR FIN
ET,1,70
ET,2,57
KXX,1,0.0006
DENS,1,0.284
C,1,0.11
KXX,2,0.003
DENS,2,0.0978
C,2,0.216
R,1,0.0755
N,1
N,3,,0.12
FILL
NGEN,3,3,1,3,1,,,0.06
NGEN,2,9,1,9,1,0.06
NGEN,5,10,11,17,3,0.06
E,1,2,5,4,10,11,14,13
EGEN,2,1,1
EGEN,2,3,-2
TYPE,2
MAT,2
E,11,14,24,21
EGEN,2,3,-1
EGEN,4,10,-2
CVSF,0,1,0,0.036,75
CVSF,0,1,0.06,0.15,75
ESEL,TYPE,2
EC,ALL,1,0.15,75
EC,ALL,2,0.15,75
EALL
LWRITE
TIME,15
ITER,-2500,0
CVSF,0,1,0,0.036,247
CVSF,0,1,0.06,0.15,85
ERSEL,TYPE,2
EC,ALL,1,0.15,85
EC,ALL,2,0.15,85
EALL
LWRITE
/VIEW,1,1,2,3
EPLOT
AFWRIT
FINISH
```

**Figure 9.10**   ANSYS-PC/THERMAL input listing
for the radiator fin problem.

command such as EALL is used to reselect all elements.

The EALL command reactivates all elements, and the LWRITE command writes the first load step to a temporary file. Next, the transient load step is specified. The TIME command specifies the transient duration of 15 seconds. The number of iterations is set to 2500 with time step optimization (specified by using a negative number for the number of iterations). The TIME and ITERATION values result in a time step of 15/2500 = 0.006 second. You can verify this time step using Eq. (9.1) and the properties for aluminum $\alpha = KXX/(DENS \times C)$.

The transient loading conditions are specified next. The same convection coefficients are specified except that the bulk temperature at the inside surface is raised to 247°F. Unless specified as a step change, the boundary conditions of the second load step are "ramped" from the first load step. In other words, the temperature is raised from 75 (steady state) to 247°F linearly over a period of 15 seconds.

The LWRITE command saves the second load step, and the AFWRIT command saves the entire input for processing by the THERMAL module. The analysis is then performed using THERMAL. Note that we did not include an ITER command for printing out temperature results as we did in the steady-state example. The printout would be enormous for so many iterations. Instead, we can use POST to print or plot temperature plots for selected iterations.

In order to determine which iterations to use for postprocessing, we need the output from the thermal analysis run. A partial listing from this output is shown in Fig. 9.11. Notice that the time step optimization results in a total of 9 iterations out of a total of 2500 being actually stored as part of the solution. This can be read from the CUM. ITER values. The actual iteration numbers that are stored are also listed. For example, iteration number 1366 represents the temperature distribution at 8.2 seconds. Other details from this output are given in Swanson Analysis Systems, *ANSYS-PC/THERMAL User's Manual* (Ref. 1).

Using the POST postprocessor module, we can plot the temperature distribution for selected iterations using the SET command. The command SET,2,1366 stores the temperature data for load step 2, iteration 1366. This data can then be plotted using the appropriate plot commands. Note that the iteration number need not be specified for the last iteration (2500, in this case). The SET command will default to the last iteration if it is not specified.

Fig. 9.12a and b shows the temperature distribution in the fin at 8.2 and 15 seconds, respectively. The temperature change in node 14 (the middle node where the fin joins the root) is plotted in Fig. 9.13. This plot is made using the POST26 module for time history plotting. Note the starting temperature is 75°F. This is the temperature of node 14 at steady state, as calculated by the first load step.

Depending on the application of the cooling fin, the temperature results may be acceptable, or other boundary conditions and material properties could be tried. For example, in order to lower the inside surface temperature, the material of the root could be changed to aluminum, or the convection coefficients could be changed.

```
***LOAD STEP   2   ITER   1   COMPLETED.   TIME =   0.600000E-02
   TIME INC = 0.600000E-02   CUM. ITER. =   2
ELEMENT FORMATION     ELEM =   1 L.S. =   2 ITER =   2   CP =
127.65
   TRANSIENT OPTIMIZATION VALUE  =   0.99738E-02 AT NODE   8
   CRITERION  =   10.000
***LOAD STEP   2   ITER   2   COMPLETED.   TIME =   0.120000E-01
   TIME INC =   0.600000E-02   CUM. ITER. =   3
ELEMENT FORMATION   ELEM =   1 L.S. =   2 ITER =   6   CP =
160.94
   TRANSIENT OPTIMIZATION VALUE  =   0.10201  AT NODE   2
   CRITERION  =   10.000
***LOAD STEP   2   ITER   6   COMPLETED.   TIME =   0.360000E-01
   TIME INC =   0.240000E-01   CUM. ITER. =   4
ELEMENT FORMATION   ELEM =   1 L.S. =   2 ITER =   22   CP =
194.39
   TRANSIENT OPTIMIZATION VALUE  =   0.42809  AT NODE   2
   CRITERION  =   10.000
***LOAD STEP   2   ITER   22   COMPLETED.   TIME =   0.132000
   TIME INC =   0.960000E-01   CUM. ITER. =   5
ELEMENT FORMATION   ELEM =   1 L.S. =   2 ITER =   86   CP =
227.29
   TRANSIENT OPTIMIZATION VALUE  =   0.41584  AT NODE   5
   CRITERION  =   10.000
***LOAD STEP   2   ITER   86   COMPLETED.   TIME =   0.516000
   TIME INC =   0.384000   CUM. ITER. =   6
ELEMENT FORMATION   ELEM =   1 L.S. =   2 ITER =   342   CP =
260.96
   TRANSIENT OPTIMIZATION VALUE  =   0.11341  AT NODE   8
   CRITERION  =   10.000
***LOAD STEP   2   ITER   342   COMPLETED.   TIME =   2.05200
   TIME INC =   1.53600   CUM. ITER. =   7
ELEMENT FORMATION   ELEM =   1 L.S. =   2 ITER =   1366   CP =
295.34
   TRANSIENT OPTIMIZATION VALUE  =   0.83337E-01 AT NODE   5
   CRITERION  =   10.000
***LOAD STEP   2   ITER   1366   COMPLETED.   TIME =   8.19600
   TIME INC =   6.14400   CUM. ITER. =   8
ELEMENT FORMATION   ELEM =   1 L.S. =   2 ITER =   2500   CP =
330.33
   TRANSIENT OPTIMIZATION VALUE  =   0.37465E-03 AT NODE   4
   CRITERION  =   10.000
***LOAD STEP   2   ITER   2500   COMPLETED.   TIME =   15.0000
   TIME INC =   6.80400   CUM. ITER. =   9
*****END OF INPUT ENCOUNTERED ON FILE 5.   FILE 5 REWOUND
```

Figure 9.11  Output from load step 2 of the radiator fin analysis. Note that only nine total iterations are actually performed in reaching a solution.

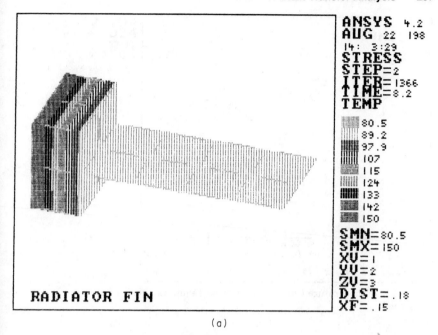

(a)

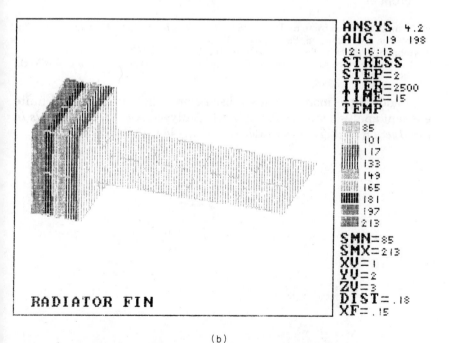

(b)

**Figure 9.12** (a) Temperature distribution of the radiator fin at 8.2 seconds. The inside surface of the root is at 150°F. (b) Temperature distribution of the radiator fin at 15 seconds. The inside surface of the root is at 213°F.

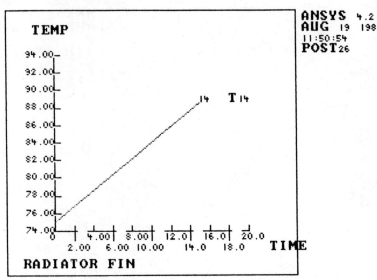

**Figure 9.13** Temperature time history of node 14 during transient of 15 seconds.

## References

1. Swanson Analysis Systems, Inc.: *ANSYS-PC/THERMAL User's Manual* (for ANSYS Revision 4. 2), Houston, Pa., March 1, 1986.
2. Holman, J. P.: *Heat Transfer*, McGraw-Hill, New York, 1976.
3. Harvey, J. F.: *Pressure Component Construction*, Van Nostrand/Reinhold, New York, 1980.

In addition, a more advanced discussion of heat transfer and finite element analysis may be found in: G. E. Myers, *Analytical Methods in Conduction Heat Transfer,* McGraw-Hill, New York, 1971.

# Files, Editors, and Graphics

In this appendix, we present general information and miscellaneous suggestions on the use of microcomputers with finite element programs. The discussion focuses on the use of IBM PC and compatible computers with the PC-DOS or MS-DOS (hereafter called simply DOS) operating system. However, some of the information in this appendix may be useful to users of other types of microcomputers. Additional general information on computers may be found in Chap. 3.

The information in this appendix should not be construed as a substitute for a thorough study of the DOS manual that accompanies your computer. In order to use finite element software efficiently, you need to have a basic understanding of the concepts and terminology contained in the DOS manual. Pay particular attention to the concepts of *paths*, *subdirectories*, and *batch files*. In addition, you will need to be familiar with the EDLIN text editor or other ASCII text editors (see Sec. A.3).

## A.1 Notes on Installing Finite Element Software

Almost all microcomputer finite element programs for the IBM PC require the following hardware configuration:

1. 512K bytes of memory (640K bytes recommended)

2. Numeric coprocessor (Intel 8087 for the PC XT, Intel 80287 for the PC AT)

3. Color graphics adapter (CGA) or enhanced-graphics adapter (EGA) and compatible graphics monitor (See Sec. A.4.)

4. 10M-byte hard disk (A minimum of 20M bytes is recommended.)

5. Dot matrix printer with graphics capability [The printer must be compatible with the DOS program GRAPHICS.COM in order to print graphic screen images using the SHIFT-PRTSC key (see Sec. A.4).]

When installing the finite element software on your hard disk, you may need to create a CONFIG.SYS file in the root directory. Most finite element programs require a CONFIG.SYS file that opens enough memory buffers and file handles for the program to operate. The CONFIG.SYS file can be created with any text editor (see Sec. A.3). The contents of a typical CONFIG.SYS file are as follows:

Files = 20

Buffers = 20

If your system already has a CONFIG.SYS file, simply edit the file to include the appropriate specifications required by your finite element program. If you have other software that specifies different file and buffer sizes, use the larger of the conflicting numbers.

If you are using a hard disk other than drive C, your finite element software may not operate properly unless you use the DOS ASSIGN command. Unfortunately, many finite element programs assume that users will always use drive C and therefore automatically read and write to this drive. If, for example, your finite element software is installed on drive D, you may need to issue the DOS command ASSIGN C = D before running the finite element program.

## A.2    Directories and Files

Most finite element programs allow you to store data in separate subdirectories on your hard disk. *Any program that does not have this capability should be avoided.* The reason this is so important is that most finite element programs *overwrite* existing data. Therefore, if you do not want to overwrite data from a previous analysis, you need to start a new problem in a new subdirectory. Otherwise, you will spend a lot of time renaming and copying files. Eventually, disaster will strike, and you will overwrite valuable data.

With the use of subdirectories, it is necessary to issue a PATH command before starting the finite element program. The PATH command can be included in your AUTOEXEC.BAT file that executes every time the computer is started up (booted). With the path specified, you can change to the subdirectory where you will store the analysis results and then call the finite element program.

For example, let us assume that you have the ANSYS-PC/LINEAR program files in a directory called C:\ANSYS. You would include this directory in your path command. The path can contain multiple directories. For example, your path may look like this:

PATH  =   C:\ANSYS;C:\WORDSTAR;C:\LOTUS;C:\W

Note that the root directory C:\ is named last. This is a good practice to follow since some programs must precede the root directory in the path. If your data directory is called CD\PROB-A, you would issue the following commands to start the ANSYS preprocessor, PREP7:

CD\PROB-A
PREP

Although the PREP program is in the ANSYS directory, it will execute since ANSYS is on the path. For ANSYS users who have both ANSYS-PC/LINEAR and ANSYS-PC/THERMAL installed on the same hard disk, you will need separate path commands for each program. Some of the files (PREP, for example) have the same names in each program. If both programs are on the path simultaneously, you may inadvertently load the wrong program.

If you use multiple path specifications, you can include them in separate batch files that you can call as needed. For example, you could create a batch file called ANSRUN.BAT with the following commands:

PATH  =  C:\ANSYS
CD\ANSYS

The command ANSRUN would automatically execute the ANSRUN.BAT file. Another batch file called THERM.BAT could include similar commands for executing ANSYS-PC/THERMAL.

A final suggestion regarding directories is to include the following command in your AUTOEXEC.BAT file:

PROMPT $P$G

This command will cause the directory name to be displayed in the DOS prompt. For example, if you are logged into the ANSYS directory, the DOS prompt would look like this:

C:\ANSYS>

This is much more informative than C>, which does not tell you what directory you are in.

### A.2.1   Backing Up Your Data

This is probably the most important section in this appendix. It is essential to regularly back up the data on your hard disk. Nothing is more frustrating than to inadvertently overwrite or delete an entire analysis including the 100 lines of commands that you labored over for an entire day.

Small files can be copied to floppy disks using the DOS COPY command. For example, your input file for an analysis might be PUMP.TXT. You can copy this file to the floppy drive as follows:

COPY PUMP.TXT A:

where A: is the floppy drive.

Large files that exceed the size of a single floppy disk may be copied using the DOS BACKUP command. However, backing up an entire 20-Mbyte hard disk with the BACKUP command is a slow, time-consuming process. The best alternative is to add a tape backup unit to your system. A 60M-byte tape backup system can be purchased for under $1000. A cheaper alternative is to purchase special disk backup software which works much faster than the DOS BACKUP command. FASTBACK, from Fifth Generation Systems, is an example of this type of software.

### A.2.2    Input and Output

Many programs allow both interactive and batch input. *Interactive input* means that you enter commands from within the finite element program and that the commands are processed as you enter them. *Batch input* means that you prepare a text file (see Sec. A.3) containing the entire set of commands for the analysis and then submit this file as input.

For example, the PREP7 module in ANSYS-PC/LINEAR can be used interactively or with batch files. For interactive use, you simply issue the command PREP. The PREP7 module executes and waits for you to enter a command. You can perform an entire analysis in this fashion, if you prefer. The commands that you issue will be saved in a file called FILE18.DAT. *Make sure that you rename the FILE18.DAT file at the end of your PREP7 session.* Otherwise, it will be overwritten the next time you run PREP7.

In batch mode, you prepare the set of commands for the analysis using a text editor and then submit the file to PREP7. You can also request an output file which will store the response of PREP7 to each command. For example, if your input file for the lug analysis is called LUG.MDL, you could execute PREP7 as follows:

PREP ‹LUG.MDL› OUTPUT.LUG

PREP7 would use the LUG.MDL as input and the file OUTPUT.LUG for output. This is how ANSYS-PC/LINEAR was used in this book. It is the author's opinion that ANSYS-PC/LINEAR and ANSYS-PC/THERMAL should be operated in batch mode for generating finite element models and interactively for using graphics and postprocessing. In addition, minor modifications of the input file using the RESUME command can be performed interactively. The problem with interactive usage is that it is very easy to overwrite the commands from your previous session. This can be frustrating indeed. It is preferable to store the commands in a text file where you can easily refer to them and modify them, if necessary.

MSC/pal 2 can also be used interactively. However, MSC/pal 2 does not keep a record of the commands you issued during the session. The use of batch files is therefore recommended for data input in MSC/pal 2. Most postprocessing operations in MSC/pal 2 can be done interactively using the VIEW2 and XYPLOT2 graphics modules.

Finite element programs generally operate in two stages. First, the preprocessing results (model generation) are stored (PREP7 in ANSYS-

PC/LINEAR or PAL2 in MSC/pal 2, for example). Then, the actual analysis is executed. When the analysis is executed, most finite element programs automatically create an output file which can be read in binary form by the program's postprocessor(s). In ANSYS-PC/LINEAR and ANSYS-PC/THERMAL, this file is always named FILE12.DAT. Other files contain important additional data (FILE4.DAT, FILE16.DAT, FILE27.DAT, etc.). In MSC/pal 2, the data is stored in a series of files with the file name PAL.DB?, where the ? represents numbers from 0 to 9.

When you complete the analysis, you can always view the results with the program's postprocessor. However, if you want printed output for the entire analysis (Fig. 6.4, for example), you must specifically request it. In ANSYS-PC/LINEAR, you request an output file as we did above with PREP7. For example, to obtain a complete ANSYS output file from the lug analysis, you would execute ANSYS as follows:

ANSYS >LUG.OUT

Note that no input file is required by ANSYS. It automatically loads the files created by the PREP7 run (FILE16.DAT). ANSYS-PC/THERMAL, on the other hand, requires an input file called FILE27.DAT. This file is automatically generated by the PREP7 module. For example, the heat transfer analysis of the fin in Chap. 9 requires the following commands:

THERMAL <FILE27.DAT >FIN.OUT

In MSC/pal 2, you can request printed output from the main menu of the STAT2 or DYNA2 module, using the DATA RECOVERY option. The output can be routed directly to the printer, to the screen, or to a disk file.

Printed output is not always desirable since, in large problems, the amount of data may be prohibitively large. You can easily tie up a printer for several hours printing output that may not be very useful. It is usually best to look at your data with the postprocessor before requesting output.

## A.3  Text Editors

DOS comes with a line editor called EDLIN. A line editor can edit only one line at a time. You cannot move the screen cursor from one line to the next as you can with a word processor, for example. You move from line to line by specifying line numbers. Line editors are fine for editing small batch files such as a CONFIG.SYS or AUTOEXEC.BAT file. However, for larger files, line editors are clumsy to use.

It is strongly recommended that you use a *full-screen editor* for preparing finite element input files. A full-screen editor is like a word processor except that it produces *ASCII text files* rather than specially formatted word processing files. Full-screen editors are also helpful for viewing the output from your analysis. You can scroll through the out put page by page rather than by line number as you would with a line editor.

Many word processors include an ASCII text mode for creating ASCII files. In this case, you can use your word processor as a full-screen editor. An example is the "nondocument mode" in Wordstar. You can also purchase excellent full screen editors for under $50, as advertised in personal computer magazines.

## A.4  Graphics

The use of graphics on the IBM PC can be somewhat confusing because there are several different standards. The original standard was the color graphics adapter (CGA) that IBM introduced when it unveiled the IBM PC. The resolution for this standard is 320 dots × 200 lines in medium mode, which is the mode used by many finite element programs. Some programs use the CGA high-resolution mode which is 640 × 200. The screens in this book from ANSYS-PC/LINEAR were generated in CGA medium-resolution mode.

The newer standard from IBM is the enhanced-graphics adapter (EGA). Medium resolution in this standard is 640 × 200, and high resolution is 640 × 350. Most of the graphics from MSC/pal 2 in this book were produced using the Japanese IBM 5550 computer, which has a resolution of 1024 × 758. Yet another standard is the Hercules graphics card, which supports a resolution of 720 × 348.

Regardless of which graphics configuration you select, it is important that your printer support the selected configuration. Many finite element programs, including ANSYS-PC/LINEAR and MSC/pal 2, use the DOS program GRAPHICS.COM to print the graphics screens. This program must be loaded into memory before you execute the finite element program. The easiest way to do this is to include the command GRAPHICS in your AUTOEXEC.BAT file. You can then use the SHIFT-PRTSC key to print graphic screens on your printer. All the computer-generated graphics in this book were printed this way.

# Finite Element Modeling with Computer-Aided Design (CAD)

As we have seen throughout this book, creating the finite element model on the computer can be a tedious task. Normally, nodes and elements are defined by a sequence of commands input as a batch file or interactively. In large problems, over 100 lines of commands may be necessary to define the finite element model. In many cases, tedious hand calculations of nodal coordinates are necessary. In addition, the entire process is highly prone to errors, which are often time-consuming and difficult to find.

An increasingly popular alternative to the traditional method of finite element modeling is to use computer-aided design (CAD) programs for designing the finite element mesh. Using a special interface program, the geometry created by the CAD program can be read by the finite element program.

In this appendix, we take a brief look at the use of CAD programs for creating finite element models. CAD programs automate many of the functions performed manually by a draftsperson. Engineering and architectural drawings are created on the computer rather than on the drafting table. The tasks of specifying dimensions, scaling, creating symbols and special shapes, hidden lines, and so forth are greatly simplified by the use of CAD programs. The details of how to use CAD programs are beyond the scope of this book. However, there are many books available on the use of a variety of CAD programs (Ref. 1).

Before proceeding any further, it is important to realize that specific CAD and finite element programs must have some sort of special interface, usually provided by the finite element program vendor. You cannot simply use any CAD program with any finite element program. In this appendix, we look at the interface between the CAD program AutoCad and MSC/pal 2. The interface, called MSC/AutoFEM, allows the geometry of AutoCad drawings to be read by MSC/pal 2. While AutoCad creates only 2-D drawings, 3-D finite element models can be made by combining two or more AutoCad drawings using MSC/AutoFEM.

The procedure for working with CAD and finite element programs together is as follows:

1. Create the geometry of the finite element model using the CAD

program (e.g., AutoCad).

2. Invoke the finite element–CAD interface program and convert the CAD drawing to an actual finite element model. (In the case of MSC/AutoFEM, this is a two-step process, as we shall see below.)

3. Perform the analysis using the finite element program (e.g., MSC/pal 2) as you would normally.

In order to illustrate the procedure, we will create the lifting lug model of Chap. 5, using AutoCad and MSC/AutoFEM. The first step is to create the geometry using AutoCad. To begin, you should have a general outline of the model as we discussed in Chap. 5 (see Fig. 5.1).

Most CAD programs recommend the use of a mouse (for example, Microsoft Mouse) or a digitizer for moving the cursor on the screen. Some programs allow you to use the keyboard cursor keys, although the cursor keys are much slower and inconvenient than the mouse or digitizer.

When you first load AutoCad and select BEGIN NEW DRAWING from the DRAW menu, you are presented with a blank screen with some options listed along the right-hand edge of the screen. You can select circles, lines, arcs, or other special shapes as objects to insert in your drawing.

For the circular portion of the lug, we select circles. Since we are creating a half-model of the lug, we simply draw the circles for the finite element mesh and then cut them in half using the BREAK option. We can either specify the center point and radius for the circle in terms of actual coordinates, or we can simply draw the radius with the mouse. In either case, AutoCad automatically draws the circle. We then select lines to draw the rectangular part of the lug.

Figure B.1 shows the lug after we have drawn the circles and the outer boundary. The important point to recognize is that we need to know only the overall dimensions of the lug. Based on the mesh refinement we want, we can simply draw in the inner circles without specifying any coordinates. In our MSC/pal 2 listing in Chap. 5, we had to specify each radial increment for the inner circles. The straight lines for the rectangular portion are also very simple to draw. As we move the mouse along a straight line, the length of the line is displayed in the upper right-hand corner of the screen (units of length are specified when you start up AutoCad).

Once the overall shape of the model has been drawn, the next step is to create the lines and curves that form the mesh. This step is necessary only for areas where the mesh is not uniformly spaced. Uniformly spaced meshes can be automatically generated with AutoFEM.

Using the ARRAY command in AutoCad, we can generate radial line

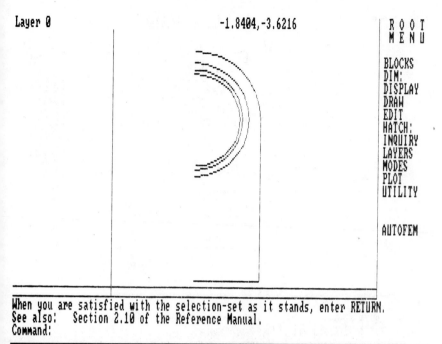

Layer 0                          -1.8404,-3.6216                    R O O T
                                                                    M E N U

                                                                    BLOCKS
                                                                    DIM:
                                                                    DISPLAY
                                                                    DRAW
                                                                    EDIT
                                                                    HATCH:
                                                                    INQUIRY
                                                                    LAYERS
                                                                    MODES
                                                                    PLOT
                                                                    UTILITY

                                                                    AUTOFEM

When you are satisfied with the selection-set as it stands, enter RETURN.
See also:    Section 2.10 of the Reference Manual.
Command:

**Figure B.1**   Lifting lug after drawing the circles and other boundary.

segments as shown in Fig. B.2. Next, we draw the lines and curves for
the rectangular portion of the lug. Curves can be drawn by simply specifying three points with the mouse. AutoCad will draw a curve through
the points. If you do not like the shape of the curve, you simply erase
it and try three new points.

After the drawing is complete, the next step is to select the Auto-
FEM option from the AutoCad main menu. Notice in Figs. B.1 and B.2
that AutoFEM is listed as an option. AutoCad allows the addition of
"user-defined programs" to its main menu. In this case, the program is
MSC/AutoFEM.

MSC/AutoFEM is operated in two steps. First, it is used within Auto-
Cad to actually build the finite element model. We then exit AutoCad
and run AutoFEM from the DOS prompt to convert the finite element
model data into MSC/pal 2 format. This second stage operates similarly to the VIEW2 module in MSC/pal 2.

In the first stage of using AutoFEM, we define the element connectivities by specifying boundary end points using the mouse. The result of
this procedure is shown in Fig. B.3. Next, we specify the element type as
a membrane-only, quadrilateral element (see Chap. 5). Finally, menu
options prompt you for the material properties and boundary condi-

Layer LINNE                                    4.1541, -3.8302

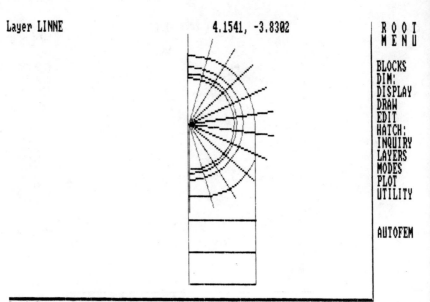

R O O T
M E N U

BLOCKS
DIM:
DISPLAY
DRAW
EDIT
HATCH:
INQUIRY
LAYERS
MODES
PLOT
UTILITY

AUTOFEM

Loaded menu C:\CAD\ACAD.mnx
Command: quit
Really want to discard all changes to drawing?

**Figure B.2** Using the ARRAY command in AutoCad, radial line segments can be generated.

Layer MODEL                          3.3106, 1.6878

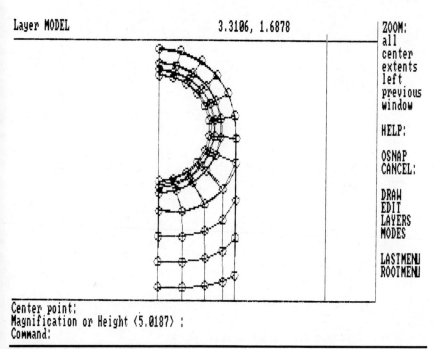

Center point:
Magnification or Height (5.0187) :
Command:

**Figure B.3**  The result of defining the element connectivities by specifying boundary and end points using the mouse.

tions. We then exit AutoCad and load the AutoFEM program from the DOS prompt.

The final step before performing the finite element analysis is to convert the model in Fig. B.3 into MSC/pal 2 format. The result is a finite element mesh similar to Fig. 5.5. Nodal coordinates and element connectivities are listed by the AutoFEM program.

AutoCad and MSC/AutoFEM together offer a much broader range of capabilities than we have covered in this brief appendix. However, it should be apparent that the combination of CAD and finite element analysis is the "wave of the future." As of this writing, the interfaces between CAD and finite element programs are in an early stage of development. Eventually, all finite element modeling will be done using CAD interfaces.

## Reference

1. Wohlers, T. T.: *Applying AutoCad: A Step-by-Step Approach*, Bennett and McKnight, Peoria, Ill., 1986.
2. Voisinet, D.D.: *AutoCad Mechanical Lab Manual*,McGraw-Hill, New York, 1987.

# Index

## About the author

Nicholas M. Baran is a technical editor at *Byte Magazine* and has a B.S. in mechanical engineering from Stanford University. Formerly a mechanical engineer and manager of computer operations for Cygna Corporation and Mark Technologies Corporation, he is the author of *Command Performance R:base* (Microsoft Press, 1987) and the coauthor of *Using R:base 4000* and *Using R:base 5000* (both Osborne/McGraw-Hill, 1985).